nation divided on the subject of race. . . . Stanton does a creditable job of recalling a signature episode in baseball history and placing it into a social context."

—Boston Herald

"Aaron's home run may have made just a small dent in America's racial quagmire . . . but it clearly helped many young fans . . . imagine a more equitable world. . . . [Hank Aaron and the Home Run That Changed America] is steeped in nostalgia and fandom. . . . Stanton's book is a laudable attempt to make our passion for the game all right again." —Austin American Statesman

"Stanton mixes sport with social commentary as he describes the racism Aaron faced, including death threats to himself and his family, hate mail, and the inexplicable indifference of baseball's commissioner Bowie Kuhn."

—BookPage

"Stanton captures the embittering and, finally, uplifting sides of Aaron's personal story from that record-breaking campaign that ended [April 8, 1974]."

—Library Journal

"A fascinating look at Henry Aaron breaking the Babe's home run record." —Publishers Weekly

"Stanton has an eye for the novelistic detail that captures the drama of Aaron's drive to the record."

—New York Times Book Review

For *The Final Season: Fathers, Sons, and One Last Season in a Classic American Ballpark*

BEST BASEBALL BOOK OF THE YEAR AS WINNER OF THE CASEY AND DAVE MOORE AWARDS

"Those who don't understand say baseball is only a game. Those who run and play it sometimes act as if it's only a business. By now, maybe they're right. But for a long time, something else was true. That something else is what Tom Stanton is getting at here."   —Bob Costas

"Stanton is part Charles Kuralt, part W. P. Kinsella."
                                        —Bookreporter.com

"It's splendid. No dad, son, or combination thereof should get through June without *The Final Season*."
                                        —*Detroit News*

"A moving portrayal of trying to hold on to the past while plunging into the future."   —*USA Today*

"A wonderful story . . . this is what real baseball is about."
                                        —Sparky Anderson

"A beautiful gem of a book, tender, perceptive, compassionate, funny, and wise. I devoured it in one sitting and am still banging my tin cup on the dining room table wanting more."   —Lawrence S. Ritter,
author of *The Glory of Their Times*

"Tom Stanton touches us with an eloquent book about fans, family, and idols as they all connect with a treasured but dying baseball landmark."

—Ernie Harwell, Hall of Fame broadcaster

FOR *The Road to Cooperstown*

"The equivalent of a tall icy glass of homemade lemonade: direct, irresistible, bittersweet."

—*Seattle Post-Intelligencer*

"Promote Tom Stanton from singles to doubles hitter. . . . True and sweet. . . . In showing baseball's power to bond, Stanton turns a phrase as deftly as Maz used to turn double plays for the Pirates." —*Richmond Times Dispatch*

"Stanton is a marvelous writer who can tell a story."

—*Library Journal*

"How baseball turns boys into men, and vice versa, considered with feeling and a bittersweet edge."

—*Kirkus Reviews*

Beth Bagley-Stanton

About the Author

TOM STANTON, an award-winning journalist of twenty-five years, is the author of two memoirs, *The Road to Cooperstown* and *The Final Season*, winner of the Casey Award for Best Baseball Book of the Year. He lives in the Detroit area with his wife and their children.

HANK AARON
AND THE | HOME RUN
THAT CHANGED AMERICA

Also by Tom Stanton

The Road to Cooperstown
The Final Season

HANK AARON

AND THE HOME RUN

THAT CHANGED AMERICA

Tom Stanton

Perennial Currents

An Imprint of HarperCollins*Publishers*

Designed by Renato Stanisic

The Library of Congress has catalogued the hardcover edition as follows:

Stanton, Tom.
 Hank Aaron and the home run that changed America / Tom Stanton.—1st ed.
  p. cm.
 Includes bibliographical references (p.) and index.
 ISBN 0-06-057976-5
 1. Aaron, Hank, 1934– 2. Baseball players—United States—Biography. 3. Racism in sports—United States. 4. Home runs (Baseball).

 GV865.A25S83 2004
 796.357'092—dc22
 [B]   2004046092

ISBN 0-06-072290-8 (pbk.)

05 06 07 08 09 ❖/RRD 10 9 8 7 6 5 4 3 2 1

For Beth

CONTENTS

A Note 1

1
Jackie's Funeral 3

2
Invincible Babe 14

3
Spring in Florida 26

4
The Quest Begins 35

5
Atlanta Heartbreak 46

6
Cal's Roscoe 62

7
The Rescue 74

8
Bowie and Mrs. Babe 86

9
Waiting for Roger 93

10
The Other Star 104

11
Sweet Home Alabama 112

12
A Hero Returns 125

13
Chicago Revival 133

14
Where Evil Lurks 139

15
Aaron's Drama 150

16
Rainy Nights in Georgia 161

17
Atlanta's Redemption 168

18
King Henry 180

19
The Hideaway 191

20
Amid a Storm 199

21
715 212

Epilogue: The Legacy 225
Bibliography: Selected Books,
Articles, and Other Sources 233
Acknowledgments 240
Index 242

HANK AARON
AND THE | HOME RUN
THAT CHANGED AMERICA

A NOTE

n the early months of the 1973 baseball season, when reports surfaced about the odious mail souring Hank Aaron's home-run pursuit, something stupendous happened. Tens of thousands of children—from San Antonio, Texas, to Salem, Oregon, from Marshfield, Wisconsin, to Mt. Vernon, New York, and myriad places between—set out individually to lift Hank Aaron's spirits. This earnest, youthful army, raised on *Brady Bunch* do-good and swayed by the words of Top 40 philosophers like Bill Withers ("Lean on me . . . I'll help you carry on"), rallied to Aaron's side.

Through the eyes of these children, it seemed a simple morality play, the line dividing right from wrong as sharp and crisp as the one separating fair territory from foul on the ball diamonds of our youths. The solution seemed just as simple: Write a letter. That it occurred to so many of us at once testifies to something universal in the unjaded heart. That we thought our letters alone could eradicate the evil heaped upon our hero affirms our age and naiveté.

I sent my letter that spring, in the twelfth year of my life, decorating the white envelope with red and blue markers, the patriotic colors of the Braves. In summer, a note of thanks came from Atlanta, Georgia, accompanied by a postcard signed, "To Tom. Best wishes. Hank Aaron." Of course, given the quantity of mail, there was no human way for Aaron to have personally answered my letter. But I was convinced he had, and his words endeared him to me. It's not a unique story. That year, Hank Aaron received more mail than anyone but the president. You may have sent one of those letters yourself, and you may have gotten one of those postcards, too. If so, you—like me and tens of millions of others—were probably watching when he stepped to the plate on April 8, 1974.

Some shared moments touch us so deeply that they become part of our national fabric: John F. Kennedy waving from the backseat of a limousine in Dallas; Neil Armstrong stepping onto the moon; the space shuttle *Challenger* exploding in sunny skies over Cape Canaveral. Rarely do sporting events transcend athletics and resonate for the country in such a powerful way.

Yet, three decades later, we still see the stands packed, the field aglow, Hank Aaron swinging, the ball rising, the crowd standing, the humble trot around the bases, two exuberant college-age intruders, the embrace at home plate, a wet-eyed smile, and a white ball clenched and held aloft by a black hand. The images remain indelible.

This book tells the story. It is about Hank Aaron's pursuit of the national pastime's most cherished record. It is about a chase that provoked bigotry, shattered prejudice, and shook stereotypes. It is about a quiet, private man who endured hatred, suffered death threats, and grew more determined to achieve his goal. It is also about heroes and friends and family—and a brief span of time that helped America define itself.

Our story begins in 1972.

—Tom Stanton
January 2004

JACKIE'S FUNERAL

hey came in silence and in somber suits. Thousands of them, many famous, most not, politicians and sports stars and civil rights leaders alongside schoolchildren and factory workers and fans of a team that long ago played in Brooklyn. They came from across the country, by plane and train and limousine, from Washington and Chicago, from Pasadena, California, and Mobile, Alabama, and every borough of New York City, a river of people flowing through the heavy, etched doors of the Neo-Gothic Riverside Church near Harlem, flowing beneath a dingy row of granite angels into the cool, solemn darkness of a sanctuary where the Rev. Martin Luther King once pleaded for peace.

They came for Jackie Robinson.

It was warm for late October, a Friday in 1972, the presidential election just days away. Outside, the sky was bright with sunshine, the crowded pavement drenched in the shadows of the twenty-one-story church. Inside, light filtered through stained-glass windows and touched the wooden pews as mourners strode past the open, gray-blue casket of the man who in 1947 had become the first black to play baseball in the major leagues.

A young preacher, the Reverend Jesse Jackson, gave the eulogy that morning. Standing tall in a full Afro that fell upon the back collar of his black-and-red robe, he spoke of the former ballplayer, his cadenced, deliberate voice buffed by a South Carolina accent. "His powerful arms lifted not only bats but barriers," said Jackson. He looked out at more than three thousand mourners. Among them were Robinson's family; entertainers, activists, and athletes like Joe Louis, Roberta Flack, and Bill Russell; an entourage of forty representing President Richard Nixon; baseball executives; white Dodger teammates such as Pee Wee Reese and Ralph Branca; and a roster of black ballplayers who, within a decade of Robinson's debut, had followed him into the major leagues: Larry Doby, Roy Campanella, Don Newcombe, Monte Irvin, Willie Mays, Joe Black, Junior Gilliam, Ernie Banks, Elston Howard, and Hank Aaron.

They formed a fraternity of sorts, most having played together in the Negro leagues and on barnstorming teams and all-star squads. They had all experienced the indignity of being refused service at restaurants where their white teammates ate, of being forced to stay at seedy hotels and boardinghouses, of playing with and against athletes who preferred they be invisible. They all knew firsthand the wickedness Jackie Robinson had endured. To varying degrees, they had all endured it themselves. And they all had stories to tell.

"He was a tremendous competitor," said Campanella, in a wheelchair since the car accident that ended his career. "The more you got on him, the more he was going to hurt you. Others might have gotten upset in a situation like this but not Jackie. He got better."

"We're all very sad," said Gilliam. "He was one of the greatest all-around athletes I've ever known on any athletic field. I was very close to him, and I learned a great deal from him on the field and off."

Joe Black and Larry Doby had been with Robinson nine days earlier when he was honored before the second game of the World Series. His friends knew he was ill. Diabetes and heart trouble had ravaged him. Though only fifty-three years old, Robinson had white hair, walked with a cane, was blind in one eye and losing sight in the other. He couldn't see well enough to recognize old friends.

Beneath the grandstands in Cincinnati that afternoon, a fan approached Robinson and asked him to autograph a ball. "I'm sorry," Robinson said. "I can't see it. I'd be sure to mess up the other names you have on it."

"There are no other names," the man said. "I only want yours."

When first invited to the World Series, Robinson had declined. He felt estranged from baseball, angry that the sport offered so few post-playing opportunities to minorities. He had been public in his criticism. A quarter century after Robinson broke the color barrier for players, the major leagues still had not hired a black manager. The biases that labeled blacks unqualified for such leadership positions persisted. "If you people expect me to change my thinking, or my speech, you're mistaken because I'm simply not going to do it," he warned the commissioner's office before agreeing to appear. "If the reporters ask me how I feel about baseball still not having any black managers, I'm going to tell them."

But he did not wait for anyone to ask.

Standing before the pitcher's mound with his wife beside him and dignitaries and a military color guard behind him, Robinson acknowledged the applause of the packed stadium. He thanked baseball for recognizing the anniversary of his debut and then concluded by reiterating the dream that he knew he would not live to see. He told a television audience of millions, "I am extremely proud and pleased to be here this afternoon but must admit I'm going to be tremendously more pleased and more proud when I look at that third base coaching line one day and see a black face managing in baseball."

After the game, Robinson visited the clubhouse of the victorious Oakland A's. Some witnesses said he looked out of place, a shadow of the strong man he once was. Some said he looked sad, his eyes glassy. Others noted the indifference of the players to whom he was being introduced. Only John "Blue Moon" Odom lavished attention on Robinson. "There seems to be a feeling among the current black players that they owe Jackie nothing," remarked one observer. It was a notion that Robinson's peers embraced as true—and one that upset them, for they had tried to pass on an appreciation for the sacrifices of Robinson and the other pioneers, just as they had passed their wisdom to them.

Of the more than one hundred black players active in the major leagues in 1972, a mere handful attended the funeral: Aaron, Mays, Willie Stargell, Vida Blue, catcher Earl Williams, and probably a couple of others who went unnoticed. Williams, twenty-four, was a member of the Atlanta Braves and, like teammate Dusty Baker, had heard Hank Aaron talk about Jackie Robinson. Williams had learned of Robinson as a boy, and in 1971, after Williams was named rookie of the year, Robinson had spoken at a banquet honoring him. Williams was dismayed that so few players his age came to the funeral. Baker wanted to be there but his duties as a marine reserve prevented him. He called Williams after the service, and Williams gave him a detailed account.

He might have told him how in Riverside Church that day the Rev. Jackson alluded to the dash that appears on grave markers, separating the year of birth from the year of death. "On that dash is where we live," said Jackson. "And for everyone there is a dash of possibility, to choose the high road or the low road; to make things better or to make things worse. . . . Progress does not roll in on the wheels of inevitability. In order for an ideal to become a reality, there must be a person, a personality, to translate it."

When Henry Louis Aaron—all twelve pounds, some ounces of him—arrived on a Monday in February 1934, no one noticed that his birth date preceded by a day that of one of the most famous men in America, Babe Ruth. Henry had been born into the harshly segregated world of Mobile, Alabama, a port town where the last illicit slave ship docked. He drew his first breath in a poor section of the city called Down the Bay, during the crushing poverty of the Great Depression. Save for his family, no one took much note.

Across an ocean, the ominous rise of Adolf Hitler had begun to grip a nation and alarm a continent. But black Alabamans needed not look to foreign shores to see the face of evil. It flashed in their everyday lives, sometimes before the eyes of the whole country, as in the Scottsboro Case of nine black youths unjustly charged, convicted by an all-white jury, and sentenced to death for a rape they did not commit. It was into this world that Henry Aaron came, and to understand him, one must understand that.

Herbert Aaron, Henry's daddy, loved his sports. But any dreams he harbored for his sons would have been tempered by the realities of the time and the vastly different opportunities afforded black and white athletes. The city of Mobile, after all, had given the world "Satchel" Paige, one of baseball's finest pitchers. But despite his immense talents and because of his dark skin, he spent his prime years competing everywhere other than in the major leagues.

In spring and often in autumn, white players from the American and National circuits would visit Mobile. When Babe Ruth came, it was always news. No star was bigger. A local judge even dismissed his courtroom on a day in 1924 to see the Bambino play. Perhaps it was in that contest that Herbert

Aaron witnessed the great, lumbering, soft-bellied Yankee slug a ball over the fence at Hartwell Field.

Herbert Aaron could not have known that a future son, born on nearly the same date as Ruth (and thirty-nine years later), would someday challenge him for the title of all-time home-run king. On February 5, 1934, he could not have dreamed how the life of his newborn, Henry Louis, would, four decades on, collide with the game's greatest legend—and change his country and its people.

Hank Aaron was a boy of eleven when in 1945 Jackie Robinson sparked the dreams of hundreds of thousands of black children across America by signing with the Brooklyn Dodgers. The next year, Robinson played with the Montreal Royals, a Dodger farm team, and a year later crossed what had been an infinite chasm into the major leagues.

Aaron grew up in Toulminville, in a black section of Mobile. He was the third of eight children born to Herbert and Estella Aaron, one of five boys and three girls over a span of twenty years. His mother, a religious woman who was raised on a farm and permitted no cussing, smoking, or drinking, labored at home, cooking, cleaning, and keeping her kids on the right and righteous path. His father worked on Pinto Island as a rivet bucker at Alabama Drydock and Shipbuilding Company, which during World War II produced Liberty ships. On the side in his spare time, he made moonshine and ran a private nightspot, the Black Cat Club, next to their modest brick home at 2010 Edwards Street. He loved baseball, having played in and around Mobile at roughly the same time as Leroy "Satchel" Paige, Ted "Double Duty" Radcliffe, and other Negro league stars. He had even started the Toulminville Whippets sandlot team. Most of Herbert Aaron's children loved baseball, too, but none more than Henry. The younger Aaron practiced variations of the game every chance he got, slapping at bottle caps with mop sticks, fielding grounders off walls, and hurling lit kerosene-soaked rag balls into the night sky and chasing after them as they fell like meteors. But it was mostly just a joyous way to pass time—until Jackie Robinson. Then it became something more.

The Alabama of Hank Aaron's youth braided a world of contrasts: the poor-folk shacks of Magazine Point with the antebellum mansions of the Old South; the untamed, moss-draped wilderness of Chickasabogue with the preened and proper Azalea Trail; Mardi Gras partiers with gospel singers; creamy magnolia blossoms with orchards of hard-shelled pecans; salt water with fresh water; the Klan with the NAACP. There was at the time no contrast greater than that between the worlds of blacks and whites. Mobile was a place not unlike the one portrayed by Harper Lee in *To Kill a Mockingbird*, and of an era when the word "nigger" flowed as freely as breath from the mouths of many whites. Blacks went to separate, unequal schools and libraries. They stayed in separate hospital wards. They ate in different restaurants, lived in different neighborhoods, sipped from different water fountains, and rode in segregated sections of buses driven by white men armed with guns. "You were never the same after living there," wrote novelist Eugene Walter.

The Dodgers had a Double-A farm team, the Bears, in Mobile, and some springs the team came to town with Jackie Robinson to scrimmage against the minor leaguers. Other years, Robinson came south in September or October with his own group of barnstorming stars. His appearances rated as major events in the city's black community, which doubled in population during Aaron's youth.

Robinson visited on April 3, 1950. An unrelenting rain drenched the city at game time. But it didn't deter the fans waiting outside Hartwell park to enter the "coloreds section" near right field. With strong demand for tickets, officials were reluctant to cancel the game. They waited five hours before making the decision that disheartened the soaked crowd. Jackie Robinson had that kind of following: loyal, committed, enthusiastic.

In autumn he returned to Mobile for a Halloween game with his barnstorming stars, including Roy Campanella and Larry Doby. This time, the weather cooperated. An almost entirely black crowd of 8,000 jammed into Hartwell Field, which bordered railroad tracks and a cemetery. Robinson rounded out his team with Negro league players and did battle with the Indianapolis Clowns, featuring a wispy nineteen-year-old shortstop, Ernie Banks.

Aaron was sixteen. Given his admiration for the Dodger star and his desire to follow Robinson to fame, he probably witnessed that contest. Robinson singled, doubled, and tripled, scoring twice and leading his troupe to a 3–2 victory. At such appearances, Robinson gave talks from the ball field. He introduced the players, thanked the audience, and expressed his pride and joy at being able to perform before a packed house. He frequently had words of advice for the youngest attendees.

Aaron saw Robinson play several times. "He was always crazy about playing baseball," Herbert Aaron said of his son. "But I'd never thought about him becoming a player until the Brooklyn Dodgers came to Mobile for an exhibition game. I took him out to see the game and he told me that night at the ballpark, 'I'm going to be in the big leagues myself, Daddy, before Jackie Robinson is through playing.'" Aaron wouldn't have been the only child making that pledge that game, for Jackie Robinson inspired a generation. When Robinson reached Brooklyn, black children and their parents saw a panorama of promises unfold like a postcard accordion. A ballplayer, huh? No longer could the question be automatically dismissed. Because of Robinson, the possibilities glistened like the yellow bricks to Oz.

Maybe that's what Aaron thought about—that long ago game—at the funeral in Riverside Church, with his brother Tommie beside him. Or maybe his mind wandered to Davis Avenue. Life in Mobile's African-American community centered around Davis. A section of it ran less than a mile from the

Aaron home. They called it simply the Avenue. Black-owned businesses dominated the street, everything from cleaners to clothing stores: the Pike Theater, Jim's Old Fashion Barbecue with its Barq root beer sign, Abrams Barber Shop, Klondike Shoe Shine Parlor, the Gomez Auditorium, Big Mama's Cafe. There were churches along Davis Avenue, a cemetery, the NAACP offices, and the hall of the International Longshoremen Association. When Robinson's travels brought him to the city, he would head over to Davis and walk the Avenue, creating a stir as he did. Aaron not only saw him play, but he heard him speak—always at a place along Davis: Central High School one time, an auditorium another.

At the funeral, maybe Aaron recalled the morning decades prior when rumor spread that Robinson would be uptown that day. Aaron skipped school. A group of young men, aspiring ballplayers, congregated outside a drugstore along the Avenue, waiting for Robinson. He came in suit and tie and told the fellows that they couldn't all make it to the majors. "Stay in school," he said. "Stay in school." It was advice Aaron failed to heed. He cut classes regularly, landing in trouble at Central High, where he got expelled. A year later, after baseball discovered him, Aaron fulfilled a promise to his mother and finished his secondary education at a private school, Josephine Allen Institute. "They sort of walked him through the front door and out the back and—surprise!—his diploma was waiting," said a Mobile scout, Bill Menton.

As a teen, Aaron played sandlot ball and fast-pitch softball. His break came one evening in 1951 when a Negro league scout, Ed Scott, decided to escape the choking heat of his home by taking in a local softball game. He discovered the slender Aaron lashing the ball across the diamond. Aaron's style was unconventional. He swung cross-handed, gripping the bat with his left hand above his right, and he hit with his weight on his front foot rather than his back. But he connected, spraying the field with authority. Scott invited Aaron to play with the Black

Bears, a semi-pro team comprised of older athletes. It took some convincing before Estella Aaron consented, but when she did Aaron blossomed on the field. Scott brought him to the attention of the Indianapolis Clowns, a traveling Negro league team, which the following spring brought him aboard.

At eighteen, as the youngest member of the Clowns, Aaron roomed with Jackie Robinson one night before an exhibition game. It was 1952, and the Korean War raged in Asia. An international figure, Robinson teased the quiet Aaron. "He said he would tell the draft board about me if I got too many hits against his team," Aaron said.

Major league scouts soon began noticing Aaron, too. That summer, he made the leap to professional baseball, signing with the Braves, and he began to bridge the huge gulf between hero-worshiper and ball-playing peer. After impressive stints with the Braves minor league teams in Eau Claire, Wisconsin, and Jacksonville, Florida, Aaron was a rookie with the Milwaukee Braves in 1954, heading north after spring training. The Braves traveled with the Dodgers, and often Aaron would sit in the same hotel rooms as Robinson, keeping his mouth shut as the young players were expected to do, soaking in the words and wisdom as Robinson and Campanella and Newcombe and other black veterans played pinochle and talked. From those conversations, Aaron took away one overriding lesson: "For a black player in our day and age, true success could not be an individual thing."

During his first Milwaukee season, when Aaron suffered bigots, Robinson urged him to be calm. "Don't let a few crazy people bother you," he said. "Just play hard." Maybe Aaron thought about that in Riverside Church. Or the game in 1955 when Robinson, a runner at third base, tricked Aaron, playing second, into relaxing his throwing arm long enough to allow him to score. "Before I knew it, he was sliding into home," Aaron said. "He was a fierce competitor. He told me, 'You don't play baseball once a week. You play every day. First thing you do is try to get on first. Then on second. Then third and then home.' Every time he put on a uniform, he went out to win."

Over two decades, Aaron and Robinson shared other conversations by phone and in person at games and functions. The talks grew longer and more personal in Robinson's last years. At a 1971 exhibition in honor of Martin Luther King, Robinson steeled Aaron's will for the pursuit that lie ahead—the final push to surpass the legendary Babe Ruth, to better his record 714 home runs, and claim the exalted title of all-time home-run king. "I will never forget," Aaron said, "that he told me to keep talking about what makes me unhappy, to keep the pressure on. Otherwise, people will think you're satisfied with the situation." Hank Aaron took that advice to heart. But could either of them truly have envisioned the troubles rising on a hazy horizon?

In Riverside Church, the Rev. Jesse Jackson said that Robinson was not a puppet of God. "He had options. He didn't have to do what he did," Jackson said. "He said 'yes' in 1947 when he wanted to say 'no.' He could not hold out for himself. . . . Pride in the black community welled up when he took the field. He reminded us of our birthright to be free." Some in the church called out in agreement. Jackson said the greatest tribute to Jackie Robinson would be for baseball to fulfill his last request and name a black manager. Listening to the eulogy, Hank Aaron realized that with the sports world focusing on his home-run pursuit, he would be in a position to push the issue.

"History," Jackson implored, "calls on all of us to do something."

INVINCIBLE BABE

abe Ruth did not invent the home run. It just seemed as if he had. When Ruth debuted with Boston in 1914, Roger Connor reigned as champion, but it wasn't a vaunted throne. Connor, who retired before the Wright Brothers took flight, never led the National League in home runs. But over his eighteen-year career he accumulated 138 of them. The game was then, and in George Herman Ruth's early years, played in a slap-and-dash style. During the Dead Ball era, men like Ty Cobb, Honus Wagner, Tris Speaker, and Eddie Collins set the tone with their wild-on-the-bases, hit-for-high-average, speed-oriented play. It was an age in which a hitter, Frank Baker, could earn the nickname "Home Run" by knocking out eleven or twelve balls in a year.

Ruth changed everything. He began as a pitcher—and a successful one, winning seventy-eight games in a four-season span. But his batting skills electrified fans. By 1919, he was playing almost full-time as an outfielder. He hit 29 home runs that year, nearly three times more than any other American Leaguer. Baseball officials had earlier introduced a livelier, cork-core baseball. In 1920, they aided hitters further by banning spitballs and other "freak" pitches. Ruth, by then a Yankee, clubbed 54 home runs. George Sisler of St. Louis was next closest with 19.

That season marked a turning point. Though Ty Cobb and other players of his time viewed Ruth's showy, prodigious blasts as detracting from the sport's gamesmanship, spectators loved the long ball. Attendance rose dramatically, by nearly 40 percent. The Yankees saw their figures more than double. The next year, 1921, in the wake of gambling indictments against members of the Chicago White Sox, Ruth scorched another 59 home runs, surpassed Connor, and, according to historians, saved the sport from its betting disgrace. From 1918 to 1931, Ruth led the American League in home runs all but two years, endearing himself to the public as no other athlete had ever done. They affectionately called him the Bambino or the Sultan of Swat or by such less-inspired alliterative efforts as the Behemoth of Bust or the Rajah of Rap. Reporters portrayed him as boyish at heart, a true Horatio Alger "rags-to-riches" character, a touch naughtier and a tad less industrious. Ruth's insatiable appetites for food, liquor, and women—earning the same kind of wink as Prohibition beer—seemed proportionate to the size of his home runs. He epitomized the Roaring Twenties. They even named a candy bar, Baby Ruth, for him. (Yes, the company claimed it was in honor of President Cleveland's daughter Ruth, but that was a transparent lie. Ruth Cleveland had died in 1904, seventeen years earlier.) Babe Ruth was a rollicking soul whose fame exceeded athletics. Valentino, Lindbergh, Henry Ford, Al Capone—Ruth toiled in no one's shadow. He shone as a sun among smaller stars, and neither time nor death would diminish him.

In the decades after Babe Ruth retired in 1935, fans and writers mused about which players, if any, might challenge his most famous record. It was a dreamy exercise, for Ruth's 714 home runs were viewed as untouchable. The fun was in the fanciful speculation. Maybe Jimmie Foxx will do it, they said in 1938 after he hit 50 home runs a second time. Or how about Hank Greenberg, who hit 58 the same year? But Foxx faded in his early thirties, and Greenberg struggled with injuries—and enlisted in a world war. Ted Williams? Perhaps, but for those five years of military service. Ralph Kiner? He didn't last long enough. Mickey Mantle? Plagued by bad knees. Willie Mays? Possibly, if not for San Francisco winds and Candlestick Park.

Few prophesized that Hank Aaron would unseat Babe Ruth. He seemed to sneak up on the record, which was fitting. Since his youth, Aaron had been exceeding others' expectations. Aaron's father thought another son, Herbert, would be the better ballplayer, but it was Henry who persisted. When a slightly built teenage Aaron showed up for a Brooklyn Dodgers tryout, organizers quickly dismissed him in favor of more confident, athletic-looking prospects. His high school coach had mentally tabbed another player as his third baseman until he saw Aaron swing a bat, and a Mobile-based scout, who should have known every prospect in his region, wasn't aware of Aaron until his team got word that the Braves were interested. Aaron's sandlot peers respected his abilities but none thought him the area's richest talent. Even when he rose to the major leagues—promoted not because he had pushed a regular out of the lineup but because the regular, Bobby Thomson, had injured himself—Aaron played for years before upstaging teammates Eddie Mathews and Warren Spahn. Aaron set goals, refused to bask in his successes, worked hard to improve himself, and methodically pursued his unspoken ambitions until—surprise!—someone would suddenly discover him near the finish line. He was the tortoise, not the hare; a marathoner, not a sprinter. "My father once told me," he said, "to never run any faster than you have to to get the job done."

Aaron had always been a quiet star, a shade of gray against a rainbow of Mays, Mantle, and Duke Snider. He spent his career in small markets, Atlanta and Milwaukee, away from the national spotlight. He lacked the flamboyance of his better-known peers. While others flashed like fireworks, Aaron burned like a candle. Prior to 1973, he annually averaged—averaged—104 runs, 35 home runs, 178 hits, and 107 RBIs. He was a testament to consistency, never hitting 50 home runs in a campaign but usually topping 30. And they weren't Harmon Killebrew–sized monsters, they were line drives that often just cleared the fences and left the pitchers who surrendered them feeling ambushed.

But Aaron did not play in anonymity. Through 1972, he had appeared in twenty All-Star Games. He wasn't invisible. He rated among the game's dominant players; there was no denying it. But into the late 1950s and most of the 1960s, he could not step from the soaring reputations of the two men— Mays and Mantle—whose names danced on dreams and flirted with fans' fantasies. In acclaim, Aaron fell far short of both. The monthly magazine *Baseball Digest* featured Mantle on its cover five times in the decades of Eisenhower and Kennedy. Mays made it three times, as did Ernie Banks. Even Pittsburgh shortstop Dick Groat captured a pair of covers. But Aaron didn't make it once in that period. With *Sport* magazine, Mays landed on the front seventeen times; Mantle, sixteen; Aaron, twice before 1970. Mays and Mantle struck *Sports Illustrated* a combined eight times before Aaron found his way there—a decade and a half into his career.

The differences in attention weren't easily attributed to performance. In their first seven seasons, Mantle, Mays, and Aaron compiled similar records. They hit a comparable amount of home runs (Aaron had a slight edge), and they led their leagues in the crucial categories roughly the same amount of times. Other factors—visibility, personality, explosiveness— accounted for the difference. Mantle spent his entire career in New York with a team that dominated the World Series. He hit powerful, awe-inspiring blasts. Mays played in New York and San Francisco, captivating crowds with his charismatic style. Aaron's quiet nature didn't divert attention from his better-known peers, but eventually his numbers did.

His fine seasons—of 34 home runs here and of 45 there and

of 39 and 40 and 44 and . . . —accumulated inconspicuously. Then, in the long summer after the assassinations of Martin Luther King and Robert Kennedy, Aaron recorded home run 500 and realized that if he stayed healthy he would have a shot at the record. Aaron passed Mantle in 1969 and then Mays in 1972. "While all of you were talking about them, I was wondering about me," he said. The media had begun to pay attention, too. "Unsung Hero," read a headline in the *Wall Street Journal*. "The Finest Hours of a Quiet Legend," said *Sport* magazine. Aaron finished 1972 with 673 career home runs, 41 shy of Babe Ruth, 41 shy of what the *Saturday Evening Post* termed "the mountain . . . the most glamorous jewel in the crown of sports achievement."

"From here in," proclaimed the *Sporting News*, "Aaron is the number-one story in sports."

Maybe, but not everyone was impressed. Writers and fans alike picked at Hank Aaron's statistics, noting that it had taken him thousands more swings to approach the same plateau as Babe Ruth. Aaron averaged a home run every sixteen at-bats; Ruth, one every twelve. Babe's boosters sniped that though Aaron might hit more home runs, he would never be the true champion. "With Aaron," wrote Tom Boswell of the *Washington Post*, "conventional figures are paradoxical—they seem to say he is the foremost offensive player when most fans sense that, great as he is, Aaron has not been able to pull away from contemporaries Mays and Mantle, let alone challenge Ruth. . . ."

The sport had changed since the 1920s and 1930s, and the changes benefited pitchers, not batters, making Aaron's numbers all the more remarkable. Ruth hit his home runs during daylight; Aaron played mostly night games. In Ruth's day, there were no cross-country flights to regular-season contests in a time zone three hours away. The major leagues had expanded no farther west than St. Louis, and the trains that transported players at least had sleeping berths (not that Ruth used his much). Aaron also played during an era that saw the rise of relief specialists. In 1927, when Ruth hit 60 home runs, starting pitchers completed nearly half of their games, meaning batters were more likely to face tired arms in the late innings. A half century later in 1967, starters finished about a fourth of their games. Pitchers dominated, allowing almost a run less per game, and batters' averages dropped thirty to forty points.

But, Ruth's supporters asked, what of those seasons in Boston when the Babe was primarily a pitcher? What if he had been hitting home runs then? What chance would Aaron have now?

Well, others countered, how about Yankee Stadium, a park with cozy dimensions—295 feet down the right-field line—tailored to Ruth's abilities? What about the slider, which was developed later?

"It's all pointless," Aaron said of the comparisons. "We're two very different players from different times."

But it wasn't just about numbers. There was a sense, too, that the man who deposed the great Babe Ruth should be as colorful a personality, able to win hearts and sway crowds with a chummy wave and a sanguine grin. He should inspire whimsical articles about his gluttonous exploits and be pictured in newspaper photos making funny faces at babies and be seen at the ballpark pointing to the outfield fence, as if revealing the flight of his next missile. But Hank Aaron did none of those things. He hardly even smiled after hitting a home run.

Babe Ruth's admirers were scattered throughout the baseball world in 1973, happily reliving his exploits and achievements. Aaron triggered not only their memories of Ruth, but also their myths about him. Ruth "was so powerful," said Buzzie Bavasi, a longtime executive, "that when he whipped a bat you could see the hickory bend." Yankee teammate Waite Hoyt described him "as one of a kind. . . . If he had never played ball, if you had never heard of him and passed him on Broadway, you'd turn around and look." Houston manager Leo Durocher, who had once roomed with the Bambino, recalled, "Ruth hit balls so high that the infielders would lose sight of them . . . and when they dropped Ruth would be standing on third with a triple hit no farther than fifteen feet beyond second base." Another cohort remembered how after a night of drinking Ruth would show up in the clubhouse, guzzle a glass of bicarbonate of soda, and burp so powerfully that "all the loose water in the showers would fall down."

Contrasted against such legend, Hank Aaron seemed as plain as raisin-less oatmeal. Reporters could spend days with him in hopes of discovering a telling detail that might capture the essence of the man or provide a bit of color to bring him to life for readers (or, at least, make him more interesting). But Aaron didn't gulp six hot dogs at a sitting or mix a dish of Ma Gehrig's pickled eels with chocolate ice cream or go on drinking binges or wear full-length camel-hair coats or appear in movies or in Vaudeville or spend his nights cavorting with a half-dozen showgirls, staying out until dawn. You wouldn't find Aaron doing "the bump" at a happening dance club. He was a man of moderation, a half-pack-a-day smoker who enjoyed an occasional beer and took care of himself, getting plenty of rest, exercising in the off-season, eating light on game days. He was of average height and build and old-fashioned in ways, preferring, for example, plain leather cleats to the new, fancier, plastic-soled Adidas variety. Aaron drove a Chevy Caprice, for God's sake, and, as one reporter who followed him to lunch discovered, drank two glasses of ice water with his meal and liked the lima beans. No one had ever named a candy bar after him.

But Babe Ruth, that lovable lug, now he was a story. A true hero. A giant of a man. Looked like a pear on chopsticks, but wow, could he hit that ball. Stood out like a cardinal in snow. Such an inspiration. Who would have guessed? And what a beginning, what a tale . . .

In truth, George Herman Ruth's reputation hid a sad, sorry start. Ruth was born to neglectful, abusive parents who lived above, and worked at, a rough Baltimore bar, where young George picked up the bad habits, crude manners, and profane language that would last him a short lifetime. His parents surrendered him at age seven to St. Mary's Industrial School for Boys, a combination reformatory/orphanage, and rarely visited him. It was a harsh beginning. His parents died before he reached age twenty. His mother went first, and his father followed in 1918, his skull cracked in a street fight after Ruth had established himself in the big leagues. By most accounts, he had gone to one of his son's games. The sentimental, soft-hearted man that Babe Ruth became—best illustrated in his undying affection for children—sprung as a reaction to his own miserable boyhood. "His love for children was genuine," said his daughter, Dorothy.

Hank Aaron also grew up in poverty but he was surrounded by a close, nurturing family, where he was expected to behave, respect elders, cut firewood, and go to church on Sundays. "Teach good words," said his mother, Estella, "and they don't know nothing else to say." His father, Herbert, said he and his wife raised their children "with love, with good in mind." The Aarons were "home folks." Henry, in particular, preferred to stay near the house and around his mother—except for baseball. "My children," said Mrs. Aaron, "liked to be together. In the yard, put them by themselves, they liked to stay with themselves." Though Aaron, a Boy Scout, got along with others, he had few close buddies and, through high school, only one girlfriend that anyone remembered.

For both Aaron and Ruth, baseball provided a path to unlimited possibilities and prosperity—a road to a wider world neither knew. At age nineteen, after a few months in the minor leagues, Ruth was promoted to the Boston Red Sox. A year later, his team won the World Series. It all happened so quickly for him. One minute in a reform school, the next, playing with Harry Hooper. The Sox won the championship again in 1916 and 1918. Ruth was just twenty-three, and the star of the team by that point, an extrovert with an unquenchable lust for the fast life. The fact that he was already married to Helen Woodford, the teenage waitress to whom he had proposed while she served him breakfast at a diner, made little difference to him. The saga had begun.

Aaron was eighteen in 1952 when the Braves signed him and sent him to their Class-C farm team in Eau Claire, Wisconsin, where for the first time he played with and against white athletes. It provided his introduction to integration, something he had only heard about. A shy soul, stricken with homesickness, Aaron stayed at the YMCA with teammates. He impressed quickly, earning a spot on the league all-star team and winning rookie of the year honors. His sophomore season took him closer to home, to Jacksonville, Florida, another Braves' affiliate, where years earlier Jackie Robinson had been barred from playing. Aaron led his team to a pennant and won the batting title, RBI crown, and most valuable player award while integrating the Sally League with teammates Felix Mantilla and Horace Garner (and two opposing players, Fleming "Junior" Reedy and Al Israel). Initially, white fans refused to applaud them. Everywhere, hecklers peppered them with racist names. In Montgomery, Alabama, they threatened to bring rifles to games and shoot them. In Savannah, Georgia, police poured onto the field to prevent a race riot after Mantilla had been pegged by a white pitcher in retaliation for a home run by Aaron.

"Playing in the Sally League was quite a bad experience for me," Aaron said in 1964. "Some of the names I was called, I never had heard them in my life ... Jigaboo, burr-head—I'd never heard down home, or maybe I heard them but they went in one ear and came out the other. Maybe I was too dumb as a kid to get mad. I'm not hot-tempered. I wouldn't think about what a fan would say to me from the stands. He could never get my temper up to where I'd go in the stands after him."

Babe Ruth also endured racial slurs. Because of his facial features, he was called "Nig," or "Nigger," by the boys at St. Mary's. The nickname followed him into the professional leagues, where opponents like Ty Cobb learned that they could quickly rile him with the insult. Though no proof ever surfaced to indicate that Ruth was of African descent—his parents were believed to be German—the rumor persisted. (In defending Aaron from racist taunts in 1973, incidentally, the *Chicago Crusader,* a black newspaper, even alluded to it: "Check the pictures of him and you will notice the broad nose and the lips that are attributed to the black people.... Are you not making too much fuss over the possibility of one black man breaking the record of possibly another black man?")

In Jacksonville, Aaron became enamored with a black, green-eyed beauty, Barbara Lucas, a college student who lived with her parents in the projects near the ballpark. They married after the season, and their daughter Gaile arrived about the same time. Aaron was nineteen and not making much money on a minor leaguer's salary. His mother offered to help raise Gaile. She spent much of her early childhood in Mobile with her grandparents.

The next spring, Aaron trained with the Braves in Bradenton, Florida. He seemed destined to be headed back to the minor leagues when Bobby Thomson, known for hitting what to that point had been baseball's most famous home run, broke an ankle. Aaron replaced Thomson and stayed with the team, his .280 average hinting at his promise. By his second season, he had become a National League All-Star, driving in more than 100 runs. He won his first batting title the year after, and in the following summer clinched a pennant with an eleventh-inning home run, assuring him a place in the heart of Milwaukee baseball fans. The Braves upset the Yankees in the World Series. Aaron contributed three home runs, knocked in seven, and scored five.

That same year, 1957, brought the birth of three more Aaron children: Hank, Jr., in March and twins Lary and Gary prematurely in December. Gary died in the hospital, and Lary, who was sickly, soon went to live in Mobile with his grandparents and sister. Another child, Dorinda, arrived in 1962 on her father's birthday.

Babe Ruth had at least one child, Dorothy. She was not

born to either Helen or his second wife, Claire Hodgson. But both women helped raise her. Ruth had become involved with Hodgson—and a harem of other women—while married to Helen. For him, infidelity was not a rare indiscretion. It was a lifestyle, which in 1925 earned him a serious case of syphilis and a hospital stay. (Indigestion, the newspapers reported.) Ruth wed Hodgson after Helen died in a fire.

The Babe was better with other people's children than his own. His visits to hospital wards were sincere (and well publicized). "He could be so communicative with total strangers yet so distant from his own family," said Dorothy Ruth Pirone. "The public knew my father as an emotional, uninhibited individual: rejoicing after home runs, arguing with umpires, and weeping openly at the funerals of close friends. . . . Babe was no saint, but then he never tried to be someone or something that he wasn't."

In the public's mind, he remained boyish all his life.

By the time the Braves moved to Atlanta in 1966, Hank and Barbara Aaron had begun to drift apart, their teenage marriage strained by the changes in both of them. Soon, he was toying with the wilder side of the ball-playing life. Aaron was, in his own words, "losing my innocence." He and Barbara divorced quietly in February 1971. The children continued to live with their mother. To escape the pain of being separated from them, Aaron immersed himself in his work—baseball—and hit more home runs than he ever had before.

Aaron's four children were never far from his mind. He talked to them almost daily. In 1973, the oldest, Gaile, was studying journalism in college. Sons Hank, Jr., and Lary, were attending Marist High, a Catholic school where they played sports, and, like youngest daughter Dorinda, living in Atlanta. Aaron frequently drove them to school, and at times the kids stayed with him. "They don't look at Aaron as if he's a superstar," said their mother. "He's just their dad. . . . He really misses them. Aaron's out at school every day, watching them practice. The boys are good athletes."

When he had been their age, Hank Aaron knew little of Babe Ruth. "For years, the only way I related to him was as the guy with the big stomach," he said. "I didn't think anymore about him." Of course, that had changed.

Ruth died in 1948. But a quarter century later, his wife Claire still resided in their eleven-room, parquet-floored apartment at 110 Riverside Drive, overlooking the Hudson River in New York. Mementoes from his playing days decorated the place: honey-colored baseballs, tarnished batting trophies, a needlepoint portrait of her husband, black-and-white photos of him and Lou Gehrig. It looked like a museum. Mrs. Ruth had even kept piles of yellowed newspapers. "I don't care how many home runs Aaron or anyone else hits," she said that winter of 1973. "They cannot replace the Babe. Lindbergh was the first man to fly nonstop across the Atlantic. Nobody remembers who was the second or the third. So it is with the Babe."

've worked awfully hard to get my name up front," noted Hank Aaron before spring training. "I've waited for my time, and it's just now coming."

While some painted Aaron's quiet demeanor as monk-like humility, he was a proud man. He did not boast or brag or gloat, but he pursued his goals until he reached them. And he did intend to topple Ruth's record. It would have been nearly inhuman to be so close to the prize and not be driven to achieve it. But it wasn't merely pride that motivated him. By shattering the home-run mark, Aaron would show there were no limits to the achievements of black players. He would slam an exclamation point on the accomplishments of his predecessors, and maybe, like Jackie Robinson, impact the larger world.

"I could do it this year," he said.

3

SPRING IN FLORIDA

pring training opened under sunny skies Thursday, March 1, in West Palm Beach, Florida, and thirty-nine-year-old Hank Aaron was there on the first morning of drills, running with rookies half his age. Eddie Mathews watched from the dugout at Municipal Stadium, his eyes hidden behind metal-rimmed sunglasses. Mathews, beginning his first full season as manager, appreciated that Aaron was trying to set an example for the young ballplayers, but he didn't like the sight of his star sprinting across the grass. He didn't need Aaron pulling a muscle.

"Hank!" Mathews bellowed. "Aaron! Get in here right now."

Aaron jogged off the field smiling.

"What in hell do you think you're doing?" Mathews blustered.

"I was running with Curt Blefary," Aaron said. "We're not going to outrun the young ones."

Blefary was one of several veterans in camp getting a last shot at the major leagues. He had been American League Rookie of the Year in 1965. Now he was twenty-nine, his career almost over. Like Blefary, most guys in camp had been born in the 1940s or early 1950s. Aaron was the only player whose days stretched back to the mid-1930s and the final seasons of Babe Ruth.

Aaron was of the same generation as his manager, and he and Mathews knew each other well from having played thirteen seasons as teammates, often hitting together in the order. Though their personalities contrasted—Mathews was a drinker, rowdier, more temperamental than Aaron—they got along well and appreciated one another. When Aaron ascended to the major leagues in 1954, Mathews was already an all-star third baseman and the National League's defending home-run champion. That August he would become the first subject to appear on the cover of *Sports Illustrated*. In 1959, if you had asked a baseball fan whether Mathews or Aaron was the more likely to challenge Babe Ruth's record, most would have picked Mathews. One annual heralded him as "Bambino of the Braves"; another, as "Babe in Beer Land." But injuries hampered Mathews. He finished playing at age thirty-seven in 1968 with 512 home runs, sixth on the all-time list behind Ruth, Willie Mays, Mickey Mantle, Jimmie Foxx, and Ted Williams. Together, Mathews and Aaron hit more home runs than any pair of teammates. That was Eddie Mathews' proudest achievement as a major leaguer.

By 1971, Mathews had been out of the sport a few years, selling bonds. He hated it. "You don't realize how you're going to miss baseball," he said. "It's all you've ever known, really, and you never quite realize how important the game, the players, the association, and the fans were to you." Mathews returned as a Braves coach under manager Lum Harris and replaced him late in the 1972 season. The team finished fourth with a 70–84 record, twenty-five games behind first-place Cincinnati.

Mathews set few rules, his philosophy being "the more rules you have, the more trouble you've got." He was a tough taskmaster, hard-nosed and with an ironclad sense of right and wrong, and he could come off as an arrogant know-it-all. He disliked players who did not give their best and had little tolerance for complainers and whiners. "You just have to get to know the guy," Aaron said. "He's one of the finest people I've ever met." Mathews' promotion meant that Aaron had a friend and ally in the manager's office as the countdown to 714 began. He could relate to Aaron on several levels. He had been a star. He knew the toll the game took on older players and, most important, he knew Aaron well enough to anticipate Aaron's concerns. Evidence of that surfaced early at camp.

Baseball wisdom says the legs go first. As a player ages, he slows. To compensate, a team will move a veteran slugger to first base. The Braves tried it with Hank Aaron in 1971, in part to preserve Aaron but also because of injuries to Orlando Cepeda, the regular at the position. It was a major change for Aaron, who had been a right fielder since 1955, and he performed well in seventy-one games at first. In 1972, with their outfield crowded with talent, the Braves made the change permanent, selling Cepeda to Oakland. Aaron played more than a hundred games at first base. Though he managed 34 home runs, Aaron watched his average spiral downward to .265—his worst yet and forty points below his norm. He knocked in just 77 runs, his lowest total since his rookie year, and he made 14 errors, second highest in the league behind Willie Stargell. Aaron disliked playing first base, and coming in to camp he intended to ask Mathews if he could return to the outfield. But Mathews asked him first.

"I'm through making a fool out of myself," Aaron said. "I'm sure that when the Braves put me in the lineup as a first baseman, they figured it would save my legs. Maybe that's true. But that's all it saves. It almost ran my head crazy. When I'm in right field, I can relax between pitches. It gives me time to reflect."

Mathews planned to move Darrell Evans from third to first, giving twenty-year-old Rod Gilbreath a shot at the hot corner. A month into the season, Gilbreath would lose the job, Evans would be back at third, and outfielder Mike Lum would be at first.

Mickey Mantle, who spent his last seasons as an infielder, empathized with Aaron. Playing outfield had become second nature after fifteen years. First base, however, drained him mentally. There was one glimmering benefit, though. "At first base, you're so involved in the game that you don't notice the fans so much," Mantle said. "The outfield is the worst place for that. . . . You can hear about everything those people in the bleachers say."

Which had never posed a problem for Aaron.

Prior to the 1972 season, Hank Aaron signed a three-year contract with the Braves. At $200,000 a year, it made him the highest-paid player in baseball. Dick Allen had since surpassed the figure, but no one on the Braves earned half as much. The average major leaguer took in $36,500 a year, and some players got as little as $15,000. Aaron made three to thirteen times more than his teammates, a fact he suspected aroused secret jealousies in the locker room.

Several Braves players—Evans, Pat Dobson, John Oates, Paul Casanova, Marty Perez, and Dusty Baker—missed the March 1 start of training camp. While Evans was on duty with the marines, the others were holdouts, playing their hands for more money, a common negotiating practice in the days before free agency.

Dusty Baker, twenty-three, felt he deserved a raise. He had batted .321 in his first full season and been named Brave of the Year. But for him the absence was not just about dollars. Independent and stubborn, Baker chafed under a club policy that prevented his girlfriend from sharing a room with him at team headquarters. So while his friends stretched and ran and threw in Florida, he stewed in Georgia—and got married. Baker wed Harriet Washington, whom he had met through teammate Ralph Garr in Louisiana. It was a small, hastily planned affair. He couldn't invite his ball-playing buddies, seeing as they were otherwise occupied, and he certainly didn't tell his strict parents. When he finally reported to Braves' camp a week late, Baker brought his new wife and they stayed at the Ramada Inn—together.

Since 1963, the Braves had been training in West Palm Beach, a town larger and farther inland than its affluent, better known, oceanfront neighbor. On windy days, the smell of the sea salted the air around Municipal Stadium, the centerpiece of the baseball complex. Beyond its right-field fence sat three fields for minor leaguers, mostly prospects not long out of high school, plus a few veterans like Tommie Aaron, Hank's brother.

On the map of baseball, Hank and Tommie lived worlds apart. Though both played in Georgia—one in Atlanta, the other in Savannah—their day-to-day lives couldn't have been more different. Hank had reached the zenith of the sport. He traveled on planes, stayed in suites, made great money, and lived in the spotlight. Tommie Aaron, who had tasted the major-league life over parts of seven seasons, worked in the Double-A minors, struggling as a thirty-three-year-old for one last un-likely shot at the Show. For him, it was low pay, bus rides, and occasional hotel stays. No room service. Once a man has played in the big parks, he has trouble surrendering the dream. Tom-mie Aaron—"T-Bone" to friends—wasn't alone in that respect.

Had it been a typical year, reporters might have focused on the latest comeback of one-time Tiger standout (and gambler) Denny McLain or the emergence of Garr and Baker among the league's top hitters or the team's newest members: catcher Oates, second baseman Davey Johnson, and pitchers Dobson, Roric Harrison, Danny Frisella, Gary Gentry, and Carl Morton, whom the Braves hoped would invigorate their weak mound staff.

But there was nothing typical about the year. Hank Aaron, on the cusp of his grand pursuit, dominated all coverage. Jour-nalists flew in from New York, Boston, Chicago, and Los An-geles to talk with Aaron, and he granted interviews to even those from the smallest papers. "Guys are coming out of the woodwork," he said. "Now, they want to know everything.

Where the hell were they twenty years ago? Now, they're here and they want me to drop everything I'm doing and talk to them." And frequently he did. Everywhere Aaron went cameras snapped and flashed, reporters with microphones followed, and crowds gathered. His teammates recognized that this season would be different from any they had witnessed. So did Eddie Mathews. The slogan he chose for his club—"We're all in this together"—seemed more a resignation of what was to come than an affirmation of team unity.

For weeks through spring training, interview followed interview—one observer counted fifteen in one day—the questions frequently the same.

"Do you think you'll break Babe Ruth's record?"

"Can you pass Ruth this year?"

"Will you play next season if you top Ruth this year?"

"What did you hear about Babe Ruth while growing up?"

"Do you think you're better than Ruth?"

Their names—Aaron and Ruth—were as inseparable as characters in a book. Stories regularly reported that Aaron was chasing Babe Ruth's ghost. In truth, it was the other way around. The ghost trailed Aaron. "There's not a day that goes by that I'm not reminded of Babe Ruth," he said. By May, Aaron would be exasperated by the comparisons. "This Babe Ruth thing is something I would like to get away from," he would say.

As spring progressed, Aaron grew weary of interviews. He felt hounded, and it was just beginning. "Hell, pretty soon I ain't going to be able to go the bathroom without someone watching me," he noted.

The title of all-time home-run king threatened to redefine Hank Aaron in ways he didn't appreciate. He considered himself well-rounded and multiskilled, and his achievements confirmed it. He had led the league not only in power categories (home runs, runs batted in, slugging percentage), but also in runs, average, hits, and doubles. He had stolen at least twenty bases in six seasons. He had won Gold Gloves for his fielding. But increasingly fans measured him only by his ability to hit home runs, which perturbed him. Aaron had never been a traditional long-ball slugger. He hit line drives, not towering cloud scrapers. He had never popped more than 47 in one season. What Aaron did was play with unparalleled consistency and amass a brilliant record in numerous areas.

Worried that the home runs would overshadow him, Aaron downplayed their importance, going to almost ridiculous lengths to show that Ruth's feat didn't mean all that much to him personally. He said that he viewed Ty Cobb's hits record as more significant. He contended that nailing a runner with an excellent throw brought him greater gratification than clouting a home run. Belting a triple, he said, rated as the most exciting event in baseball. It bothered him to be thought of as merely a home-run hitter. "I like to think of myself as a complete player," he said. "I feel I do have to prove something."

That Aaron, approaching baseball's pinnacle, still felt he had something to prove spoke to his deeply held sense that he had not yet received proper recognition for his talents and contributions. A pamphlet issued in the spring by the Baseball Hall of Fame corroborated his view. A year prior, the hall had published a flyer that highlighted artifacts contributed by Willie Mays and others not yet inducted. Through the years, Aaron had donated several items to the Cooperstown institution. He had given the museum his 3,000-hit ball and the bats with which he registered home runs 500 and 600. Aaron had complained in writing in 1972 when the pamphlet ignored his donations but hyped those of Mays. Now, a year later, with Aaron permanently ahead of Mays in the home-run tally, the new edition of the publication had been released—with no mention of Aaron. And he was upset. "With all of the things I have done, I think they should at least include my name in that magazine," he said. Aaron said his days of donating to the museum might be over. "To hell with it all."

When Aaron spoke—even when angry—he used a calm, reasoned voice that in person softened his sharp words. He made his point without yelling or thumping his fist. He took pride in his ability to control his emotions. After home runs, he trotted the bases somberly. After strikeouts, he returned calmly to the bench. As far as anyone could remember, Aaron had been tossed from only one game. In 1966, after being called out on strikes, he gave the umpire his bat. "You've been taking the bat out of my hands all day," Aaron said. "You want it so bad, take it." When perturbed, Aaron usually responded with silence. Initially, anyway. He simmered and sometimes boiled, and once angry, once offended, he held grudges. He never forgot. On the rare occasions when his gathering steam erupted in fury, he would regret his actions. Aaron got into a fistfight with Rico Carty on a 1967 team flight after Carty had called him "black slick." "It was the most embarrassing thing that ever happened to me," he was still saying years later.

"Things do bother me but I react differently from other people," he said. "Some guys go 4–0 and throw their helmets or kick things. But I think, 'Why did I pop up? Why did I strike out?' This is how I try to teach my kids—to sit down and figure it out. . . . I always feel there's room for improvement. Like if I hit two homers and double, I wonder why I wasn't able to hit three homers. In a way, I'm never satisfied."

Atlanta hitters struggled through the early weeks of spring training. By mid-March, the Braves had lost nine straight. Mathews ordered extra batting practice for his starters but that produced no results. "I've had about enough of this character building," he said. "It's getting to be a damn joke."

Finally, on a wet and stormy Wednesday, Hank Aaron walloped his first home run and lit a rally. "He was the one who finally showed us the light," said Mathews. Aaron guided the Braves to a 5–2 victory over the Dodgers and clipped Atlanta's losing streak. "Everything's going to be all right, skip," said Ralph Garr, beaming at Mathews. But Garr's assessment was premature. The team kept losing, and Mathews called a meeting to straighten out his players. "Hell, three and fourteen will get to anyone after a while," he said. "We should have at least, the very least, eight wins right now."

The losses didn't deflate the fans, preoccupied as they were with Hank Aaron and the prospect of getting his signature. One morning, as Aaron chatted in the shade of the Braves dugout, a boy popped his head over the edge and asked, "May I have your autograph, Mr. Aaron?" Aaron obliged but stayed out of sight. Soon, two more children leaned over the edge. "I guess I should stand on the steps or one of these young fellows might fall in here," Aaron said. He autographed a few more items. "It's a small thing to sign your name on a piece of paper. I can remember driving around Atlanta looking for the Jackson Five rock group because my kids wanted their autographs. I know how kids feel when they want mine."

Which didn't mean that Aaron signed tirelessly or indiscriminately. He turned down requests. Like all athletes, he frequently ignored the calling fans out of necessity. "It's just impossible to sign autographs for fifteen hundred kids in a crowd," he said. Aaron picked his moments, which, given his popularity, were never numerous enough to satisfy the demand. Inevitably, he left a trail of disappointment. When he refused at a spring game in St. Petersburg, a fan hurled an orange at him.

Aaron felt relief when spring training ended and the Braves headed north to begin their regular season. "Really, spring training is the hardest part for a player after you've been around this long," he said. "Mainly you're concerned about getting in shape when you're my age. . . . I think I'm ready."

4

THE QUEST BEGINS

n New York, Newsday greeted the 1973 season with a huge photo of Hank Aaron on the front of its sports section. "The most exciting chase in all of baseball history!!" announced the headline.

Despite his team's lousy spring record, Eddie Mathews talked optimistically. "There were a lot of years in Milwaukee when we had bad spring training records, and then would come back and win during the season," he said. Mathews felt this might be one of them. He had a solid, improved club. He liked his lineup. He knew that the Braves had plenty of hitters, and he felt that the perennial question—pitching?—had been answered through trades for Pat Dobson, Carl Morton, and Danny Frisella. Plus, his guys were excited and enthusiastic. Hank Aaron agreed. "Don't let those games in Florida fool you," he said. "It has been a long time since we have had a team with the attitude this team has."

What Aaron wanted most from the new season wasn't a home-run record, he said, but a return to the World Series. Team before self—he had always played the game that way. It had been almost fifteen years since the Braves faced the Yankees in October 1958. The Braves lost that rematch. A decade and a half later, three key members of the team—Aaron, manager Mathews, and pitching coach Lew Burdette—had reunited with the Braves, a reminder of distant glories. Aaron wanted to taste victory once more. "I've known Eddie Mathews for more than twenty years," he said, "and he is going to be a successful manager."

The Braves launched their 1973 season on April 6, a Friday night. It was in the first game that Aaron noticed some boos, which surprised him. His $200,000 salary seemed to irritate some fans. But the season had just begun. "What was my crime?" he would ask. Aaron went hitless, and the Braves lost to Houston in thirteen innings. It was not the start Aaron or Mathews had envisioned.

Atlanta slumped early in the season. After twelve at-bats, Aaron had nothing to show but a line of zeroes. In the fifth game, he broke his streak against San Diego, welcoming rookie Rich Troedson to the majors with a blast over the left-field fence. But the lead of the United Press International recap didn't mention the hit. "Henry Aaron says he isn't thinking about home runs," the story began, "but there are signs that the pressure is already getting to the Atlanta Brave star in his quest to become baseball's all-time home-run king."

"I try not to think about the record," Aaron said. "I just go up there and do the best I can."

Aaron got his second home run, number 675 of his career, the next night. "It was a low slider that was going to hit him in the ankle," said pitcher Fred Norman. "I thought he was fooled by the pitch, he started to swing so early. But he still hit it over the fence."

The Braves headed north to Los Angeles Friday, where manager Walt Alston and his staff decided to pitch around

Aaron. "We've made up our minds that we simply won't pitch to Henry when the game is on the line," said left-hander Tommy John. "It's silly to give one of the game's great hitters anything good."

John walked Aaron twice. Claude Osteen, who had surrendered more homers to Aaron (13) than any pitcher other than Don Drysdale, also walked Aaron twice the following day. Los Angeles fans booed when Osteen did it on four straight pitches in Aaron's last appearance. In the third game, Aaron walked once but teed off against Al Downing in the ninth inning for his third hit—and third home run—of the year.

I t was cold in San Francisco. Fans in turtlenecks, leather jackets, and fur-hooded coats clumped around the edges of the Braves dugout Tuesday in the chilled confines of Candlestick Park, awaiting Hank Aaron. When he emerged, they called to him and drew him to a corner of the dugout. He stood on the steps, out of sight to all but the nearest smiling patrons. One artist-fan gave Aaron a three-foot portrait of him striding into a pitch. Aaron dutifully signed programs and scraps of paper and handed them back to their owners, making little eye contact, aloof as usual. He looked tired and glum.

Maybe it was his team's performance. The Dodgers had swept the Braves, dropping them into last place. Or maybe it was his growing sense, accurate or not, that most fans wanted him to fail. Or maybe—and this seemed more likely—it was his slump. He had three hits in twenty-six at-bats. All were home runs. Observers wondered if Aaron, who had been the consummate team player, was now swinging selfishly for himself. He said he wasn't but his performance pointed to a different conclusion. And it frustrated him. For a man trying to remind the world that there was more to him than home runs, he was failing miserably.

At least in Candlestick Park, Aaron didn't need to worry about adding to that perception. The place had been stingy with him in recent years. Since 1968, he had recorded only two home runs there. The stadium's wild wind gusts killed long balls. It had, by most accounts, reduced the career numbers of Willie McCovey and Willie Mays, who played more of their games there than anywhere.

Mays had departed for New York in 1972, but McCovey remained in San Francisco. He and Aaron often talked before games. Like Aaron, McCovey had been raised in Mobile, Alabama, an area that produced a disproportionate number of quality players for a city of 200,000. Billy Williams, Cleon Jones, Tommie Agee, and Amos Otis all came from Mobile. The connection wasn't lost on any of them. Aaron called them his "homeboys." They sometimes socialized together. Aaron always chatted with Jones when the Braves played the Mets, and he enjoyed meals at Agee's home.

McCovey, born four years after Aaron, admired him. He had seen him play as a boy when both lived in Mobile. As a tribute to Aaron, McCovey wore the same uniform number, 44. The number had proven magical for Aaron. Four times in his career he hit 44 home runs in a season, and in one of those years, 1963, he and McCovey tied for the league lead, both reaching that figure.

At six-foot-four, McCovey was taller and more powerful than the six-foot, 190-pound Aaron. His physical presence— his ability to deliver enormous blasts—intimidated pitchers. Baseball fans liked to speculate what McCovey might have accomplished had he avoided injury. Only four times did McCovey exceed five hundred official at-bats in a season. Aaron did it sixteen times—ten of those surpassing the six-hundred mark. "Two to three years ago," said Aaron, "I would have told you Willie McCovey would be the greatest home-run hitter in the game. If he hadn't hurt himself, he'd have topped all the records."

McCovey's output had dropped dramatically by 1973. He still wielded a dangerous club, but another San Francisco Giant attracted more praise. Twenty-seven-year-old Bobby Bonds, beginning his sixth season, qualified as an oddity: a leadoff hitter who combined speed with power. Hank Aaron was undeniably the biggest news in baseball but even he thought Bonds was the best all-around performer.

Bonds and Dusty Baker were no strangers. They knew each other well. Baker's father had coached Bonds in Riverside, California, and Dusty, a few years younger, viewed him as a big brother. By 1973, Bonds had become one of the Giant team leaders. It was common for him to bring his eight-year-old son, Barry, to the park. He had been doing it for years. Bonds' teammates enjoyed pitching to Barry, and detected in him at an early age an unflagging confidence and heavy dose of cockiness. Some guys even threw the youngster fake brushbacks. In the clubhouse, players maneuvered carefully around the boy when he wielded a bat, for Barry Bonds would swing it without paying heed to who was walking near him.

Over the three-game set against Atlanta, Bobby Bonds got six hits, scored five runs, and led his team to a sweep of the Braves with a dramatic extra-inning blast in the final contest. Hank Aaron finally stroked his first non-home-run hit of the season, a double, in the cold Tuesday nightcap. When the Braves flew out of San Francisco for Cincinnati, Aaron's average lay at .122. He felt terrible. The team's mark had sunk to 3–9. Nothing was going right.

And it wasn't just Aaron. No one was hitting. Not Ralph Garr or Dusty Baker, who had finished second and third in the league in batting in 1972. Not Darrell Evans. Not the new guys. Not even the scrubs. No one.

Of his teammates, Aaron felt closest to Garr, Baker, and Paul Casanova. They had nicknames for one another. Garr and Baker, both African-American, frequently called Aaron "Supe," short for superstar. Casanova, a dark-skinned

Cuban, called him "Ham," an abbreviated version of "Hammer" (which the catcher had difficulty pronouncing). Garr was "Gator," Casanova was "Cassie," and Dusty, born as Johnnie B. Baker, Jr., was, well, Dusty, or "Bake."

Baker and Garr came as a pair—"loud and louder," one teammate tagged them. They had adjoining lockers. They roomed together. They played beside one another in the outfield, along with Aaron, and after road games hung out or hit the town as a duo. Both had signed with the Braves in 1967. Garr was four years older, having gone to Grambling for his bachelor's degree. Despite the age difference, Garr and Baker had come through the farm system at the same time, starting with Austin in the Texas League. Both debuted in the majors in September 1968 and bounced between Richmond and Atlanta in the years after. Garr stuck with the Braves in 1971; Baker in 1972. They both had something else in common, as well: Hank Aaron had watched over them from their earliest days with the club.

When Garr came to his first training camp, the Braves matched him with Aaron, one of his heroes growing up in Louisiana. Young Hispanic and African-American players often got paired with Aaron. The Braves felt he would be a good influence, personally and professionally. Garr, a jokester, connected easily with others, and he hit it off immediately with Aaron, who loved to laugh. "People would see us knocking around together and I liked that," Garr said. In camp, Aaron used to give Garr his old gloves, and Garr accepted them as if blessed by God. The Braves liked the sway Aaron had with Garr and asked him to tutor him on defense one winter. "Hank will talk to you all day about baseball if you ask him about something," he said. "But he does not think it's his place to come to you. If you're interested, you go to him."

Aaron appreciated that he had a serious student. "Of all the ballplayers I've seen, Garr has the best, smartest attitude," he said. "If Ralph thinks he can learn something from you he will sit and listen and learn and use it. . . . When I came up I just sat in a corner and listened. Today, I sit with a bunch of rookies and I got to wind up listening to them. . . . Often, you find a talented kid coming up and he has that little bit of resentment toward you for the simple reason that you're at the level he wants to be. He feels, 'Hell, he made it his way, I want to make it my own way' and he doesn't want to take advice."

Enter Dusty Baker, touted as the next Hank Aaron.

Baker grew up in California and had a reputation for being rebellious and not taking advice well. In camp, before being cut, Denny McLain had called him a "know-it-all smart-ass." (Not that McLain was a respected arbiter of character.) Baker's relationship with his father defined him. John Baker, Sr., was a stern authoritarian, who cut Dusty from a team he coached for not chasing a fly ball. Dusty's parents divorced while he was in high school, back in the days when he would sand the name off the barrel of his bat and etch it with his own, Dusty "The Hammer" Baker.

Baker's father, a civilian military employee, wanted Dusty to go to college on a basketball or football scholarship, so he discouraged baseball teams from drafting his son. As the oldest of five children, Dusty felt he should contribute income to his mother. Signing a baseball contract offered one way. "The night before the draft, I prayed I wouldn't get picked by the Atlanta Braves," Baker said. He despised everything he thought he knew about the South: the Klan, the racism, George Wallace and Lester Maddox, the civil rights killings. He had attended high school in Carmichael, a short drive to San Francisco's Haight-Ashbury Hippie Haven and the music he so loved—Jimi Hendrix, Carlos Santana, Janis Joplin. The South seemed the antithesis of his free spirit. But the Braves hooked him in the twenty-fifth round, and in that summer of 1967 invited him to a workout at Dodger Stadium.

It was difficult for a seventeen-year-old not to be impressed on that warm afternoon. Here he was just weeks out of high school, standing on the diamond where Sandy Koufax and the

1965 World Champion Dodgers had played, taking batting practice with National League stars like Rico Carty and being paid attention by one of the team's top hitters, Felipe Alou, who gave him a game-used bat. And then there was Hank Aaron. The famous Hank Aaron. Baker asked him whether he should choose college or baseball. Both, Aaron recommended. If you think you have the talent, pursue baseball with everything you've got, Aaron said—and get the team to agree to pay for your college education. But the pivotal moment came when Baker's mother, Christine, sought a pledge from Aaron. She worried about Dusty playing in the South and asked Aaron a favor. Would he watch over Dusty as if he were his own son?

If Aaron, as the defending National League home-run champion, felt the request out of line, he did not let on. He simply agreed to keep an eye on Dusty, and Baker and his mother signed a contract with the Braves—against the wishes of his father, who contested in court. The battle prompted Dusty to cut his father from his life.

Baker ate meals regularly with Aaron's family. He was four years older than Aaron's daughter Gaile—closer in age to any of the four kids than to their daddy. As he worked his way through the minor leagues, Baker discovered that Aaron had friends and family watching him. Aaron's brother-in-law at the time, Bill Lucas, was a minor league administrator with the Braves, and Tommie Aaron was playing in the system. "When I got to the big leagues, people said I knew everybody," said Baker. "But it was because I was with Hank."

Aaron's relationship with Casanova was different from Garr's and Baker's. Casanova wasn't among Aaron's protégés. He was closer in age and had established himself as a top defensive catcher with the Washington Senators before coming to the Braves in 1972. Born and raised in Cuba, he had followed baseball in the newspapers. In 1957, when Aaron and the Braves played the Yankees in the World Series, Casanova watched the games with two hundred other fans on a television that had been dragged into the streets of Colon. Within two years, he had come to America to pursue baseball dreams. For a while, he played with the Indianapolis Clowns, the traveling Negro league team on which Aaron had been discovered.

F ew places match the dynamics of a clubhouse. In baseball, you start with twenty-five guys who come from different regions and backgrounds. Some have graduated from college, others barely escaped high school. Some grew up well off, some poor. They may speak different languages and even vary in age by as much as two decades. Further, while vying against one another for playing time, they must also compete as a team to succeed. Humor helps bridge the differences, keep the atmosphere light, and create camaraderie.

In a radio interview one evening, Davey Johnson had blamed his poor batting performance in 1972 on an arm injury that he said effectively left him disabled. The next afternoon, a teammate, finding the alibi humorous, replaced the name above Johnson's locker with that of a single-armed outfielder who had played for St. Louis in 1945. "Pete Gray," read the tag. Such teasing abounded in the clubhouse, most of it good-natured: shoes filled with shaving cream, a locker wrapped with toilet paper. After Ed Kranepool spiked Dusty Baker's foot, Baker's teammates draped his stall with a cane and a large bandaged rabbit's foot.

One night, Baker and Garr had stayed out too late after a game. Baker arrived at the clubhouse the next day exhausted. "I'm going to Hank and see if he has anything to help me," he told Garr. He thought Aaron might know of an energy juice, a vitamin shot, or a pill that would provide pep.

"Yeah, I got something to help you," Aaron said. He gave Baker a tablet. "This will take care of you, baby."

Baker took it with coffee. Soon, after a trip to the restroom, he returned, his face flushed with alarm. Baker pulled them into the john and showed them the toilet water, which was red.

"You think I'm dying?" he asked.

Aaron and Garr burst out laughing. Aaron's pill had produced the desired effect, discoloring Baker's urine. Aaron laughed so hard that he cried.

The Braves locker room granted little privacy. Players stripped and dressed in the open. They hung their streetclothes in stalls that had no doors. They showered in a common area. They heard of one another's troubles and indiscretions. They saw when Mathews had words for a teammate. "What you see here, what you say here, what you hear here, let it stay here when you leave here," read a sign posted on the white cinderblock wall.

What all of the Braves knew in the final week of April—what everyone who watched the team knew—was that Hank Aaron was struggling. The home runs were coming at a fast pace but his average was no higher than a hot day in Havana. Early in his career, Aaron had been a line-drive hitter who scattered shots across the field. But in latter years, he had become a pull hitter. He shortened his swing by pulling his hands down and closer to his body. (Mathews had left the Braves as their third baseman, and Aaron felt he needed to swing for the fences more than ever.) Now, teams were using a shift against him, sliding the shortstop closer to the third baseman and anchoring the second baseman behind the base. The shift closed holes on the left side of the infield, which meant Aaron either had to hit the ball over the infielders' heads or be content to put it in the opposite field, where he no longer hit for power.

Aaron himself felt ashamed of his low average. Critics said that he was swinging for home runs. He chafed at the suggestion. Worse, he suspected that his teammates felt sorry for him. "I don't ever want anyone feeling sorry for me," he said. He also didn't want to put Eddie Mathews in the awkward position of having to bench him. Mathews deflected such talk, labeling it as premature. But the thought did occur to him. How could it not? His star hitter's average languished a hundred points lower than that of the other starters. Home runs or not, Aaron's performance was hindering the team. Mathews knew that if the situation didn't improve he would have to consider all options.

Aaron realized that he must turn his season around. But his slump had him baffled. "There's no real explanation for it," he said. But maybe there was, maybe he just hadn't admitted it to anyone—or even himself. Aaron had learned from his father that you keep some things to yourself. "I worked in a shipyard for twenty-nine years and never made a fuss about anything," said Herbert Aaron. "I think one of the reasons Henry has done so well is that he has kept his mouth shut."

5

ATLANTA HEARTBREAK

ver 42,000 exuberant fans piled into Riverfront Stadium on a Friday in April, a record for a non-opener in Cincinnati. More than half of them walked up to crowded ticket booths an hour or two before the evening's game, securing seats for a surprisingly large homecoming for the defending National League champions, who had been on the road for ten days. Even in spring it looked like Christmas at the park, the pristine emerald-green Astro-Turf serving as a backdrop for Cincinnati's ornament-red uniforms. The team had enough stars to decorate a tree. Pete Rose, Joe Morgan, Johnny Bench, and Tony Perez formed the nucleus of a squad that dazzled fans with energy, excitement, and talent.

The Reds overwhelmed the Braves with superb defense. Bobby Tolan made what some described as the best catch ever at Riverfront, diving all-out to prevent a base-clearing hit. Rose nailed a Brave at the plate and robbed another of a run-producing drive, and Bench landed one of his signature single-handed tags on a close play. The lone Atlanta highlight occurred in the third inning when Hank Aaron followed a Dusty Baker double with his fourth home run. It came off twenty-two-year-old Don Gullett, the seventh he had given to Aaron in three-plus seasons. The Braves lost their tenth game. "It takes a strong man to go through what we're going through," said Baker.

The crowds in Cincinnati provided a discouraging contrast for the Braves when they returned home. In Atlanta, attendance was dismal: 3,400 one evening, 2,800 the next. They were the kind of nights where, in Ralph Garr's words, "You could throw a bomb in the place and not kill anyone." And they were becoming common. At half of their first ten home games, the Braves drew fewer than 4,000 fans—abysmal for an ordinary year, shameful given Aaron's pursuit.

In that respect, the season had begun ominously weeks earlier when the Braves started their home schedule with a poorly attended clunker: a Friday night contest before the smallest opening-day crowd in the National League. In most cities, the opener set off a daylong celebration that saw executives and line workers call in sick and children beg their way out of school. It was like that in Cincinnati, where 51,579 witnessed the festive start of the National League schedule, and in Cleveland, where 74,420 packed the city's cavernous stadium beside Lake Erie. Pittsburgh drew 51,695 to its opener, and Chicago attracted 40,273 to Wrigley Field. In Detroit, the bars around Michigan and Trumbull overflowed with joyous revelers. But in Atlanta, a gathering of only 23,385 had watched Hank Aaron begin his march to immortality. The club would top that figure a meager five times over the next eighty home games. Weak numbers would plague the Braves throughout the season. They would average 11,774 per gate in Atlanta, with annual attendance hobbling past the 800,000 mark in a league where the median approached 1.4 million. If Atlanta fans cared about Hank Aaron's pursuit, they weren't proving it with ticket sales.

The Braves had moved from Milwaukee to Atlanta in 1966, lured by Mayor Ivan Allen, who had built a stadium as an enticement for some club—any club—to move south and anoint the region. The city had welcomed the Braves, the first major league franchise to call the South home. It seemed an ideal fit. The Braves had fallen on hard times in Wisconsin, and Atlanta—birthplace of Martin Luther King, Jr., and the heart of the civil rights movement—yearned to prove itself leader of the enlightened New South. More than 50,000 fans cheered the Braves' 1966 debut. Over that inaugural year, 1.5 million sampled the attraction. The move to Atlanta appeared a success. But as the novelty wore off, attendance decreased. It dropped every year with one exception, 1969, when the Braves won their division. By 1972, turnout had fallen beneath a million. Some of it was simply a matter of performance. Often, the Braves had been lackluster. But other factors contributed as well. At least part of the explanation lay deeper in the psyche of the city through which General Sherman had marched a century past. Old sentiments seethed in the New South.

When the Braves relocated to Atlanta, half of their everyday players were white, including two stars, Mathews and Joe Torre. By 1971, the team had a noticeably darker complexion, and, aside from pitchers, all of the prominent players—Aaron, Garr, Rico Carty, Orlando Cepeda, Earl Williams—were black or Hispanic. The club contended for a division title that year, finishing eight games out, but fan support slipped further. "They could have put eight top-rated black ballplayers on the field when they chose to," said San Francisco's Bobby Bonds. "They were a competitive team because of these men. And yet, for no obvious reason, most of these players were not with the Braves the next year." Bonds accused the Braves of rebalancing the team racially to make it more palatable to white fans. The Braves did unload regulars Carty, Cepeda, Williams, and Felix Milan in 1972. But in fairness, injuries plagued Carty and Cepeda, and Williams and Milan were sacrificed for direly needed pitching. Still, the result was a lighter-looking lineup.

Color mattered to a considerable block of Georgians. Aaron had worried about it when the Braves first talked of leaving Milwaukee. Like other blacks on the team, he had no desire to move to Georgia. The memories of his rough times in Jacksonville were fresh enough, and life in Wisconsin was good. His family had settled comfortably in a suburb, Mequon, and the kids were doing well in school. Life was rougher for blacks in the South, and Aaron's children had never experienced the kind of segregation that still existed there. He announced that he didn't want to play in Atlanta. But when the team's transfer became unavoidable, Aaron, realizing he had no choice, muted his objections. "It doesn't make any difference where I play," he said. "I've got to play somewhere." Still, he and Eddie Mathews kept their families in Wisconsin at first, renting apartments in Atlanta during the season.

It undoubtedly upset some Southerners that the team's franchise player was an African-American. Mayor Allen argued that Aaron's race wasn't an issue. "The first time he knocked one over that left-field fence, everyone forgot what color he was," said Allen. But Aaron knew better—or would learn. White residents departed his Atlanta neighborhood after he moved in; white parents squelched backyard games of football with his sons; a white police officer pointed a gun at his wife and threatened her life; a white referee targeted his son on the basketball court. Aaron knew better even if he didn't often raise the subject.

Aaron had never been a lightning rod in racial disputes. He was not radical or militant. Though he spoke out on issues, particularly related to baseball, he took care to distinguish himself from the Stoakley Carmichaels and Eldridge Cleavers of the world. He wasn't a Black Panther. He didn't subscribe to the views of Malcolm X. He never riled the conservative soul the way Cassius Clay had by becoming Muhammad Ali, a Black Muslim and conscientious objector. He wasn't Tommy Smith or John Carlos at the 1968 Olympics thrusting his fist in a Black Power salute. Aaron did not wear gargantuan orange Super Fly hats as Joe Frazier did or bold polyester-print jumpsuits with spangled belts as Wilt Chamberlain might. He dressed smartly but conservatively in coats and ties. He sported a clean-shaven face and a short haircut. He was a devoted father and a person of faith, not ashamed in his later years to carry a Bible to the ballpark. Aaron seemed an appropriate match for Atlanta.

But now, at the zenith of his career, as he approached the game's ultimate record, local fans avoided the ballpark. It ate at Aaron, and in a rare moment he admitted it. He said he preferred playing on the road and suggested that the Braves' poor attendance stemmed from bigotry. "Here I am with all these records behind me and the big one so close in front of me and no one really cares," he said. "If I were a white man going for the record, the place would have fifteen to twenty thousand every night."

Team president Bill Bartholomay, caught in an awkward position, wore an understanding public face. He didn't blame his potential customers, the fans; he blamed the team's performance. "The won-lost record has dimmed the enthusiasm," he said, and there was a scent of truth in those words. Besides, what else could he say—that large sections of the state of Georgia, which as late as 1971 had a segregationist governor, might not be thrilled by Aaron's progress? Otherwise, regardless of the team's mediocrity, wouldn't crowds eventually materialize as Aaron neared important plateaus? At some point, presumably, local fans would feel compelled to witness the drama being hosted in their town, to capture a glimpse of a season that promised history, to root Aaron toward his goal, to honor him.

Perhaps it would happen on Hank Aaron Poster Day. The first 20,000 youngsters, after all, would get a free Aaron poster. But fewer than 12,200 people came out for the game. Plenty of posters were left over. And then on a pretty Saturday evening in the summer—the day after Aaron hit number 699 and stood poised to join Ruth on the 700-home-run pedestal—two-thirds of the park was empty. Aaron delivered the momentous blast before 16,200 fans.

The story played out differently on the road, where Aaron and the Braves drew enthusiastic crowds: 37,000 in New York, 40,000 in Cincinnati, 60,000 in Philadelphia, 35,000 in Los Angeles. Aaron was not the sole draw, but his presence boosted attendance. Fans everywhere else showed their appreciation, frequently greeting him with standing ovations. They booed their own pitchers for walking Aaron. They cheered Aaron even when his hits cost their home teams victories.

"The fans here are so nice to me," Aaron said in Montreal.

"I've always enjoyed it here," he said in San Diego.

"Pittsburgh has always been one of my favorite cities," Aaron proclaimed between games against the Pirates.

"It was good to hear the applause when I came to bat here," he said at Wrigley Field. "Chicago fans have always been fair to me."

In Milwaukee, Brewers fans gave him a long-distance standing ovation after it was announced that he had belted two home runs—in Montreal. Two cities even staged Hank Aaron days, and in Los Angeles, Dodger management promised to reward any fan who retrieved an Aaron home-run ball with free tickets, an autograph, and a photo with the slugger. Atlanta might not appreciate Aaron, but other towns did.

In early June, Chicago was enjoying new acclaim. The recently completed Sears Tower had marked it as home to the world's tallest building, and Chicago baseball fans were intent on demonstrating that they too could rise to such heights. Callers to radio stations urged listeners to give Aaron a massive welcome. The papers got on board, too.

At Wrigley Field, fans stood amid the box seats behind the dark brick wall and between and around the dugouts to watch Hank Aaron take batting practice on a Saturday. Aaron stepped into the cage. But before he managed a swing, the spectators did something they rarely did at batting practice. They cheered. He hadn't yet hit the ball and they were cheering. Those who had been seated stood and applauded. It was spontaneous, unprovoked, and genuine. Aaron popped some balls into left field before depositing one among the bleacher bums beyond the ivy-covered outfield wall. They cheered again.

Aaron did not start. But in the eighth inning, with his team down by one run and pitcher Ron Schueler due up, Aaron got the nod from Eddie Mathews. The crowd—30,702 fans, the vast majority white—"showered an ovation on the magnificent slugger that probably no enemy player here has ever received," reported the *Tribune*.

"It was a very moving thing, and there's no question he deserves it," said Cubs manager Whitey Lockman.

With the game close, pitcher Rick Reuschel didn't want to walk Aaron. But "I wasn't going to give him a good pitch," he said. Reuschel served Aaron three straight balls. The booing intensified with each one. Aaron took one strike, fouled off a second, and then watched the third go by. He locked eyes in quiet protest with umpire Ed Vargo.

In 1973, the Braves would set a record while visiting other parks, attracting 1.5 million—their highest road draw in their eight Atlanta seasons. "I'm a lot more comfortable on the road," Aaron said. "I feel I'm playing in front of people who appreciate me.... I don't know why it's come to this. I've never really been any trouble to anybody before."

H ad the home crowds simply been small, Atlanta's ambivalence toward Aaron's quest might have provided a ripple. But among the few fans attending were some who were growing more vocal.

On a Friday in late April, Tom Seaver of the Mets opened a

series against the Braves that would change the tone of Aaron's season. Seaver wasted no pitches, mixing fastballs, curves, and sliders with precision, speeding through the Braves lineup with barely a bump. Arguably baseball's most-prized pitcher, he retired the first nine Braves. In the fourth, he got Ralph Garr to fly out to Willie Mays, who with just one hit on the season was struggling more than Aaron. Seaver enticed catcher John Oates to slap a harmless grounder to second, which brought Aaron to the plate.

A major leaguer since 1967, Seaver experienced a slight twinge each time Aaron strode toward the batter's box. As a youth in California, he had rooted for the Milwaukee Braves and idolized Aaron. He was a boy the year Aaron and the Braves upset the Yankees in the 1957 World Series. "I lived and died with them every day of the season, and Aaron was my hero," he said. "I used to play that I was Henry Aaron in my backyard when I was twelve years old, imitating his swing and his mannerisms." Now, as an adult, Seaver continued to follow Aaron's career, checking the Atlanta box score each morning to see whether he had gained ground on Babe Ruth.

The first time Seaver encountered Aaron was as a rookie. He was twenty-two, Aaron was thirty-three. "As he approached the plate, I knew so well what his every action would be—how he'd put on his batting helmet with both hands, how he'd carry his bat, how he'd walk, what the expression on his face would be—that I deliberately turned away from him and stared out to the outfield." In their initial meeting, Seaver got Aaron to ground into a double play. The next time, though, Aaron drove one over the fence. He had adjusted to Seaver, outsmarted him. Seaver learned that pitchers weren't the only thinking athletes on the ball field.

Hank Aaron wasn't endowed only with famously quick wrists. Equally important, he had an encyclopedic knowledge of pitchers. He knew their strengths and weaknesses. He remembered how they approached him, how they got him out, and which pitches they liked to use in specific situations. He realized that a young pitcher who struck him out on a curveball would likely go to his curveball at the crucial moment the next time he faced him, and he would be waiting. He knew that an experienced pitcher would be wilier in such situations. Through much of his career, Aaron would relive his at-bats after games, mentally logging the information and learning from his mistakes. Ted Williams, one of the game's foremost experts on hitting, praised Aaron as a serious student. "He knows more about the pitchers in the National League than anyone playing today," Williams said.

In Atlanta on Friday night, with 7,500 fans in the seats, Aaron stepped to the plate and performed the intimidating routine that Seaver knew so well. He carried his helmet to the plate, staring at Seaver while pulling it onto his head. He always wanted the pitcher to get a good look at the enemy. After Aaron settled into the box and looked out to the mound, Seaver pinched the bill of his blue cap and skated his fingers across the brim of it. He tugged the back of his hat, rocked into his rhythmic motion, and delivered a hanging curveball. Aaron popped it unceremoniously into the left-field stands. Seaver's no-hit shutout vanished with the ball. Darrell Evans followed Aaron to the plate. He was thinking, too. "After the mistake he made to Hank, I figured he might be a little upset and rear back and throw it extra hard." Evans guessed fastball, and Seaver delivered one. Evans put it out as well. With two consecutive pitches, the Braves were ahead 2–0, providing the only margin they would need. After the game—it took merely an hour and thirty-six minutes—Seaver was gruff. "Get away from me," he snapped at a writer. "Get away before I start yelling."

Despite Aaron's winning performance, a few spectators in the right-field seats needled him throughout the night. It was a taste of what was to come.

Even heroes get booed. Players know to expect it. Fans pay their admission and buy the right to have their say. Sometimes they cheer and clap and whistle and sometimes they vent. Usually, they direct their venom at visitors, at opponents from other towns. But not always. Boston fans belittled Ted Williams. Philadelphia fans savaged Pennsylvania-born Richie Allen. Even Babe Ruth endured rough times in New York.

In twenty seasons, Hank Aaron had heard the occasional catcalls of leather-lunged critics. It was particularly rough when he played in the minors in Jacksonville, Florida, breaking the Southern League color barrier. But as a National League veteran with a clean reputation free of controversy, Aaron provoked little ire. Aaron was like Willie Mays in New York, Brooks Robinson in Baltimore, and Al Kaline in Detroit—one of the sport's respected senior statesmen. Fans treated him well. Except in Atlanta as he approached Babe Ruth.

The hecklers' words turned harsher and more personal the day after the Braves beat Seaver. Stationed in the outfield stands, a few men yelled that Aaron was no Babe Ruth. They told him that he wasn't worth the $200,000 he got paid. They insulted his family. They called him "son of a bitch." They called him "nigger." The abuse spanned innings. By the end of the game, Aaron, hitless, had taken all that he could tolerate. He approached the outfield fence with fists clenched and challenged one man, threatening to kick his ass if he didn't shut his damn mouth. The man continued until security intervened.

In the meantime, criticism of Aaron's play mounted. A letter writer to a local paper urged Mathews to bench his "bunch of old cripples." He complained, "One Atlanta star charges the fans some three hundred dollars every time he carefully places that blue batting helmet on his head."

The *New York Daily News*' Dick Young, one of the nation's best-known sports columnists, had been in Atlanta for the Mets series and asked Aaron about the abuse being directed his way. Aaron said that he could handle criticism of his play but would no longer endure "loudmouth redneck" bigotry. "I don't have to take that crap," Aaron said.

"Just as it was with Roger Maris," wrote Young, "the beauty of baseball is turning to something ugly for Hank Aaron, something inexplicably hostile, something he feels the urge to flee from." Aaron expounded on the subject over the next weeks. "All there is" in Atlanta, he said, "is hatred and resentment. It's getting to be pretty nasty already and you know the closer I get, the nastier it's going to get. . . . They seem to sense I'm getting into an area where no black man has a place to be. . . . All I want is to be treated like a human being. . . . Five years ago, I probably would have walked away from it but now I just feel I've taken all I can."

Aaron's words resonated with Jackie Robinson's advice: Speak about what makes you unhappy. And he did.

"These people start in and never let up," Aaron said. "Some loudmouth keeps hollering I'm not as good as Babe Ruth. Hell, this guy doing all the hollering, he ain't half as good as me. I take one look at him, see he's about my age, and know he never saw Babe Ruth in his life. Then they get on this thing about me not being worth the money I'm getting. I've always earned what I got. Nobody ever gave me anything for nothing. The only thing I can figure is this guy's old lady kicks him out of the house on Saturday, and he says to himself I'll go out there and get on the boy in right field. I'm sure he doesn't call me Aaron. He probably calls me 'that boy.' "

The controversy triggered a flood of compassionate publicity for Aaron, who found he had plenty of defenders. They just didn't come to the park in big numbers. One Atlanta editor confessed that Aaron had become a "whipping boy" for folks who still believed in separate but equal water fountains.

"It is inconceivable," wrote another, "that the player who has been cheered elsewhere more than any Brave in history should be cursed in his own park."

Eddie Mathews vowed that the club would protect Aaron. Chairman Bill Bartholomay pledged the same. "There's no question we will do anything we can," he said. "Unfortunately, this is something Henry, or any great black athlete, has had to face all his life. It's something that began with Jackie Robinson and apparently still goes on today." Sam Massell, mayor of "the city too busy to hate," wrote an open letter to Aaron. "You're a hero—Atlanta's hero. . . . Don't let the bums get you down," he said. Massell led an entourage to a Braves game and sat in the outfield near Aaron to ensure that no one berated him. In print, one fan publicly implored Aaron to ignore the jibes. The bigoted comments were human nature, he said. "If it were Babe Ruth out there the fans would be throwing out insults about his obesity or Joe DiMaggio's Italian ancestry or Mickey Mantle's crippled legs or even Lou Gehrig's fatal disease," he wrote.

In Philadelphia, the Braves were engaged in the longest game in their Atlanta history. It went twenty innings before the Phillies won. Ralph Garr batted eleven times and got one hit, and his team stranded a record twenty-seven runners. But it was Dusty Baker who squandered an apparent victory by dropping an easy fly ball. "Man, this is the freakiest year I've ever seen in my life," he said.

Mathews, livid over a close call at home plate, slammed his fist on a locker-room desk. "Damn it!" The defeat dropped the team's record to 7–16. The next day, Mathews benched Garr. Partly obscured in details of the marathon game was a major lineup change. Mathews had started Hank Aaron in left field, not right. "I'm moving him because of his arm," he said. "He simply can't make the throw from right field any more." Aaron admitted as much. He suspected that he hadn't gotten in good shape at spring camp. His legs felt weak, and his arm had lost strength. Over the winter, Atlanta had moved back its right-field fence, creating more territory to cover. The move made sense for the reasons Mathews stated, but observers suspected an ulterior motive: Mathews switched Aaron to insulate him from name-callers. He denied it. But in left field Aaron would have the Braves bullpen directly behind him, providing a cushion between him and the fans. He would be in friendlier territory.

Amid the uproar, one Atlanta newspaper ran a lighthearted and ill-timed feature about quirky baseball fans. Its title: "Those Crazy Fans: They Keep the Players Laughing."

News of Aaron's troubles did not boost attendance at Atlanta Stadium, and sympathetic public support did not end the racist comments. The two problems, in fact, fed each other. Sparse crowds meant that a lone voice could carry to the field undisturbed and into the ears of a superstar—or a $10-a-day batboy like Gary Stensland. From his spot near the dugout, Stensland heard Aaron taunted almost nightly. The sixteen-year-old had grown up in Atlanta and had friends whose fathers belonged to the Ku Klux Klan. The verbal bombs didn't surprise him. "There was a lot of animosity about a black man chasing Babe Ruth in the South," he said.

When Aaron took the field May 24 (a day after Eddie Mathews had strummed and sung a pregame rendition of "You Are My Sunshine" with country artist Loretta Lynn), he nodded to the fans. Most cheered him, but not all. Over the innings, a pair of rowdy men attempted to instigate a fight with Aaron. But they found themselves outnumbered by his supporters. When the men departed, the crowd applauded and whistled.

In June, at a home game against the Cubs, Aaron found himself targeted again.

"Hey, jigaboo," yelled a redneck in the stands. "How much is two hundred grand in bananas? That's what they use where you come from, ain't it? Bananas? . . . Hey, Aaron. What are you going to do with all that money you get for hitting them homers? Buy a Cadillac and go on welfare?"

Aaron glared at the instigator.

The run-ins did nothing to promote Atlanta's reputation as leader of the New South. "Atlanta is the most prejudiced town I've ever been to in my life," said Pat Dobson after he had been traded to the Yankees. "Can you imagine guys coming to the ballpark just to boo a nice guy like Hank Aaron?"

Aaron could at least always depend on seeing the friendly faces of two women seated near the Braves dugout: his secretary, Carla Koplin, and television personality Billye Williams.

A single woman in her early twenties, Koplin had a taste for stylish clothes: flared slacks, bold, colorful tops, stacked-heel platform shoes. She also had a friendly, polished demeanor, a blend of her Macon, Georgia, childhood and her formal secretarial training in New York City at the renowned Katharine Gibbs School. Koplin had started with the Braves in the late 1960s, assisting with the team's youth camp. Her office was in the stadium tunnel next to the clubhouse. During off-season, players passed her desk to get into the facility.

That's how she got to know Hank Aaron, who soon asked her help in drafting letters and responding to fan mail. Koplin enjoyed working with Aaron, whom she found modest and kind, traits foreign to some athletes. But as Aaron's mail increased and demands on his time became numerous, he requested Koplin's assistance more frequently. Koplin finally let him know that while she liked helping him she couldn't handle two jobs at once. When Aaron signed a three-year contract in 1972, he sought a stipulation almost unheard of at the time. Aaron negotiated for his own secretary, and he chose Carla Koplin, who moved into the administrative area on the third floor. She and Aaron got an office to share, with desks and phones for each and an IBM Selectric typewriter for her. Everything, it seemed, went through Koplin: She coordinated his schedule, requests for interviews, invitations to benefits, pleas on behalf of sick children.

After working at the park all day, Koplin capped her evenings by watching the game with thirty-six-year-old Williams, a semi-celebrity in Atlanta as one of the hosts of WSB-TV's *Today in Georgia* morning show. Williams joined the station staff in 1968, becoming the first black woman to appear regularly on a Georgia television station as on-air talent. At the time, she was married to prominent civil rights leader Samuel Williams. A professor at Morehouse College, he was a mentor and friend to Martin Luther King, Jr., and one of four men to preside over King's 1948 ordination at Ebenezer Church. Williams also cofounded the Southern Christian Leadership Conference. When King was assassinated in 1968, Sam Williams was considered to lead the conference.

Billye Williams, a native of Texas and a graduate of Atlanta University, had directed community relations at Morehouse College and taught English literature at her alma mater. She was astute and knowledgeable on civil rights issues. She and Sam Williams met, married, and adopted a daughter, Ceci, who was four when Sam died unexpectedly in 1970 during routine surgery.

Hank Aaron and Billye Williams crossed paths at WSB-TV. Williams was not a sports fan but had heard of Aaron. In 1971, she hosted a series of lighthearted segments called "Billye at the Bat" and arranged to interview Aaron live on the air. The station teased his appearance days in advance, but Aaron failed to show. He slept through the engagement. Given the advance promotion, Williams was embarrassed but she rescheduled Aaron. On the morning of that show, she went to his apartment and rang the bell until he woke. Aaron appeared as promised.

"Henry called me the next day and asked me out for dinner," Williams said. A year hadn't passed since the death of her husband, Sam. "I was having problems. I was in no frame of mind for dating." She declined the invitation. Aaron was patient. "We kept in touch and he helped me contact other ballplayers and got them to appear on the show," she said. "We became friends and, finally, we did get together."

Quietly—an adverb that fits nicely with much of Aaron's private life—they became engaged around Easter. Their romance thrilled Koplin. Williams really brings something to the table, she thought—a nice match for the "sweetest, kindest, gentlest man you'll ever meet." Williams brought a missing sparkle to Aaron's eyes. She was educated, articulate, pretty, caring, elegant, and, perhaps more important, someone to whom he could vent and confide his deepest, most private thoughts, concerns, and worries. Koplin knew better than most that Aaron had his share of worries.

6

CAL'S ROSCOE

At Atlanta Stadium *in* an office decorated with Hank Aaron posters, Carla Koplin sorted through bundles of letters covering her desk. Thousands of notes, postcards, and packages were arriving weekly, the volume growing continually. Envelopes addressed with nothing more than the name "Hank" found their way to Aaron. One fan didn't even use the name, putting a picture of a hammer in its place. The mail load had been increasing throughout 1972 as the world recognized that Aaron would someday pass Babe Ruth.

By spring 1973, the Braves, Aaron, and Koplin were inundated. There were all sorts of letters. They came from everywhere, not just each state in the nation but from Europe and Africa and Japan and the Mideast. They asked for autographed photos and gum cards and baseballs. They invited Aaron to company picnics and high school graduations and benefit dinners. They sought his old gloves and snips of his hair and patches from his uniforms. They solicited advice—what size bat should I use?—and proffered it as well—tighten your stance, hit to all fields, lift your back shoulder. There was too much mail for Koplin to answer individually, so she and Aaron devised a form letter. It got sent to tens of thousands of fans in a packet with an autographed photo. In the beginning, Aaron signed the pictures. Later, the duty fell to a machine. Touching letters with special requests got his personal attention.

Aaron had noticed early on that many letter writers supported Babe Ruth. "They send figures and statistics to me about Ruth, showing what he did," Aaron said. "It's not vicious." Or so he said. Contrary to Aaron's assurances, some of it was vicious. For months before the racial encounters with Atlanta fans, Aaron said nothing. He kept it secret, and others were unaware, believing—wanting to believe?—that Aaron's pursuit of Ruth was being universally embraced, seeing it as evidence of how far the country had come in racial matters. It demonstrated, after all, that some things were going right in America. A Los Angeles columnist noted warmly that Aaron was leading the world in fan mail and motivating more missives than Valentine's Day. He quoted from lighthearted letters from children. "I don't really like the Braves," one said. "But you are the greatest player I have ever seen in all my life on this earth of six-and-a-half years."

"Everybody's for Hank Aaron," declared Milton Richman of United Press International. "Nobody wants him to fail."

But there had been signs at training camp in West Palm Beach that not all was perfect in Hank Aaron's world. Even at that stage, with his secret intact, Aaron had dropped a major hint that something was wrong. Two weeks into camp, his team slumping and his first home run yet to come, Aaron held court with a half-dozen reporters near the field. Squinting into the sun, he leaned against a slatted, wooden bench. His legs were crossed, and his arms stretched out, crucifix style. The blue 44 of his uniform, outlined in red, leaped off his white jersey. Aaron seemed relaxed, no hint that anything was amiss. But his words prompted wonder. "If I should get extra lucky and hit forty-two home runs this season, I'm planning on quitting," he said. His comment raised curiosity. Aaron's contract ran for two more years, and for the first time he was suggesting he might not fulfill it. What could make Aaron consider walking away from $200,000?

Part of the answer could be found in his mail. When in Atlanta, Aaron often popped into the office to read the letters. To his disappointment, he discovered that they were mostly negative. Six out of ten writers didn't want him to pass Babe Ruth.

Koplin noticed an alarming change in the tone of the correspondence. How could she not? Amid the adoring proclamations of love decorated with red hearts and striped with magic markers and pasted with gold stars were the other kind. "Dear Nigger," they began. They came from across the country, from New York and Chicago and Atlanta. They were typewritten and handwritten and scrawled on postcards. They included sketches of Klan hoods and angry exclamation marks scratched fiercely into paper. At first, they accounted for just a trickle. Then they grew meaner and more frequent. Some suggested that Aaron simply quit or retire; others warned that he would die if he didn't. When the threats surfaced, Koplin took the letters to her boss. He called the FBI, and privately agents fingerprinted Aaron and Koplin to better isolate the prints of those penning the threats.

"Martin Luther King was a troublemaker and had a short life span," someone wrote.

"If you do not retire from the baseball scene," said another, "your family will inherit a great bit of trouble."

And, "My gun is watching your every black move."

Aaron didn't tell even his closest teammates until May, when he broke his silence with Paul Casanova. The two went for a late breakfast Saturday morning in the restaurant of the Marriott Motor Hotel, where the Braves stayed in Philadelphia. The hotel was on City Line Road, near Schuylkill Expressway, a short drive from Veterans Stadium. Casanova could tell something was wrong. Aaron wasn't an easy person to read, leaving friends to measure his moods by degrees of silence. This time, he lay bare his worries. Aaron told Casanova about the letters. He told him about threats against him and his family. Casanova knew that for a strong man like Aaron to reveal such concerns testified to the depth of his despair.

"Cassie, these people are crazy," Aaron said.

"It wigged me out," Casanova said. "It made me sad."

The revelation surfaced in the media about the same time. Suddenly, wherever he went, Aaron was asked about his hate mail. For a long while, he didn't reveal the specific nature of the threats.

"You have to be black in America to realize how sick it is," he said in one town.

"If I were a white boy, it'd be fine," he said in another. "If this were someone like Killebrew or Mantle doing it, everything would be all right. But they can't accept the fact I'm black and I've got this chance to do it."

ABC, NBC, CBS, *Time*, *Newsweek*, the *New York Times*, the *Washington Post*—media outlets everywhere reported on Aaron's ordeal. *Sports Illustrated* wondered how 1973 would fare in history. "Is this to be the year in which Aaron, at the age of thirty-nine, takes a moon walk above one of the most hallowed individual records in American sport . . . ? Or will it be remembered as the season in which Aaron, the most dignified of athletes, was besieged with hate mail and trapped by the cobwebs and goblins that lurk in baseball's attic?"

Aaron's troubles touched millions. Charles Schulz, whose *Peanuts* strip had the largest readership in the country, devoted two weeks to the topic, with Snoopy playing the role of Aaron, lying atop his doghouse reading wicked letters. "If you break the Babe's home-run record, we'll break you!" one said. "We'll run you out of the country. We hate your kind." (Snoopy fell short because of a Charlie Brown blunder.) A writer in Boston wondered whether it was Aaron's destiny to "be shepherded through the crowds of admiring children after a game lest some forlorn and demented soul lurk in the shadows, intent on an act of sheer insanity." Jim Murray, the renowned *Los Angeles*

Times columnist, tried to add levity to the discourse. "Write a poison letter to Henry Aaron? Not me!" he said. "I'm saving mine for a dirty-faced little kid hitting stones with a barrel stave somewhere in Mississippi or Alabama or Texas or California today who will one day hit 750 big league home runs and topple the idol of my middle years, Good Henry Aaron."

News stories often featured a photo of Koplin sorting Aaron's mail, which elicited a reaction of its own. She got filth-filled diatribes condemning her for working for a black man. Some rants came from prison inmates. Those who accurately surmised from her last name that she was Jewish spewed anti-Semitism, as well.

Aaron acknowledged that the threats were probably idle and innocuous. But how could he be sure? "It bothers me," he admitted. "I have seen a president shot and his brother shot. The man who murdered Dr. Martin Luther King is in jail, but that isn't doing Dr. King much good, is it? I have four children and I have to be concerned about their welfare." As a precaution when he came to the ballpark, Aaron drove his car into the bowels of Atlanta Stadium, parking in the tunnel near the clubhouse rather than in the players' lot.

The menacing letters emanated from all states. The Mason-Dixon Line provided no barrier, but Aaron spent most of his time in Atlanta. He played and lived in the city. If anything were to happen to him, it would likely happen there, where a stalker could more easily chart his comings and goings.

Atlanta had a history that was difficult for Aaron to ignore. In 1949, the grand wizard of the Ku Klux Klan had warned of violence when Jackie Robinson played at Ponce de Leon Park against the Atlanta Crackers. And during the civil rights turmoil of the late 1960s, the FBI had checked fans coming into Atlanta Stadium after getting a tip that a sniper might take aim at Aaron. Nothing happened in either case. But in 1970, when Muhammad Ali was about to return to boxing with a match in

Atlanta, he received a package warning him to stay out of Georgia. It contained a decapitated black Chihuahua. All of it made Aaron's ordeal seem like another incident in an unseemly list.

The Braves viewed the threats as significant and took action, hiring two off-duty city police officers to sit in the outfield stands above Hank Aaron. Lamar Harris and Calvin Wardlaw agreed to take on the extra job. They handled their usual departmental duties during the day and worked for the Braves on nights and weekends in Atlanta. In plainclothes, they watched over Aaron from their perch a good thirty to forty feet above the playing field, scanning the crowd for suspicious characters, looking and listening for trouble.

Early on, Harris and Wardlaw went down to the clubhouse to introduce themselves. Wardlaw, a casual baseball fan, had never seen Aaron up close, and he was surprised to discover a wide-chested man. He hadn't gotten that impression watching him on the diamond. He also noticed Aaron's wrists, roughly eight inches in diameter, nearly as big as the barrel of a baseball bat. Aaron had strengthened his wrists as an adolescent working part-time in Mobile delivering blocks of refrigerator ice, hauling them up flights of stairs while gripping them with large tongs. More than any other, that physical feature—the wrists—differentiated Aaron.

Wardlaw visited the locker room frequently and became a familiar sight. Raised in Atlanta, he went into law enforcement late. He joined the force in 1971 at age thirty after stints with Ford and the air force military police. He worked in homicide and internal affairs and belonged to the city's first SWAT team. He also had experience with the bomb squad.

At the ballpark Wardlaw carried his gun, a .38 Smith-Wesson detective special, in a brown binoculars case.

"Calvin, would you use that Roscoe?" Eddie Mathews asked him once.

"If I have to," Wardlaw answered.

Braves officials held weekly meetings to discuss Hank Aaron and began requesting other teams provide extra security for Aaron when he visited their ballparks. The security was in place when the Braves rolled into New York for the start of a weekend series. Aaron had been warned that his life was in jeopardy. The stream of threats covered almost every game. "You'll be in Shea Stadium July 6–8 and in Philly July 9–11," said this one. "You will die in one of those games. I'll shoot you."

For an assassin intent on killing Aaron as a public statement, New York provided maximum exposure. It reigned as the nation's media capital, headquartering the news operations of all three networks and serving as home to more daily papers than any other American city, among them the country's most prestigious, the *New York Times*. No major league player had ever been shot on a professional ball field. But what would stop a person so motivated? Some fans brought fifths of whiskey into stadiums. A handgun would be easier to conceal. No metal detectors stood beyond ticket takers, and few, if any, police officers patrolled stands.

Aaron loved the outdoors and liked to hunt. He shot elk and deer and pheasant. He traveled across the country to pursue his hobby in the off-season. He had handled all sorts of guns, and he knew that the easiest shot provided clear sight of a stationary target. That description fit a ballplayer on the field. Whether awaiting a pitch or standing in the outfield, a player offered an easy mark.

Cleon Jones maneuvered his black Chrysler through traffic in East Elmhurst, glancing at Hank Aaron, his friend, as they talked. They weren't far from Shea Stadium or the Out-

fielders Lounge, a bar and grill that Jones owned with former
Mets teammate Tommie Agee, when Aaron confessed that he
was thinking of quitting baseball.

As Jones drove, Aaron said he was weary of the threats,
tired of the incessant demands, discouraged that so many people opposed him, and "sick of living in a prison." He wanted
the freedom to leave his hotel room for a beer with his teammates or to go to dinner in a popular restaurant without being
overwhelmed by fans. He wanted a more normal life. This
record, he said, was no longer worth the personal sacrifices. His
health and family were far more important. Whether or not he
passed Babe Ruth, this might be his last year, he said.

It pained Jones to hear Aaron say such things. Aaron was
his idol, after all, a big-brother figure eight years senior who
had watched out for him when he arrived in the majors. In high
school in Mobile, Jones had played against Tommie Aaron and
they had become friends. The friendship expanded to include
Hank Aaron.

Jones listened to his friend; he could relate. He had experienced something similar, though on a smaller scale, in 1969
when the Miracle Mets overtook the Chicago Cubs. Jones received an explicit death threat, vowing that he would be shot at
Wrigley Field. He had intended to keep the letter to himself,
but Agee discovered it and eventually the FBI became involved,
tracking down the writer, who turned out to be a minor.

Aaron quit? The words didn't belong together, and Jones
let him know.

"All of the people that you see hate you, there are a lot
more that love you," Jones said. "You're not just chasing Babe
Ruth's record. You're chasing lots of records, and that's because
of the hard work and dedication you gave the game of baseball.
No one has been as consistent as you have. And no one has
been as great as you are. You need to rethink."

There were no tears, no whining. Just two friends being

honest with each other. Jones reminded Aaron about Jackie Robinson's sacrifices. "What you're doing, it's not just for you anymore," he said.

Aaron lit up the ball diamond in early May, going on a tear by hitting safely 40 percent of the time. With the Montreal Expos in town, he began May with two home runs in the first game, and followed with two singles in the next. Facing Philadelphia, Aaron got three hits one night, including a home run off Steve Carlton. Against San Diego, he slapped home runs in both games of a doubleheader, vaulting him to within thirty-one of Babe Ruth. "I wish they would give Aaron the record and let him retire," joked Padre manager Don Zimmer. Ralph Garr also emerged from his slump, returning to the lineup after a week on the bench and getting eight hits in two days. In the midst of his own troubles, Aaron had made time to help Garr. "Hank talked to me," Garr said. "He was like a brother. . . . Everybody on the team was pulling for me. That's the way these guys are."

Aaron had ten home runs and was contending for the league lead with Willie Stargell when the Braves visited Houston for a four-game set starting May 14. Houston played in the Astrodome, the first enclosed park in the majors. When it opened with President Lyndon Johnson on hand for the festivities, it was considered futuristic. More than 4,700 panels provided the dome, which peaked at 208 feet. The turf was synthetic; the climate controlled. "It reminds me of what my first ride would be like in a flying saucer," Mickey Mantle said. Purists viewed it as an abomination.

The Astrodome had a grand scoreboard on which Houston officials sometimes posted partisan messages. In 1969, after umpire John Kibler made the second of two questionable calls, Astros management flashed this criticism: "Kibler did it again!" The league fined the team. But for Hank Aaron in May

1973, the scoreboard offered a message of support. "Mr. Aaron," it stated, "for every one of those bad letters you receive, there are thousands pulling for you. Good luck in your homer quest . . . after you leave the Astrodome."

The Braves swept the first three games, and Aaron hit number 684, putting him on pace to pass Ruth that season. In the fourth matchup, the Astros clung to a 2–1 lead with two outs in the ninth inning and Aaron coming to bat. Ken Forsch, twenty-six, had pitched to Aaron several times in his brief career. He had surrendered a home run to Aaron two years earlier. But Forsch had been sharp all night. He had allowed only four hits, and his fastball was popping.

With no one on base, Forsch turned on the heat and tried to blow one past Aaron. The pitch was inside, and Aaron drove it down the left-field line into the upper deck, a few feet foul. As Aaron walked back to home plate for another try, he caught Forsch's eye and smiled at him. "When I saw him smiling, I decided that was the end of the challenge," Forsch said. "No way was I going to throw him a fastball again." He pitched around him. Aaron walked.

Pitchers and managers employed that strategy more often as Aaron found his timing. They wouldn't announce their intention to walk him—and suffer the boos of fans who had come to see Aaron swing—but they would feed him balls away from the plate that Aaron would find unpalatable. "As I get closer, I'm getting fewer pitches to hit," he noted. "Pitchers seem more conscious of the home runs." Aaron wanted to pass Ruth in 1973. But he needed the at-bats to have a shot. Walks didn't help.

A day after Forsch's close call in Houston, the Dodgers came to Atlanta. They walked Aaron three times in the first game. They walked him again the next game. Walt Alston, one of baseball's best skippers, had been with the Dodgers since the Jackie Robinson days in Brooklyn. Like many successful managers, Alston had a lousy career as a player. He had come to bat just once in the major leagues, striking out in 1936 with St. Louis. But as leader of the Dodgers, he had earned respect. Aaron himself rated Alston as the league's top manager.

In the tenth inning Sunday, with the game tied at two and speedy Ralph Garr on second base, Alston had pitcher George Culver give Darrell Evans a free ride to get to Hank Aaron. With Evans on first, Aaron might ground into a double play. Besides, Evans, who was hitting home runs as often as Aaron, batted left-handed, which theoretically gave him an edge over the right-handed pitcher. Not since the days when Eddie Mathews preceded Aaron in the lineup had a manager walked a hitter to challenge Aaron.

Aaron had gotten a home run off Culver in 1970, bulleting the ball up the middle. Culver had flinched, thinking it was coming at him. But it kept rising. It stopped when it struck the wall beyond the fence in deep center. Culver wanted to avoid that outcome now. With the game on the line, he and catcher Joe Ferguson shied away from starting Aaron with a fastball. Instead, Culver opened with an off-speed pitch. Aaron was waiting and rapped the ball to left. Garr scored, and the Braves won.

Between games of the doubleheader the mood in the Atlanta clubhouse was joyous, with the hub of activity centered, as usual, at the neighboring lockers of the three outfielders: Aaron, Garr, and Baker.

"This game sure is fun when you win," said Garr.

Baker teased Garr, who had fallen rounding third.

"I was going so fast that my legs had to catch up with my body," Garr said.

The victory accounted for the one hundredth of Phil Niekro's career. "Hammer not only knocked in the winning run," said Niekro, "but he saved a homer with his catch in left field," robbing Manny Mota.

Aaron continued on his mission Tuesday, May 22, with the Giants visiting Atlanta. He drove a sixth-inning slider off Juan Marichal into the left-field stands. It gave him 12 home runs for the season, tying him with Willie Stargell. "It's just one more closer to where I want go," he said.

If the threats were meant to distract Aaron and throw him off his game, they failed, for they strengthened his resolve. He was more determined than ever to break the record—"for Jackie and my people and myself and for everybody who ever called me nigger." Aaron, at age thirty-nine, was now hitting home runs at a faster pace than in any other year.

If his assailants wanted to silence him, to make him think twice before speaking out, they failed in that, too, for the racism they threw his way gave him an opportunity to respond and be heard. That summer, Aaron talked about his admiration for Dr. Martin Luther King, who had been assassinated five years earlier: "He could walk with kings and talk with presidents. He wasn't for lootings and bombings and fights but he wasn't afraid of violence, either." Aaron finally admitted that he received death threats on his life nearly every day. "But I can't think about that," he said. "If I'm a target, then I'm a target. I can only worry about doing my job and doing it good."

7

THE RESCUE

Above Three Rivers Stadium, the sky had darkened, twilight evolving into nighttime. From outside, the ballpark appeared to wear a radiant crown, its top basked in light, some of it falling on the Allegheny River that ran beyond right field and nearby merged with the Monongahela to form the Ohio. When built in July 1970, Three Rivers ushered in a streak of success for the Pirates that included three consecutive division titles, one culminating in a world championship. The ballpark had been built on an Indian burial ground, a fact that provided no karmic benefit for the Atlanta Braves, who had a losing record there. The place didn't stoke Hank Aaron's power either. He had hit only three home runs at the stadium.

Aaron played in the series opener on May 29. His performance—three strikeouts and a single—brought a headline for the pitcher who fanned him twice. Even Aaron's outs had become noteworthy. "I didn't mean for that pitch to be so high but it just took off and must have caught him by surprise," said Luke Walker. The Braves lost the game and the one that followed. The third meeting brought a duel between Gary Gentry and Nellie Briles. Combined, they allowed five hits through seven innings. The Braves, ahead 1–0, thought themselves on the crest of ending a six-game slide. Gentry needed two strong innings to beat Pittsburgh. But trouble materialized in the eighth when Manny Sanguillen singled and Richie Hebner walked, bringing Aaron's friend Willie Stargell to bat.

Aaron was in the dugout beside veteran reliever Joe Hoerner when Stargell appeared. In the absurdly far-off right-field upper deck, Aaron could see three seats that had been painted blue and numbered, noting where Herculean home runs had struck—all of them Stargell's. The Pirate slugger, thirty to forty pounds heavier than Aaron, windmilled his bat toward Gentry, repeating the gesture several times, glaring at the man on the mound, holding the bat briefly at the two o'clock position before reeling it back into place. It looked as if he were forecasting the skyward path of the ball. Gentry's first pitch missed, fastball outside.

Aaron nudged Hoerner. "Just how hard do you have to hit the ball to put it in that upper deck?" he asked.

Stargell twirled his bat and pulled it back into place, above his muscular shoulders. Gentry delivered, and Stargell launched the pitch 468 feet into the yellow seats.

"About that hard," Hoerner said.

The Pirates won.

Stargell and Aaron were battling for the league lead in home runs, a potential harbinger given what had happened the last time they vied for the title in 1971. Stargell hit 48, and Aaron, while falling one shy, logged his most productive season. The two men had known each other since the early 1960s when Stargell, a struggling prospect, mustered the nerve to ask Aaron for advice. Aaron obliged, as he always did. Ever since, Stargell had held him in awe. "I thought he was just a very special person to take time out with a guy he didn't even know, and from another club," he said. During the Pittsburgh series, Aaron presented his friend with a $2,500 check to benefit the Black

Athletes Foundation, an organization headed by Stargell to fight sickle cell anemia. The money represented a portion of the proceeds from a celebrity bowling tournament that Aaron had organized. The two men had played against each other now in twelve seasons, and several times joined up as National All-Stars. Stargell's respect for Aaron remained undiminished. He rooted for Aaron in his pursuit of the record.

Throughout the leagues, Aaron found support from fellow players. Some knew what he was going through. Others could guess. "Tell him to stop reading his mail," said Dodger pitcher Don Sutton, a buddy.

Aaron's ordeal elicited encouragement from both black and white players, but his troubles particularly resonated with fellow African-Americans. Reggie Jackson of Oakland telephoned Aaron one day. "I want you to know that all the young black players in the American League realize what the older blacks in the National have done for us," said Jackson. "You know what I'm trying to say, don't you? Baby, I'm pulling for you." Top prospects like Dave Winfield made a point of visiting Aaron when he came to their town. In Los Angeles, Anthony Davis, the University of Southern California football standout, stood near Aaron in the Braves clubhouse before a gaggle of reporters. "It's too bad that a guy of his caliber has to take that stuff," Davis said.

But it wasn't just ballplayers. The black community at large began to rally around Aaron, and a wave of support swelled, particularly from near the banks of Lake Michigan in Chicago, national headquarters to a preacher of rising prominence, the Rev. Jesse Jackson. Earlier in the year as spring training neared an end, Jackson had announced a national effort to push for equal rights in the sports world. A former college athlete, Jackson said the group, part of his Operation PUSH (People United to Save Humanity), would demand the hiring of black managers, coaches, and executives. He reiterated the concerns of Jackie Robinson, Aaron, and other ballplayers. Baseball, he said, does not provide black athletes with the same post-career opportunities as white athletes. "We're not looking for breaks," he said. "We're looking for justice."

The Braves' postgame flight from Pittsburgh arrived at Chicago's O'Hare Airport around midnight. It had been a somber trip, following the team's seventh straight loss. At that late hour, the terminal was usually empty. But this time, the players found a surprise: An enthusiastic, mostly black crowd of more than two hundred awaited them—or, more accurately, awaited Hank Aaron. Charged with energy and excited by the occasion, the gathering of children and adults erupted in cheers and applause when Aaron appeared at the gate. They waved signs and called out their affection. Jackson, who had orchestrated the affair, greeted Aaron with warm words. The children sang songs. It was a hero's welcome, and it was the start of a weekend's worth that would shape Aaron's outlook and inspire in him a sense of destiny. Later, Aaron would refer to this moment as his "rescue."

Chicago played in the afternoon at Wrigley Field. Opened in 1914, the park clung to tradition. Unlike every other venue in the major leagues, Wrigley Field had no lights, which meant, among other things, that ballplayers had their evenings free. That night, after the Braves disposed of the Cubs, Jesse Jackson hosted a party at his home to honor Aaron. Familiar faces enlivened the place, not only black ballplayers from the Braves and Cubs but other well-known figures like Walt Frazier, Gale Sayers, and Billy Preston. Aaron got to know Jackson better and liked what he heard and saw. Jackson told Aaron that he was in a unique position to make a difference, that the world's attention would be on him and that if he wanted to use that opportunity to improve the lives of others he would have a chance. The tribute continued the next morning, with Jackson leading a celebration of Aaron before a group of nearly two thousand at PUSH headquarters. Amid signs and posters, Jackson told those gathered—and the more than half a million tuning in to his radio broadcast—that Aaron had inspired blacks of all generations. "He has achieved a level of excellence ... few men in athletics have," said Jackson, "and yet he has not been recognized in proportion to his worth and his greatness."

At the podium with the crowd exuberant, Jackson hoisted Aaron's left hand above his head and championed him. Aaron grinned. Separated by seven years, they looked of different generations: Jackson with a bushy Afro, a pirate-striped T-shirt, and an unzipped jacket, collar flipped Elvis-style; Aaron in a conservative solid sport coat and dark tie. Jackson spoke in flourishes; Aaron was more subdued but his words were heartfelt and revealing. "The last two days," Aaron said, "I can say I've been happier than I have been in my life."

He thanked Jackson for his support and then used the platform to decry baseball's slow progress in racial matters, picking up where Jackie Robinson had left off, spotlighting baseball's flagrant lack of a black manager. "About the only strides we've made is that we've been able to get to coach first base," he said. "When our careers are done and we're no longer needed, then they send us to the back of the bus."

Aaron had begun speaking on the issue regularly. Now that he was the biggest story in sports, reporters were asking him about it more frequently, too. His heightened exposure caused murmurs about Aaron's outspokenness. Some hinted, privately at first, that Aaron's concerns sprung from Jackson, the vocal preacher, and Billye Williams, Aaron's articulate fiancée, widow of a civil rights leader. Such talk rankled Aaron for obvious reasons—the implication being that he was a puppet able only to mouth other peoples' words. Jackson did encourage Aaron to speak his heart and make a difference. And Williams, an educator, had in fact fed his desire to become more knowledgeable on civil rights, encouraging him to read the writings of Martin Luther King. But Aaron's feelings about blacks' limited management opportunities were well documented. He had been speaking his mind for a decade. Now more people listened.

In 1965, Aaron expressed hope that progress was near. "Personally, I don't think there is any general manager in baseball today who would be afraid to hire a Negro manager," he said. "People in sports have learned that you forget who's white and who's black. You go with the man who does the best job."

In 1968, after the assassination of King, Aaron sounded less confident. He said baseball had failed by not hiring men like Jackie Robinson, Larry Doby, and Monte Irvin. His words upset Paul Richards, the Braves general manager, who chided Aaron publicly, saying that he should think before speaking. "That's the way I feel," Aaron responded. "But if that's stepping on somebody's toes, then they can go to hell. I'm a Negro first. It would be wrong if I didn't speak out."

In 1970, Aaron lamented the status quo. "Unfortunately, no owner has had the guts up to this point to hire a black manager," he said. "In fact, I wouldn't even call it guts; I'd call it common sense. . . . It burns me up a little that there's this kind of—what would you call it?—managerial club, whereby the owners seem to have gotten together and decided that certain men, white men, should be hired and rehired no matter what kind of failures they have been. . . . Surely no one thinks at this point that white fans are going to boycott a team because it has a Negro in a front office or managerial position. So why not just do it?"

In 1971, Aaron raised the issue again: "Qualified people obviously have been bypassed," he said. "If you don't say anything, it's no good. I suppose most blacks feel the way I do. I wouldn't look for them to say anything because there are a lot of them who are out there scuffling, trying to make a living. . . . I believe things are going to change. They have to change."

It was no stretch for him to be talking about the issue in 1973, too.

Aaron's activism evolved over the years, not overnight.

Early on, in the 1950s, Jackie Robinson confessed to Howard Cosell that he had no sense of where Aaron stood as a black man. Cosell said, "Robinson could see that Aaron was coming out of the shell . . . and beginning to try, at least, to deal with the issues that Robinson felt every black was compelled to."

By the early 1970s, Aaron was taking a more active role in Atlanta's civic affairs. Behind the scenes and away from baseball, Aaron and other prominent blacks were meeting privately to plan ways to exert influence. Aaron invited Dusty Baker and Ralph Garr to some meetings, which drew athletes from the Falcons football and Hawks basketball teams, as well as men like Andrew Young, in 1972 the first black to be elected to Congress from Georgia since Reconstruction; Maynard Jackson, who would soon launch a successful candidacy for mayor of Atlanta; and self-made multimillionaire Herman Russell, the first black member of the city's chamber of commerce. The goal of the low-key gatherings was to create a network of support for African-American leaders.

In public, Aaron kept his activism focused on baseball and management. Frank Robinson had been pressing the same issue for years. "There really isn't much use talking about it anymore," Robinson noted in 1973. "It's no secret that I want to manage in the big leagues. . . . When my playing days are over, which I think will be in about two or three years, I'll see what happens."

Aaron, on the other hand, had no desire to manage. He envisioned himself in the upper echelons of baseball administration, like Stan Musial, who had left the playing field and prospered as a Cardinals executive. Aaron had gotten to know Musial in 1966–67 when they spent six weeks together visiting soldiers and touring Vietnam. He wanted the same opportunity, but few blacks worked in the top administrative tier.

Hank and Tommie Aaron hadn't seen each other since training camp in March. In the months after, Tommie had written his brother several letters but Hank hadn't responded. "He's a busy man," Tommie said. "He just probably read them and forgot about them."

It took a Thursday scrimmage in mid-June to bring the Aarons together. Between games with Pittsburgh and Chicago, the Braves traveled to Savannah to take on the Southern League All-Stars. Tommie Aaron, who was a player-coach with Atlanta's Double-A Savannah squad, served as designated hitter for the minor leaguers. Hank played the same role for the Braves. Neither got a hit in the rain-shortened game. But they spent time with one another, catching up on family, health, and happenings in Mobile, Alabama. "We talked about a lot of different things . . . but nothing about the record," said Tommie.

Five and a half years separated the brothers. By the time Tommie turned fifteen, Hank had been in the National League for most of a season. They played together with the Braves sporadically through the 1960s and early 1970s. Hank felt his brother, a first baseman and outfielder, never got a solid chance to prove himself. But in 944 at-bats over parts of seven seasons, Tommie, whom Hank called "Porkchop" as a boy, hit .229 with 13 home runs. He had the desire and the work ethic but not enough talent. "We're two different style ballplayers," Tommie once said. "He is the complete ballplayer. He can do just about anything. I had to scuffle."

Tommie followed Hank's home-run pursuit in the newspapers, checking daily to see whether he had hit one. Hank often made the headlines. Soon, it would be Tommie's turn.

The day after their visit, the Braves promoted Savannah skipper Clint "Old Scrap Iron" Courtney to the Triple-A job in Richmond, Virginia, and awarded the Savannah opening to

Tommie Aaron. The promotion made Aaron the top black manager in professional baseball, a sad confirmation of the sport's lack of progress. Double-A was, after all, a long way from the major leagues. Only two other blacks, Deacon Jones and Bernie Williams, were managing, and they were at lower levels.

For a change, it was Hank's chance to congratulate his brother. "I wish him all the luck in the world," he said. "I'm happy for him, I really am. It's a thrill for me, and just a heck of a thing for him. He deserves something after playing all these years and I think he'll do a good job."

Tommie Aaron's offer of advancement came from Atlanta vice president Eddie Robinson and minor-league administrator Bill Lucas (Aaron's ex-brother-in-law). Was it mere coincidence that the new manager, Aaron, and one of baseball's highest-ranking black executives, Lucas, both had family ties to Aaron and were promoted by the team on which he starred? Hank Aaron tried to dispel the speculation related to his brother. "I just hope the people won't get the idea that the Braves gave him the job because of me," he said. "That's not the way it was. Tommie earned it on his own and he'll hold it on his own." Jackie Robinson, however, had once said that Aaron pressured the Braves to give Bill Lucas an opportunity.

It was progress, though agonizingly slow.

ank Aaron's pursuit did not dominate the front page in the American spring of 1973. Banner headlines went to a deepening scandal that was eroding Americans' confidence in their government. The Watergate saga had begun as a story about a burglary at Democratic Party national headquarters. But as the tale unfolded, its tentacles entangled the president. By mid-May Congress had opened hearings into the matter, and Richard Nixon's popularity had begun to plummet. The investigation came in the wake of another debacle that also changed how Americans viewed themselves: the Vietnam War. Nixon had promised peace with honor when he announced the end of American involvement. But the lengthy, costly conflict in Southeast Asia remained a raw wound for Americans accustomed to winning the wars they waged. It must have seemed to some as if the very landscape of the country was being transformed. And it was.

The Equal Rights Amendment, passed a year earlier by Congress, was being considered in state houses, as *Ms.* magazine, founded by Gloria Steinem, approached its first anniversary. Relations between blacks and whites were strained over many issues, including desegregation of schools through cross-district busing. For seventy-one days through early May, armed Native American activists occupied Wounded Knee, South Dakota, the site of an 1890 conflict in which two hundred Sioux died. In Florida, a race riot flared at Sumter prison. "It looks like the whites and blacks declared war on each other," said one official. On the radio, singer Helen Reddy was proclaiming, "I Am Woman," and at the Academy Awards Marlon Brando, named best actor for his role in *The Godfather*, had Sacheen Littlefeather appear on his behalf in protest of government treatment of Indians.

Nowhere were old assumptions being challenged more than in the sports world. In Ypsilanti, Michigan, a twelve-year-old girl played in a Little League baseball game, her debut provoking controversy and lawsuits. In tennis, ex-champion and fifty-five-year-old hustler Bobby Riggs beat the top women's player, Margaret Court, in a Mother's Day match, prompting Billie Jean King to accept Riggs' invitation to a September Battle of the Sexes. A study of the NFL chided the league for its lack of black second-string players—"mediocrity is a white luxury"—and for its reluctance to place blacks in "intelligence" positions, such as quarterback and middle linebacker. Every week, it seemed, some news item pointed to a racial dispute: black Pirate pitcher Dock Ellis fighting his manager and, he presumed, the commissioner over wearing curlers in his hair on the field before the game; lounges in Baton Rouge, Louisiana, refusing to serve black coaches in town for an NCAA track event; former Brave Rico Carty trying to incite trouble by accusing Eddie Mathews of treating blacks poorly (a charge dismissed as ludicrous by Aaron and others).

In Arlington, Rod Carew found himself the target of racial taunts when the Twins played the Rangers on June 28. A posse of Texans sent a tirade of insults toward the Panama-born second baseman. "Hey, I didn't think that black stuff came off," one guy yelled after Carew stole home. Frank Quilici, Carew's manager, emerged from the dugout and turned to confront the men, threatening to lead a group of his players into the stands before umpires intervened. "They said we might all be suspended," said Quilici. "But we didn't care. We were ready to take them on." Carew agreed. "They were ready for a fight and, frankly, so was I," he said.

Hank Aaron came to see that the home-run record carried significance beyond baseball. The civil rights movement had shifted its focus from legislation to altering the attitudes of whites, and Aaron gave that goal a jolt. What better way of forcing a change in perception than in a black man dethroning the country's most idolized white sports legend as king of the national pastime?

Aaron rated as the biggest name in sports. Anyone who read the papers or watched television knew about him, Babe Ruth, and the chase. But soon America would become enamored with another hero, a fresh name with neither a word to say nor a complaint to air. Secretariat bounded into the public conscience with an easy victory in the Kentucky Derby. He followed it two weeks later with a magnificent, winning performance at the Preakness, and then in New York at the Belmont Stakes won by thirty-seven lengths, setting a new course record and capturing the Triple Crown, the first horse to do so since Citation in 1948. With not a hint of controversy (and little possibility of creating one), the colt conjured only warm feelings. He was neither black nor white nor Native American, and to most people he was genderless. Secretariat was the ideal antidote for tense, tumultuous times. Hank Aaron, on the other hand, was human.

"I have never lived a day in my life that in some way—some small way, somewhere—someone didn't remind me that I'm black," he said.

Aaron received letters from children and realized that, like Jackie Robinson, he was inspiring a younger generation. He dedicated his pursuit to kids—black and white—"because they're the ones who have shown me the greatest support." Achieving the record, he said, would give "children hope that no matter how high the mountain, they can climb it."

In Atlanta in June, Carla Koplin noticed changes in Aaron's mail. For one thing, the already high volume had increased dramatically. For another, even more letters than usual were coming from children. And, most important, their words were overwhelmingly kind and supportive. I'm sorry for the nasty letters, many said. A child in Pennsylvania wrote, "I hope you break the Babe's record by 100,000,000,000." In St. Paul, Minnesota, a thousand children signed petitions supporting Aaron. In Los Angeles, students at the Thirty-second Street School sent Aaron "I Am Somebody" essays. It felt as if every baseball-loving kid in America was writing Hank Aaron, urging him ahead, begging that he ignore the critics, apologizing for the name-callers, telling him that they wanted him to topple the record, that he was the best, that he was their favorite, and that they, by the way, would really appreciate an autographed picture. Thank you, Mr. Aaron. Thank you, they said.

It was no coincidence that whenever Aaron visited Chicago his friend Jesse Jackson surrounded him with children. It filled Aaron with a sense of purpose.

8

BOWIE AND MRS. BABE

Hank Aaron awoke on a Sunday morning in June to find himself embroiled in a controversy of someone else's doing. "Pitchers Say They'd Groove Aaron's 715"—the headline ran in papers throughout the nation. "Henry Aaron has worked very hard for his home runs but if some pitchers have their way, number 715, the one that breaks Babe Ruth's career mark, will be his easiest." So began an Associated Press story by Fred Rothenberg, who asked a dozen pitchers whether they would mind surrendering the historic hit.

The pitchers were divided. Andy Messersmith, Reggie Cleveland, and Larry Dierker said they'd serve a fastball over the center of the plate. Phil Hennigan said he would alert Aaron in advance. "It will be like batting practice," he said. Tug McGraw pledged to throw his best pitch "and hope like hell he hits it." Pete Richert said he wouldn't be bothered being remembered for the home run. And Juan Marichal, a six-time twenty-game winner, remarked, "If Aaron broke the record off me, it would be maybe like a trophy." Four pitchers vowed not to become Aaron trivia. Prophetically, two of them—Jack Billingham and Dave Roberts—would be in a position to become what they hoped to avoid. How they handled the challenge would vary.

Having faced pitchers all season who were reluctant to even put the ball over the plate, Aaron detected lightheartedness in the statements and he responded in kind: "No one has done anything like that for me so far, and I wish if they were going to do that they would start doing it right now."

Commissioner Bowie Kuhn, however, found nothing comical in the story. He viewed the pitchers' comments as an assault on the integrity of the game. If a pitcher would throw a fluff ball to Aaron, what would prevent him from throwing a game? The office of baseball commissioner had been borne out of an effort to sanitize the sport after the Black Sox scandal. All commissioners served in the long shadow of the first man to hold the job, Kenesaw Mountain Landis. Kuhn was no exception. Landis, a former federal judge whose baseball powers bordered on dictatorial, held the job for nearly a quarter century—his death ending his tenure.

At six-foot-five, Bowie Kuhn cut an impressive profile even in the clubhouse among athletes. He looked like the stereotype of a corporate attorney. He wore wingtips and suits to ball games, and his hair, with hints of gray, was slicked back. Full, graying Captain Kangaroo–sideburns gave his face a paunchy appearance. Kuhn had attended college through a naval officers training program, earning an economics degree from Princeton and a law degree at the University of Virginia. He represented the National League when Milwaukee interests sued to prevent the Braves from moving to Atlanta. In 1969, he ascended to the commissioner's seat.

Describing himself as "greatly disturbed" by the pitchers' comments, Kuhn fired off a warning from the Manhattan offices of Major League Baseball. Rather than call the offending players first to gauge the veracity of the quotes or to weigh the spirit in which they gave them, Kuhn responded as if the sport were on the cusp of imminent and irreparable harm. He threatened a long-term suspension for any player who "intentionally fails to give his best effort." "Nothing will be permitted which will tarnish the achievements of a truly great player such as Henry Aaron," he said. Kuhn may have hoped to reinforce the serious nature of the matter, but his strong, no-nonsense stance would have other repercussions.

His reaction baffled the pitchers. Hennigan said he was only joking: "It was said in jest." McGraw noted that he had pledged to throw "my best pitch." A surprised Messersmith sighed. "I can't believe the commissioner could take this seriously."

Aaron apologized at first. "I'm sorry this came up," he said. "But I don't really believe they meant it."

Though there had not been a scent of evidence that anyone had served Aaron easy pitches—the facts pointed to the opposite conclusion—the pitchers' comments and Kuhn's reply hung like an accusation over Aaron, who was hitting home runs so frequently that he stood a decent shot at passing Ruth before October. It became one more issue on which he had to comment.

By week's end in San Diego, Aaron faced a nervous rookie, Randy Jones, making his debut as a starter. Jones, a lefty, had appeared in one other game and had given up a home run to Willie Mays. In his first confrontation with Aaron he let the count go to three balls, one strike. "I didn't want to walk him," Jones said. In the tradition of overconfident rookies everywhere, he tried to smoke a fastball past the veteran. The guy was thirty-nine, after all. No matter, Aaron smoked the ball past Jones—440 feet into the center-field bleachers. He walked Aaron the next time. Jones said that Aaron and Mays had taught him a lesson: "You can't get behind in the count on hitters like those two."

In the clubhouse, Aaron was asked if the home run had

been a gift, the kind Bowie Kuhn had warned against. Aaron measured the question, as if gauging whether to be offended, and then, noticing the reporter's light expression, laughed it off: "It's silly. Fat pitches! I haven't seen many fat pitches. I've seen some pitches down the middle all right. But it wasn't because anyone was trying to throw them there. . . . What's the commissioner going to do, start following me around?"

Yes, actually. But not for two months.

When hot, Hank Aaron could impact games without playing. Steve Arlin of San Diego had an impressive three-hitter in progress on Sunday as the eighth inning began with his team ahead 1–0. But Arlin, twenty-seven, promptly fell into trouble, loading the bases on a single to John Oates and walks to Darrell Evans and Dusty Baker. Ralph Garr was due to bat. Manager Don Zimmer would normally have brought in Mike Caldwell, a left-hander, to pitch to the left-handed Garr. But Zimmer surmised that Eddie Mathews would then introduce Aaron as a pinch hitter. So he stuck with Arlin, and Garr belted the first pitch for a grand slam. The Braves won.

"Either way I went," said Zimmer, "I knew people would blame me if we lost." Fans did blame Zimmer. But Garr thought he made the right decision. "I heard all of the boos," he said, "but how could anyone second-guess the man for wanting to pitch to me instead of to Aaron?"

Such successes were rare for the Braves. By the end of June, Eddie Mathews was fighting mad. His team's streak of bad play—the Braves were twelve games under .500—had him so frustrated that he yanked a phone off the dugout wall after Garr had been picked off third base. In Montreal, he instituted a midnight curfew, and another time, following a five-error performance, he blasted his players in a heated team meeting. "I've turned the other cheek so often that they're both bleeding," he said. "I can't watch it anymore. I can't take excuses anymore. From now on, every mental mistake will result in a fine."

The punishment riled some Braves. Aaron offered no comment, but, anonymously, other players called the action "stupid" and "ridiculous." On the record, Garr questioned Mathews' wisdom. "He can say what he wants," Garr said, "but it won't make us any better." Added Dusty Baker, "I guess he knows what he's doing." That was a measured response for Baker, who bristled under Mathews' authority—anyone's authority, for that matter. Baker felt Mathews disliked him, and he had evidence. Mathews once canceled the entire club's batting practice because of a Baker transgression. On a team bus he confronted Baker over music and ordered him to turn off James Brown or Zeppelin or Hendrix or whoever was blaring from his portable stereo in the wake of a Braves' loss. Another day, when Baker had tried to board the bus wearing a stylish leisure suit, Mathews ordered him to take a taxi for violating a rule that required all Braves wear collared shirts. It seemed to Baker that he couldn't do anything right in his manager's eyes.

The Kuhn controversy inspired heated words. From Mississippi, seventy-one-year-old Guy Bush, a former Pirate pitcher, said that Tug McGraw, Andy Messersmith, and those other pitchers quoted in the story should be banned from baseball. "Judge Landis would have marched those boys into his office, de-uniformed them, and sent them on their merry way with a permanent suspension," he said. Bush added that in his day he would have decked Aaron. "Anything to get him out of the game," he said. But Bush's criticism struck fans as incredible given that he had allowed Babe Ruth's final two home runs, 713 and 714. At Bush's urging, his catcher had told Ruth where the fastballs would be delivered. He didn't groove those pitches, Bush claimed. He just wanted to challenge Ruth.

Many baseball writers admonished Kuhn. A *Sporting News* columnist characterized Kuhn's decree as a "staggering over-reaction. . . . If the commissioner of baseball feels impelled to say anything at all about Aaron, how about loudly and frequently deploring the hate mail?" he asked. But the commissioner did find support in New York, from Dick Young. "Integrity is the name of the game," Young said. "It's what separates baseball from roller derby."

Fourteen days later, Aaron was still being asked about Kuhn's reaction, and his assessment was hardening. "The commissioner overreacted," he said. "He threw another log on the fire to stir up the people who've already said I've played a thousand more games than the Babe. The commissioner shouldn't have said it. He touched off a lot of unpleasant things."

It wouldn't be the last time.

The Braves headed to Shea Stadium after the July 4 holiday for Aaron's final New York appearance of the season. New York, of course, gave birth to the legend of Babe Ruth. He had been a huge part of the city since purchased from the Boston Red Sox in 1920, and he had become a household name with the Yankees, whose park carried the label "The House That Ruth Built."

In the years after her husband's death, Claire Ruth continued to receive his fan mail. It had slowed but never stopped. As Aaron edged closer to the record, she noticed that the volume had multiplied. "It's been ten times as heavy," she said. "People remember." Initially, Mrs. Ruth sounded resentful of Aaron's quest. But when Aaron's racist mail became public, Mrs. Ruth tempered her words. "I just wish there wouldn't be so much talk about that sort of stuff," she said. "There's too much hate already. Maybe he'd like to know about my mail. I get about a hundred letters a week. They all tell me how wonderful they think the Babe was, and not one mentions a word of hate for Aaron. . . . I thought he might like to hear that."

But not long after, she added, "No matter what happens, there's only one Babe. He stands alone and he always will. Roger Maris hit sixty-one home runs, but who writes about him today?"

The Braves and Mets drew 33,000 to Shea Stadium on Sunday afternoon. It was sticky and sweltering, and by the third inning Mets pitcher George Stone felt drained. Stone and Aaron had played together for parts of six seasons. Stone's new teammates figured he knew Aaron's secrets, and they pushed him for advice on how to pitch the Braves star. He said he had none and proceeded to prove it. Aaron pelted two home runs off Stone. After the second one, a fan in the upper deck unveiled a banner painted with the number 715 in green. Aaron led the Braves to victory, knocking in three of four runs. When Eddie Mathews removed him for a pinch runner, Mets fans ushered him from the field with a standing ovation.

"I hope the commissioner was watching," Aaron teased. "Neither pitch was down the middle."

9

WAITING FOR ROGER

Hank, is the pressure getting to you?" Almost every day—sometimes a dozen times a day—Aaron faced a version of the question. What's the pressure like? Can you feel the stress increasing? How do you handle it? Almost always Aaron had the same answer: There is no pressure. He said it often and with conviction. "Pressure?" he repeated. "I don't know what that is really. I've been playing this game too long to all of a sudden think . . . I've got to play under pressure. I've got to play baseball the way I know I can play it, and that's to relax and do the things that I can do best."

No pressure? Aaron seemed to believe his words, but just about everyone else doubted him. How could it be that he didn't feel the pressure with bigots telling him to go back to the plantation and I'm-going-to-kill-you letters poisoning his mailbag? How could he pretend that all the attention and the autograph-seeking fans and the gang of reporters clustering around him didn't distress him? It seemed too much to accept as true. "He doesn't show the pressure outside," said Chicago pitcher Milt Pappas, "even though we all know how it's building up in him." But Aaron acted as calm as ever, and others praised his "gracious" behavior and "unfailing good nature"—all the while wondering.

Tom Brokaw, a young White House correspondent, visited Aaron while working on a documentary for NBC. Brokaw, with long hair and open-collar shirt, walked with Aaron from the warning track in left field toward home plate.

"Do you feel like you're under a lot of pressure?" Brokaw asked.

"Tom," said Aaron, his voice as easy and reassuring as Mister Rogers', "it's no pressure on me, really."

In spring, Aaron's orthopedic surgeon had pronounced him ready for the season. "This man looks at least six or seven years younger than thirty-nine," he said. "He is a strong, vigorous man and extremely stable emotionally."

And that's what everyone was really getting at, wasn't it? How would Aaron hold up mentally? Was he going to crumble? Would he explode? Might he stop talking altogether or get tearful or paranoid? Would there be a meltdown?

"Sportswriters are convinced there must be pressure so they keep talking about it, looking for something that isn't there," said Eddie Mathews. "Outwardly at least, Henry hasn't displayed a sign of pressure.... He'll send back his eggs because they aren't done the way he wants. 'Oops! See? Pressure's getting to him.' The fact is that Henry's always been particular about his eggs. He's sent them back for years when they weren't right."

"Everyone in the world wants him to roll over and kick his feet," said Mathews. "I told him he ought to do it once and get it over with."

All that stood between Aaron and the record was death, injury, or a mental breakdown. The latter provoked the most curiosity. One newspaper hired a clinical psychologist who had never met Aaron to interpret his behavior. He speculated that Aaron's angry response to heckling fans bordered on a "paranoid reaction." A psychiatrist in a health magazine analyzed

Aaron's on-the-field calmness, crediting an altered state of consciousness. "This allows him to screen out any noise and to be completely focused on the pitcher while physically he is relaxed and natural." *Psychology Today* broached the topic in a piece titled "Henry Aaron: Countdown to an Outrage." A sporting publication contributed a story headlined, "Can Aaron Possibly Crack?"

In baseball, any talk of pressure conjured one name, that of the last man to encounter the legend of Babe Ruth on a dark, sepia alley off Memory Lane, in the town of Nostalgiaville, state of Baseball Lore.

Roger Maris. Boyish, brush-cut, gap-toothed Roger Maris was the one man on the planet who had a sense of what Aaron faced. Under intense scrutiny in 1961, he had toppled Ruth's single-season home-run record, clubbing 61 home runs in a short-sleeved jersey that showed off his muscles. But doing so made him miserable. A private person, he lost clumps of hair from the stress of dealing with the New York media and ungrateful fans. He broke out with a nasty rash on his face and struggled with mental exhaustion.

"It's the continuous thing of people wanting your time," Maris said. "And everyone insists on being first. It's wearing on you, and it isn't something that stops after a while. It keeps wearing and wearing all the time. You get tired answering the same questions. 'What kind of pitch did you hit?' 'How many more home runs do you think you can hit?' 'Did the umpire call a bad pitch on you?'"

It didn't help that much of the baseball world hoped Maris would fail. Ruth's supporters deluged him with discouraging mail. They didn't want the Bambino's record to fall to a bland, second-year Yankee from Fargo, North Dakota. They didn't want the record to fall at all. But if it had to, it should at least belong to Mickey Mantle. Yeah, maybe Mantle. But not Maris.

He had never batted .300 and had only topped 30 home runs in one prior season. He wasn't worthy of the mark.

Unlike Aaron, Maris did not read his vile letters. He tossed them. But he couldn't escape the fans in right field who blistered him with vicious comments and booed him—sometimes for hitting a home run, sometimes for not. (In Detroit, one man lobbed a folding chair at him.) Ruth's contemporaries counted the ways in which Maris fell short. Rogers Hornsby, a National League great, described Maris as a "lousy player." Babe Ruth's widow wished her husband's record would stand: "I hope he doesn't do it," she said. "Babe loved that record above all." Even the commissioner of baseball, who had ghostwritten stories for Ruth, could barely disguise his desire that Ruth remain the record holder. Ford Frick ruled that Maris, Mantle, or any challenger would need to surpass Ruth's mark of 60 home runs within the same 154-game schedule to be the undisputed record holder. (By then, the season had expanded to 162 games.) "Maybe you should use an asterisk on the new record," suggested Dick Young.

As Hank Aaron closed in on Ruth's career record, interviewers repeatedly invoked Maris' name. Will you be able to handle the pressure better than Maris? Are you losing your hair, Hank? Maris got asked about Aaron, as well. Though months younger, he had been out of baseball five years, happily shedding his pinstripes after the 1966 season, vowing never to return to Yankee Stadium. He ended his career in St. Louis with World Series appearances in 1967 and 1968. Maris played twelve seasons, but excelled in only three, 1960–62, when he collected 133 home runs and knocked in 354 runs. He retired with a .260 average and 275 home runs.

"The thing Maris was going through was entirely different," said Aaron. Maris labored under a strict deadline. He had to achieve the record by the last game of the season or the opportunity would evaporate, as it had for Jimmie Foxx and Hank

Greenberg. If Aaron didn't reach 714 in 1973, he would continue the pursuit the following April. No deadline taunted him.

There were other differences, too. Though both men were reticent, Aaron dealt well with the media. He answered questions cordially. He acted with kindness and poise. Reporters often described him as the most approachable of baseball's stars. His age and stature helped. Aaron was finishing a long, rich career. Many fans and writers appreciated him. Maris was twenty-six when the 1961 campaign began. He had been in the big leagues only four seasons. He had appeared in two All-Star games but he hadn't tasted great success yet—or won a loyal following. Plus, Maris was curt and easily agitated. When critics told him to quit complaining about the booing fans who paid his salary by attending games, Maris retorted, "I didn't ask them to come."

Aaron and Maris had met as players but didn't know each other well. Now, they found their names entwined. Soon, Maris would be paying him a visit.

Hank Aaron viewed the home-run record with a sense of inevitability. If he stayed healthy, if he could play, he would claim it. "Let's face it," he said. "Anything could happen. After you reach a certain age, you might go out there and crack an ankle tomorrow. You just don't recuperate as quickly as you did when you were eighteen."

Aaron took care of himself. He exercised during the off-season. He got ten to twelve hours of sleep a night—and an hour more in the afternoon. "He's not a carouser in any sense of the word," said Eddie Mathews. As a concession to his age, Aaron limited his game appearances to conserve energy. He no longer started both ends of a doubleheader. He usually didn't play day games that followed night games, and he sat out contests that followed coast-to-coast flights.

Throughout his career, Aaron had avoided the disabled list, his one major injury being a broken ankle near the end of his rookie campaign. In the nine seasons to follow, he never missed more than six games annually. He averaged 153 games from 1955 to 1970, and in some of those campaigns the team played only 154. There were minor ailments: a sprained ankle in 1959 and another ankle surgery in 1965 to remove bone chips. In 1970, he hurt his knee in a collision with catcher Dick Dietz. Aaron assumed that it would be the knee problem that lingered into his late years. Aaron had it drained regularly. He lifted weights in winter and wore a brace on the advice of Willie McCovey—a veteran of such troubles—and the knee improved dramatically. But now, during this momentous season, at the same time he was denying feeling any pressure, health ailments were surfacing like air bubbles in water.

In St. Louis at the end of May, trainer David Pursley worked Aaron's muscles as he lay face down on a padded table amid whirlpools and a sauna. Younger players called Pursley "Doc." Aaron called him Dave. Pursley had been with the team since 1961, rising through the minors. He knew Aaron's aches as well as anyone. He massaged Aaron's back. The pain had been with Aaron on and off since April, and he had been unable to shake it. It had plagued him for a couple of years, prompting him to change his swing to accommodate it. He lowered his bat to reduce the strain, and that eased it. But now the problem was reoccurring frequently. Aaron resigned himself to the possibility that it might trouble him through what remained of his playing days. "Nothing seems to help," he said.

Aaron was often among the first players in the clubhouse. Dusty Baker would notice him hobbling like an old man—like Fred Sanford, he said. Aaron would sit at his stall with a newspaper and stare at the pages. Not reading, just gazing at the

print, a Zen-like ritual to clear his mind, block the hurt, and focus him on the battle ahead. And then he'd go out on the ball
field and play as if nothing were wrong. Only now it was getting tougher to do.

Ralph Garr witnessed his determination. Garr had been
around at the end of the 1969 season when Aaron cut his hand
badly, requiring stitches. With the playoffs about to begin,
Aaron tried to hide his injury. The team doctor gave him shots
of novocaine between his fingers before the game. Aaron
cloaked the wound with a batting glove. The Miracle Mets
swept the Braves, but Aaron hit .357 and led his team with
three home runs. Garr was amazed. Watching Aaron, he
learned, "There's a difference between playing with pain and
performing with pain." Through his actions, Aaron reinforced
one of the nuggets he instilled in Garr, Baker, and other willing
students: "You can't help your club in the tub."

Before the St. Louis game, Pursley warmed Aaron's muscles for the competition. The soreness limited Aaron's ability to
hit outside pitches with power, but neither Scipio Spinks nor
John Andrews knew that. Each surrendered a home run. The
next night, Aaron struggled at the plate. By the ninth inning, he
had yet to get a ball out of the infield. It was an unusual day for
Aaron. He had popped to first, grounded into a double play,
dribbled to the shortstop, and fanned. Aaron had a chance for
redemption in the ninth with the Braves down by one, the bases
loaded, and two out. Red Schoendienst brought in a right-
hander, Wayne Granger, to face Aaron, and Granger fed him
slow curveballs. Twelve in a row. Aaron fouled eight pitches before plopping a harmless fly into Lou Brock's mitt.

Pittsburgh followed St. Louis into Atlanta, and on the next
evening, his back still bothering him, Aaron approached the
plate with two runners on base. Jim Rooker, who had spent all
of his previous seasons in the Aaron-less American League,
tried to work around him. But when the count drifted to 3–1, a

grand advantage for a hitter, Aaron's teammates sensed what might be coming. Pitching coach Lew Burdette snickered. "He doesn't know what he's in for now." Rooker found out. Aaron drove the ball over the fence in left-center, giving his team all the runs necessary for the win.

Aaron's bad back flared up again in Los Angeles—for the fifth time in eight weeks. He had already missed half a dozen games because of it. This time, trainer Pursley could work no magic. Aaron took to the bench for three more games. "I'm going to play when I feel like it, do the best I can, and see what happens," he said. Aaron knew better than to push it. Mathews served as a daily reminder. His quest to pass Ted Williams on the all-time list had been thwarted by back troubles. The day after his 512th home run, Mathews was sidelined and then forced to undergo back surgery. He returned for a few months but never hit another. "I thought I'd finish my career with a lot more homers," he said.

Going out in public became an ordeal for Aaron. His face had become one of the most recognized in the sports world. Wherever he went, eager fans approached for autographs. Aaron instantly sized up situations. Could he tactfully sign a few or would it be a half-hour commitment? Would that first autograph seeker trigger a swarm of others, sending the signal that it was okay to approach? A peaceful meal with friends could quickly turn into an evening of disruptions and a never-ending line of well meaning but intrusive fans. And not everyone who approached had good intentions.

On a visit to California, Aaron joined Bob Hope, the Braves' director of public relations, for postgame drinks in the lounge of the Sheraton-West. Aaron was signing autographs when another patron took offense and accosted him. "You think you're better than the rest of us," he said. The man pushed Aaron. Hope and others leaped up to restrain him. Aaron excused himself from the table and returned to the solitude of his hotel room sanctuary, where he holed up on road trips, sleeping, eating meals, and watching *Days of Our Lives*.

Despite Aaron's introverted nature—"I'm a hard person to get close to; I can ride a plane from here to Los Angeles and not talk to anyone"—the isolation was too much. Paul Casanova sensed it. A warm, gregarious man, he spent many hours with Aaron in hotel suites talking about whatever: baseball, family, the Indianapolis Clowns. Sometimes, Ralph Garr and Dusty Baker would join them, and the evening would instantly get louder and funnier. It was a lively mix of personalities. It wouldn't take much to get Garr, in his animated style, to reenact the time he had rescued Baker in the Cajun outdoors. Petrified of poisonous snakes, Baker had stumbled upon a water moccasin beside a marshy lake. Garr came to his aid, killing the snake with a cane pole. Garr's stories never failed to get Aaron laughing.

Aaron's health ailments weren't limited to what he once termed his "mysteriously sore back." He also developed a cyst on his abdomen, which had to be lanced in Los Angeles, and missed several games in Chicago with what was described as a virus. An irritated shoulder also impeded him. Against San Francisco, Aaron had to leave a game with stomach pain. Eddie Mathews sent him to the hospital. "As easygoing as Henry is, I don't think it's nerves," said Davey Johnson. "But if it is, I sure wouldn't blame him." By season's end, Aaron would have fewer than 400 official at-bats, his lowest total yet.

Hank Aaron was a wily competitor, a sly veteran with a poker face, who told younger players to be careful of their words because they never knew who might be listening. He was a cautious man, proud of his ability to react calmly, control his temper, and deliberate before making reasoned decisions. One writer nicknamed him "Mr. Patience." "That's me," he said. Aaron learned from his father to never tip his cards. Even if Hank Aaron felt pressure, he wouldn't likely have advertised it. Why give his critics the satisfaction?

Whether Aaron recognized it or cared to admit it, perhaps the death threats, the hate mail, the controversies, and the endless comparisons to Babe Ruth were affecting him. Maybe, despite his best efforts to deny its existence, the pressure was weighing on him—and punishing his body. Jackie Robinson endured much abuse in order to integrate the major leagues. Late in his career, after that goal had been reached, he began to speak out and continued to until his last days. Robinson died young. Several of his teammates thought the stress he absorbed in the late 1940s had manifested in other diseases and stolen his breath.

"I think every black person is prepared to deal with pressure because they're born under adversity, and they live under pressure every day of their lives," Aaron said. "They know damn well that they've got to go out there and do better than the average person in order to keep their job."

Finally, in July, Aaron acknowledged for the first time that he had "noticed" increasing pressure. He used the word "noticed" as if he were an observer and the pressure were someone else's burden, not his. It was as if there were a distinct, emotional difference between the Aaron standing before reporters and this other entity, the one chasing a record. Aaron seemed to have disconnected the two. "I've noticed some pressure building up in the last few weeks—more writers and broadcasters in the clubhouse," he said. "I've never talked about this with Roger Maris, but I can't believe that the pressure on me is anywhere near the pressure that was on him. . . . He played in New York and that meant people were flocking around him all the time."

Not long after, Maris brought his sons to Atlanta to see the

Braves play. His nine-year-old boy, Richard, counted himself among Aaron's legions and begged his father to bring him up from Gainesville, Florida, where Maris ran a beer distributorship. The two men got a chance to talk and shared a laugh for the cameras. Maris said that he had no desire to relive his own chase: "Once was enough. . . . I think the most privacy I had was when the game was going on." He also declined to give Aaron advice. "I don't think Hank needs any. He's a big boy and knows how to take care of himself," he said. "I hope the public will realize that he is just a man trying to do a job."

Maris wished Aaron well and said he hoped Aaron would break the record. "For all the things he has done since he came into baseball, you have to admire and respect him," Maris said.

10

THE OTHER STAR

ommercial flights from LaGuardia Airport seared the sky over Shea Stadium on Saturday, July 7, as Hank Aaron and Willie Mays made history again by stepping onto the same ball field. No pair of players with more combined home runs had ever appeared on a diamond together. Between them, they had topped 1,350. But for a couple of thousand dollars, they might have hit most of those as teammates. In 1952, the New York Giants, Mays' first team, were on the verge of signing Aaron but were outbid by the Braves, who offered a larger guarantee to the Indianapolis Clowns, with whom Aaron was under contract. How different might baseball history have been with those two Alabamans—and later a third, Willie McCovey—in the same lineup? The possibilities tantalize. Would San Francisco have been home to a baseball dynasty? Would Sandy Koufax and the Dodgers have made it to the 1965 and 1966 World Series? Would Ruth's record have been under assault two decades on? By Aaron? Or would Candlestick Park have swallowed dozens of his deep drives?

Aaron broke into the majors three years after Mays and continually found himself one step behind. Mays captured his first MVP in 1954, Aaron in 1957. Mays won a batting title in 1954, Aaron in 1956. Mays led the National League in home runs in 1955, Aaron two years later. Mays beat Aaron to the World Series and to the All-Star Game. Inevitably, Aaron was widely viewed as second to Mays. As the two most prominent African-American players of their era, they faced constant comparison. They were measured against each other. Writers painted them as rivals, and they were on paper, by the fact that they often vied for the league lead in offensive categories. From 1955 to 1959, both men finished fifth or better in batting four out of five times. For eighteen years through 1972, one or both of them ranked among the top five in home runs.

Aaron and Mays considered each other friends—not best friends, but good enough to share occasional meals when their teams played, good enough to celebrate and socialize at All-Star Games for the nearly two decades that they were mid-season teammates. Publicly, they defused talk of a rivalry. "I like to think we're the closest of friends," Aaron said. Mays agreed. "Hank and I are good friends." Still, their words and actions over the years offered evidence of a rivalry, born more of an innate competitiveness than a personal animosity, though jealousies emerged at times.

Mays and Aaron each had their supporters. Mays' friends contended he was the more complete player, faster and more thrilling to watch. Remember that over-the-shoulder, back-to-the-plate catch in the 1954 Series? Aaron's boosters responded that he could do everything Mays could—and make it look easier. He flew around the bases without losing his hat, they said, which was a dig at Mays who, according to Eddie Mathews, "looked like he was coming apart at the seams" when he ran.

Early on, Aaron pronounced Mays the better player, confirming public sentiment. But by 1968 he had modified that assessment: "Mays is a greater ballplayer, but he's been a lucky ballplayer, too," Aaron said. "He got to play in New York and in San Francisco. They can make celebrities out of a benchwarmer like Phil Linz in New York." Later still, Aaron conceded nothing to Mays, judging himself the stronger hitter, while noting that if he had one game to win "there isn't anybody I would pick to play my center field but Willie."

Through most of their careers, Mays was thought to have the better shot at dethroning Babe Ruth. By the end of 1969, he knew otherwise. His output had withered to 13 home runs, for a total of 600. Aaron belted 44, giving him 554. "Ruth's record? Forget it," Mays said. "I don't have a chance. Maybe Aaron has. He's thirty-five—three years younger than me and he should play until he's as old as I am and maybe longer."

But it bothered Mays to see Aaron's chances increase as his own diminished. Mays witnessed Aaron's 500th home run but refused to have a picture taken with him. He also was on the field for Aaron's 600th in 1971. Will Aaron pass Ruth, he was asked? "Well, he has to catch me first," Mays said.

The next spring, after a year in which he hit 18 home runs to Aaron's 47, Mays downplayed the significance of Ruth's record. "What's so important about this record being broken?" he wondered. "I'm not trying to break the record; it's been around for quite a while." When pressed, he described Aaron as "a hell of a ballplayer. . . . But I haven't done too bad myself. As far as who is the greatest, well maybe he is, I don't know. The fans will have to determine."

That summer of 1972, Aaron passed Mays. He had already erased—or soon would—Mays' advantages in numerous other categories: hits, runs, doubles, runs batted in, total bases, extra bases, batting average, most years with 40 home runs, most with 30, most with 20, most years with 100 runs batted in, most with 100 scored, most sacrifice flies, most intentional walks, and on and on.

Now, as Aaron approached the pinnacle of his career, Mays saw his own playing days lurching toward a frustrating conclusion. The season had begun so pitifully for Mays that he had wanted to retire in May, but the Mets talked him out of it. It was June before he hit his first home run. "His batting reflexes are gone, and so is his arm," wrote Roger Angell, the sport's most celebrated writer. "His failings are now so cruel to watch that I am relieved when he is not in the lineup. It is hard for the rest of us to fall apart quite on our own; heroes should depart." Fellow players noticed, too. Young pitchers could sneak the fastball past him. "He takes that big swing and it looks great," one said. "But he can't hit anymore."

Prior to Saturday's game at Shea Stadium, as the thick sounds of organ music filled the park, Aaron and Mays agreed to appear on Ralph Kiner's postgame television show. The demands on Aaron's time were constant. Autograph hunters awaited him everywhere in New York: outside the Essex House hotel, across from Central Park; near the ballpark, as the team bus rolled in; even in the dugout, where he greeted dignitaries and sick children and posed for photos.

Neither Mays nor Aaron started but both saw action. Late in the game, two Mets outfielders, Don Hahn and rookie George Theodore, crashed on the warning track while chasing Ralph Garr's fly to left-center. Hahn struck the fence. The impact dropped both men with injuries. Garr turned the collision into an inside-the-park home run. Hahn and Theodore left on stretchers. Mays replaced Hahn in center field.

In his only at bat, Mays thrilled 30,000 fans by driving in two runs that put the struggling Mets in front. Aaron, called upon to pinch-hit, contributed a single in a three-run ninth inning that permanently returned the lead to the Braves. Afterward, as promised, Aaron made his way to Ralph Kiner, the former Pirates star, to appear live on *Kiner's Korner*. But Mays did not, leaving the host to uncomfortably alibi his absence. Kiner suggested on air that the difficult loss had zapped Mays.

Aaron felt snubbed—and others wondered, too. Had Mays turned so envious that he could not stomach sharing the stage with his old friend?

For two men almost evenly matched on the ball field, Hank Aaron and Willie Mays differed greatly away from the diamond. Their styles, temperaments, and personalities contrasted. Mays was cherry-red satin; Aaron, gray flannel. Mays could ignite a room with obscene language; Aaron could smother it with a piercing glance. Mays' emotions—anger, pain, joy—could develop and dissipate as quickly as a tornado; Aaron's simmered like a slow-cooking stew. In the area of civil rights, Aaron spoke his mind while Mays kept his thoughts to himself—and suffered attacks because of it.

More than anyone else, Jackie Robinson questioned Mays' silence. For his 1964 book, *Baseball Has Done It,* Robinson asked black stars of the day to share their experiences. Aaron participated in the project, detailing bigotry he had encountered in the professional leagues: racial heckling, threatening letters, knockdown pitches. Mays declined to participate, and Robinson challenged him publicly. "No Negro in the public eye can shilly-shally any longer," he said. "There's no escape, not even for Willie . . . from being a Negro." Robinson said he hoped Mays hadn't "forgotten his shotgun house in Birmingham's slums." Robinson blasted Mays several times. "You know, you can't forget your Blackness," he said.

Mays contended that it didn't bother him that baseball hadn't hired a black manager. "Why should it?" he asked. He didn't want to manage. Near the end of his career, he objected to critics who portrayed him alternately as an Uncle Tom character and a selfish man concerned only with his financial success. "I don't picket in the streets of Birmingham," Mays said. "I'm not mad at the people who do. Maybe they shouldn't be mad at the people who don't."

Aaron never railed against Mays the way Jackie Robinson did, not by name anyway. But he did try to motivate fellow players to look past their own interests. "I think we athletes sometimes sit back and as long as things are going good for us, we don't want to disturb the applecart," said Aaron. "We forget where we came from, you know? If not for baseball, I'd just be an average black for white people to step on. We in sports get lost sometimes, wrapped up in our own little thing, and as long as we got a dollar, we forget about how there's fifteen million other blacks in America. . . ."

As players, both Mays and Aaron had come a long way. But their contrasting public stances on civil rights issues made it seem as if Aaron had vastly outgrown him as a person, as if Mays had stopped pondering these topics decades back. When Aaron had first headed to Eau Claire as a teenager, he worried that he might not be able to compete against white athletes. The differences in how society treated the races told him that white players might be superior to him. In his early years, he quietly bore the indignities of the time: a manager who referred to him in the press as "Steppin-fetchit," the "oh-I-didn't-mean-anything-by-that" jokes and comments of teammates, the news stories that described him as slow, sleepy, and shuffling; the hotels in St. Louis that never put him in a room overlooking a swimming pool. Since then, Aaron had grown greatly as a man. His pursuit of the home-run record was changing him, too.

Ten days after Mays' no-show on the Kiner segment, New York visited Atlanta. Mets reliever Tug McGraw, one of the pitchers who created the fuss with Bowie Kuhn, arrived at the park to find a new baseball in his shoe, the sign that he would be starting. McGraw had been struggling, and manager Yogi Berra, whose job was rumored vulnerable, wanted to get him back on track. So he sprung a surprise start on McGraw, one of the team's zaniest characters. McGraw had recently been spouting a slogan—"You Gotta Believe"—that would follow the Mets as they rose from last place to the World Series. But at the moment the Braves looked to be the hotter team, having won ten of twelve games. Eddie Mathews was talking as if he knew his guys could play like that all along. Aaron hoped it marked a turnaround. He yearned to make the playoffs.

Prior to the game, Aaron headed to the cages to take his cuts. Children called his name as he ambled toward the clump of players ringing the cage. Aaron and Mays would often chat before batting practice, but Aaron did not seek out Mays and Mays did not approach Aaron. Near the cage, Aaron and Cleon Jones reminisced about the year Jones served as the Mobile Black Bears batboy when Aaron played for the team.

The game against McGraw started with promise for Atlanta. Ralph Garr rocketed the opening pitch into the left-center seats. Aaron contributed home run 698, and the Braves took a cushy 7–1 lead into the ninth before 8,100 paying customers. But it proved not enough. The Mets rallied. Mays, showing a flash of brilliance, entered as a pinch-hitter. He had been hot lately, hitting .319 over the month. With two outs, he lined a single deep to right, driving in the tying and winning runs. For Atlanta, it was the kind of loss that sometimes provoked Eddie Mathews to hurl a tray of Church's Chicken at the clubhouse wall. For others, it provided a sweet reminder of the athlete Willie Mays had been—the Willie Mays who would soon depart baseball.

In late September, Mays would say good-bye to New York. On a Tuesday evening, he would soak in the applause of 53,000 fans who had come to honor him at Shea Stadium. Mays had revealed a week earlier that he would retire at season's end. At the celebration, his admirers would give him cars and golf clubs. His peers—Joe DiMaggio, Ernie Banks, Stan Musial,

Duke Snider, and others—would praise his talents. Mays would dab his eyes with a handkerchief as they spoke. When it was his turn, he would say, "This is a sad day for me. I may not look it, but it is a new experience for me to have you cheer for me and not be able to do anything about it."

In his autumn, he admitted that his only regret was not breaking Babe Ruth's record. "That's the only thing I wanted to do that I didn't do," he said. If he had not served two years in the military, Mays might have hit 75 more home runs. If he had not played in Candlestick Park, he might have hit another 75 home runs. Either way, his supporters pointed out, he would have passed Babe Ruth.

There were always what-ifs. What if Ruth hadn't been a pitcher? What if Ted Williams hadn't served his country? What if Mantle hadn't hurt his knees? Aaron could have replied with one of his own: What if Aaron had concentrated on home runs early in his career, pulling the ball from day one? How many more could he have hit?

But Aaron didn't offer a what-if in his own defense. He didn't diminish Mays—or Mantle or Williams, either. (In fact, he acknowledged that Mays might have broken the record first had he not played in Candlestick Park.) But Aaron did have a response for those Babe Ruth defenders who needled him. If blacks had been allowed to play in Ruth's era, Aaron suggested, the home-run record might have belonged to Josh Gibson, a powerful catcher with the Homestead Grays and Pittsburgh Crawfords of the Negro leagues. "Hell, a lot of those records would have been broken a long time ago," he said. And if Ruth had been forced to face the best black pitchers, might he also have been deprived of a few of those 714 home runs?

11

SWEET HOME ALABAMA

Hank Aaron slipped back home to Mobile, Alabama, on an off-day in mid-July. The city was preparing for its annual deep-sea fishing rodeo, which on the weekend would draw thousands of sportsmen to compete for prizes (the big one being a camper trailer). Almost any sea creature was fair game: shark, stingray, red snapper, blackfish, bluefish, red-fish, flounder, grouper. Since 1929, the city had been playing host to the tournament. It was one of the highlights of summer, drawing entrants from throughout Alabama, Florida, Missis-sippi, Louisiana, and beyond.

Nothing relaxed Aaron like a day of fishing on the area's rivers or in the Gulf of Mexico. He had two boats, a seventeen-footer and a twenty-seven-footer. He kept the smaller one un-der a carport at the family home in Toulminville, where his parents, several siblings, and friends still lived. Aaron had grown up not far from the Mobile River, and though his mother forbade him from going near it as a boy, he was known to sneak down to the piers or to the bayou or nearby Three Mile River. The bay shaped life in Mobile.

Aaron liked the water for its solitude. If only for a few

hours, he could escape the phone calls, the questions, the autographs, the stares, and the knocks on his door. As he approached the 700 home-run mark, Aaron was drawing more attention. Topping the 600 plateau in 1971 had placed him in an elite league with just Willie Mays and Babe Ruth. But 700 had always been the domain of only Ruth. When Aaron finally crashed that ceiling, the countdown to the ultimate prize would begin.

Trips to Mobile rejuvenated him. They grounded him, reminded him of his roots, and reconnected him to his family. For all of the Aaron children, Edwards Street remained home. Even in adulthood, even when they lived elsewhere, it was the gathering place, their momma's nest. In her home, the same rules applied whether you were a store clerk or America's most famous baseball player. If Estella Aaron's children wanted to smoke a cigarette or sip a beer, they didn't do it in her presence. They slipped into another room or outside or to the nearby family-run, private club, Aaron's Sports Page, which had been built with Hank Aaron's baseball money.

Aaron's visits never went unnoticed in Mobile. Word spread by phone and on the street. The newspaper got tips. Friends spotted him wherever he went. Ball-playing buddies, former coaches, childhood pals, schoolmates, neighbors—they popped up at the airport, in stores, and near the ball diamond. Everyone, it sometimes seemed, had tales to tell about how their lives overlapped with that of Henry Aaron, or "Man," as his mother had called him since his boyhood (a result of his birth size).

" 'Man' was raised right here, between this store and the alley and that house," the widow who ran the cornerstore would recall. "I told his momma, 'You watch, "Man" is going to make you some money someday.' We're right proud of him."

"I was a better shortstop" would boast Dr. Warren Foster, who had played ball with Aaron.

Herman "Punkin" Smith, a hotel bellman, would relate,

"We grew up together, and it was always good times. Henry was so dedicated. He'd sacrifice anything to play and to win, and everything came so natural. I'll never forget the time we . . ."

Security officer Theodore Blunt would reminisce about how Aaron hung out around ballparks as a boy. "Why, he used to carry my glove."

And Ed Scott, who discovered Aaron and brought him to the attention of the Indianapolis Clowns, would sing of the promise: "The first time he got up to the plate he drove it to the fence on a line drive. I thought this kid could hit. He was lighting them up."

The Aarons' brick home on Edwards Street was no castle but it stood out among the smaller wood-frame houses along the block. Since Hank Aaron's sandlot days, the neighborhood had deteriorated. Central High was closed now, its windows broken, its rooms empty, weeds growing high around it. "Oh, we could move to a fancy neighborhood, get a bigger house, a bigger car," Herbert Aaron acknowledged. "What for? We've been happy here many years and we can be happy here many more. This is home." During Hank Aaron's brief July visit, his father tried to persuade him to move back to Mobile after his playing days. "I think he might," his dad said. "He loves to fish and hunt, so he might come back here to live."

As Aaron neared 700 home runs, major news organizations sharpened their focus on him. NBC was filming at the ballparks, and several national magazines were preparing spreads. Aaron's fishing excursion even had an element of business to it. In addition to being accompanied by his older brother Herbert and friend Joseph Coleman, Aaron went with journalists—some invited, some not.

They tried their luck first in a reedy spot near Chickasaw. But with the bass not biting, they headed to the Spanish River and then miles out into the bay. Under a hot son, Aaron and his party fished the still waters. Seated on the stern, with long slacks folded up to his knees and a bright orange preserver latched around his neck, Aaron dangled his stocking feet off the white fiberglass boat and cast his line for croaker. His party reeled in dozens of fish. But they were not alone. Photographers from *Newsweek, Time,* and *Ebony* were in nearby boats, filling frames of Aaron at play. The Mobile *Register and Press* also had been alerted to Aaron's return. A persistent reporter from the local paper called the Aaron home a dozen times that evening. When Aaron departed for Atlanta in the morning, a photographer was waiting for him at the airport. Aaron got his picture taken presenting a flight ticket to a clerk.

The hunt resumed in Atlanta later that day, but it wasn't just Aaron's hitting prowess putting him in the news. On *Today in Georgia,* WSB-TV's live morning show, Charles Welch asked cohost Billye Williams whether the rumors swirling throughout the city held any truth: Had she and Hank Aaron become engaged? Yes, she confirmed. They had been engaged since Easter and would wed after the Braves' season. Word of the upcoming nuptials spread nationally, and Williams got swamped with calls. "It's just surprising to wake up to all this," she said. "I can't really understand it, and I'm a bit disturbed at some of it because Henry is such a private person off the field and I wouldn't want it to hurt him or his children in any way."

Aaron celebrated with a three-run homer that night, number 699. It came in the seventh inning off army reservist Wayne Twitchell, who had spent the week drilling in combat boots at Fort Drum in New York. In his last appearance at the plate, Aaron got a shot at number 700. Many of the 9,031 in attendance flooded into the left-field seats in hopes of claiming a valuable souvenir. But Phillies pitcher Mac Scarce walked Aaron. Fans booed. The home run would have to wait.

But not for long.

hose who heaped anger, bitterness, and threats upon Hank Aaron did not represent the nation. Most people wanted to celebrate Aaron's pursuit. Some did it with song. Atlanta Pops director Albert Coleman, a Frenchman who had never been to a baseball game, wrote a march, "Hank's 715." He envisioned it being performed at parades and in ballparks. Elmo Ellis, general manager of an Atlanta TV station and working under the pseudonym "Big Daddy Beaver," contributed "Hammerin' Hank" to the catalog. Louisianan Evans J. Falcon offered "714," and the Blast Furnace Band and the Grapevine Singers presented "Hammerin' Hank, Part I." But none of them made the Top 40 play list dominated by Jim Croce's "Bad, Bad Leroy Brown" and Charlie Rich's "Behind Closed Doors."

The song that received the most exposure came out of Detroit. "Move Over, Babe" combined the talents of Tigers radio announcer Ernie Harwell and pitching prospect Bill Slayback. Harwell, who had grown up in Georgia and been the paperboy for *Gone With the Wind* author Margaret Mitchell, hatched the idea. He wasn't a novice. B. J. Thomas and Homer and Jethro, among others, had recorded his songs. Slayback, who provided the music, was something of a Renaissance man. He sang, played numerous instruments, painted, sketched, and made furniture. Released in America and Japan, their song got airplay on radio and the *NBC Game of the Week*. Aaron gave his blessing to the project.

> *Move over, Babe.*
> *Here comes Henry and he's swinging mean.*
> *Move over, Babe.*
> *Hank's hit another; he'll break that 714.*

In Philadelphia, Mayor Frank Rizzo, the Black Elks, and prominent business officials feted Aaron when the Braves came to town. The Elks launched a national petition drive in support of Aaron. In Congress, representatives introduced a resolution condemning the hatred directed at Aaron. It stated in part, "Whereas today, Hank Aaron's efforts have been the target of racial slurs and insults from a small minority of individuals, it should be made clear that these utterances do not in any way reflect the feeling of the vast majority of Americans."

Aaron's chase spawned poems, posters, buttons, and contests—as well as "Aaron Is Ruth-less" bumper stickers. The *Sporting News* tapped an astrologer to chart Aaron's fortune. He went out on a limb and reported, "There is an astrological indication of considerable power in his wrists and excellent control of their use."

Billye Williams, thinking the Braves' game started at 7 P.M., rather than 6 P.M., had not yet departed for the stadium Saturday, July 21, when the opening pitch was thrown. Consequently, she missed Aaron's first appearance of the night. He got a single, which extended his streak to nine games. Two innings later en route to the park, she was listening on her car radio to Milo Hamilton's broadcast. Pitcher Ken Brett had surrendered a double to Darrell Evans, and Aaron was approaching the plate again, his step absent of swagger. He stopped outside the batter's box and looked toward the pitcher's mound while pressing his helmet onto his head. The Braves on the bench were quiet with expectation. "You knew it was going to happen. It was just a matter of time," said pitcher Phil Niekro. "It's like the sun coming up every morning. You just don't know what time."

Brett, twenty-four, had little experience against Aaron. Prior to being traded to Philadelphia, he played in the American League. He came from a baseball family (younger brother George would debut in two weeks), and he certainly knew of Aaron—who didn't? Brett realized that Aaron was on the verge of a significant plateau. As a reminder, one of his teammates taped the number 700 to his locker. In previous games against Brett, Aaron had discovered that Brett relied on his fastball. He had good luck with it against Aaron. Earlier in the evening, Brett had fed him mostly breaking balls. Aaron knew to be looking for fastballs now.

With Evans on second, the thin left-hander pitched from the set. He leaned toward catcher Bob Boone for the sign, pulled back into position, and unleashed one too high. The next pitch to Aaron also looked high and outside, but umpire Ken Burkhart called it a strike. Aaron turned his head toward him, disagreed with a subtle word or two, backed off the plate, and swept his right hand through the dirt, grabbing a palmful and rubbing it into his bat handle.

Brett's third pitch came in low, but Aaron took an uppercut and drove it toward the left-field stands. Greg Luzinski rumbled back a bit and watched it sail over a fan's long-pole fishing net. It disappeared five rows up into a thickening tangle of raised arms and wiry bodies. Robert Winborne, who had recently graduated from high school and had set down a copy of Aldous Huxley's 1928 satirical novel *Point Counter Point* in anticipation, stealthily nabbed the ball, hid it, and escaped the rowdy, chaotic scene. Aaron trotted the bases as if it were home run 227, rather than something momentous. His elbows were bent, his face blank, his pace steady. The opposing Phillies did not congratulate him as he passed; their team had just lost the lead. The fans supplied the emotion.

Brett, the pitcher, stood facing his dugout, hands propped on hips while an outfield scoreboard glowed with the number 700. As Aaron rounded third base, coach Jim Busby greeted him with one hand and swatted his rear with the other. No swarm of players waited at the plate, but Darrell Evans, who had scored, was just beyond. "Henry didn't say anything," said Evans. But when Aaron touched home, he broke into a smile. Evans noticed him tremble with excitement. It was imperceptible to the audience, but standing beside him Evans detected the flicker of emotion. Dusty Baker, Davey Johnson, and Ralph Garr welcomed Aaron as he approached the steps of the dugout. All of his teammates were on their feet applauding.

So were the fans. They gave Aaron a two-minute ovation. He emerged from the dugout twice to acknowledge their appreciation, holding his cap above his head as if it were a torch and he were the Statue of Liberty. The Phillies went on to win the game, which added to their graciousness about Aaron's achievement. "The home run didn't mean anything to me except that I can say I seen it," said manager Danny Ozark. "He can hit all he wants as long as we win."

Aaron relaxed in front of his locker, loosening the belt around his waist as reporters closed in around him. Aaron gripped the home-run ball and held it for the photographers standing on chairs behind the pack. A pile of seven hundred silver dollars set on a table in front of him, the prize the team had offered for the ball. Beside Aaron, Robert Winborne, the eighteen-year-old who had retrieved it and won the money, offered to donate the cash to charity. Aaron refused, telling the young man to keep the money for himself.

"Hank, that's about how old you were when you started," one writer interjected.

That night and over the next two days, Aaron received a flood of telegrams. Jesse Jackson sent one, as did the president of the National League. Fans, friends, and even a former teammate, Montreal pitcher Pat Jarvis, congratulated Aaron by wire. But missing from the stack of a hundred messages was an acknowledgment from the commissioner of baseball, Bowie Kuhn. He hadn't sent one, and Aaron noticed.

Eddie Mathews was disappointed at the All-Star break. His team was playing lousily again. In the last game prior to the three-day mid-summer respite, the Braves made a club-record seven errors and lost a sixth straight game. "We looked like a bunch of amateurs, for cripe's sake," he said. "You make two or three errors and it's a bad day. But seven? I still can't believe it." The team owned a 45–57 record, worse than under Lum Harris when the Braves fired him and promoted Mathews.

In April, with Aaron, Baker, and Garr slumping, Mathews had worried that hitting might be the problem. But soon the bats had heated and the pitching had cooled. Health troubles didn't help. Pitcher Mike McQueen and first baseman Jim Breazeale had been seriously hurt in a December car accident. During the season, Gary Gentry and Ron Reed, both starters, had injured their arms, and catcher John Oates had followed them on to the disabled list. Statistics placed the Braves among the top offensive teams, powered by Evans, Aaron, and Johnson. But the pitching ranked with the worst. With sixty games remaining, the Braves were nineteen out of first place. "I don't know about the rest of the club," said Mathews, "but I need the All-Star break."

The Forty-fourth All-Star Game came to Kansas City the fourth week of July 1973. For a nineteenth straight year, the National League team would feature Hank Aaron. The contest showcased baseball at its most festive. The World Series may have been a bigger production with greater historical and financial significance, but the Mid-Summer Classic offered a breezy, carefree feel that celebrated the sport and its heroes and risked nothing, save for a little pride.

In 1970, after a twelve-year run in which managers, coaches, and players chose teams, baseball returned to fans the right to select starting lineups for each league. Hank Aaron garnered the most votes that year and the next, 1971. A year later, young Johnny Bench received the highest tally, though Aaron proved to be the game favorite by slamming a dramatic, go-ahead home run before an Atlanta crowd.

This summer fans voted Aaron as the starting first baseman, a position he had abandoned in spring. With 1.3 million ballots, Aaron outpulled everyone except Bench. But controversy muddied the process. Despite remarkable half-season statistics, Bobby Bonds was not picked to start. Fans preferred an outfield of Pete Rose, Billy Williams, and Cesar Cedeno. "Who am I to say that I'm better than those other fellows?" Bonds asked. Further, Willie Mays, who had a streak of appearances nearly identical to Aaron's, had been inadvertently left off the twenty-eight man roster in what was suspected to be his final season. The leagues scrambled to correct the oversight, and created an additional spot on each team, clearing room for Mays in the National League and fire-throwing, no-hit pitcher Nolan Ryan in the American League.

Royals owner Ewing Kauffman, who had made his millions in pharmaceuticals, looked forward to introducing his sparkling new park to a television audience expected to exceed fifty million. The stadium, which had opened in April, featured fountains and waterfalls. "It's beautiful. It don't take a backseat to nobody," said Cincinnati manager Sparky Anderson. At game time, the field would be accented with All-Star emblems and bases with red, blue, and white stars.

Players worked out at the park on Monday. As had become customary, the two senior veterans, Aaron and Mays, posed together for photographers. One year, they had sat on carousel horses at a Six Flags amusement park, illustrating the neck-and-neck nature of their home-run race. This time, Aaron held a painted portrait of himself as Mays smiled and admired it, veins bulging from his arms. Their falling out seemed over.

Amid the fun and frivolity, Aaron took Jackie Robinson's advice and let the world know that he was unhappy, less it be assumed otherwise. At a formal press conference, he spoke out about the game two nights earlier and his 700th home run. "I got one hundred telegrams congratulating me," he said, his voice unexcited. "But I didn't receive a telegram from the commissioner. I would think that the commissioner would send one, too. I felt let down. I think what I did was good for baseball. I felt like he should have sent me a wire. I'm not agitating him and I'm perfectly serious. I mean this sincerely. Regardless of how small he thinks it is hitting that home run, it wasn't small to me. I feel he should have acknowledged it somehow. Frankly, it bothers me."

But the true issue lay deeper than a forgotten telegram. It wasn't just about the commissioner ignoring an historic home run. For decades, Aaron had played in the shadow of more popular and better known players, always assuming that when his time came the recognition would be his. "As I always say," he once offered, "good things come to those who wait." But how long did he need to wait? Wasn't twenty years enough? When Aaron got his 3,000th hit in 1970, the commissioner did not congratulate him. And then after he donated items to the Hall of Fame, the museum did not list his contributions in its brochure. And then in June, Bowie Kuhn responded rapidly and authoritatively to the news story about pitchers possibly serving home runs to Aaron. The lack of a telegram felt like a slam to Aaron, a step removed from a Roger Maris asterisk—a not-so-subtle statement that the official baseball world would prefer he not break Ruth's record.

Kuhn chose his words carefully when he responded to Aaron. "I'm certainly sorry that Henry Aaron was disappointed as I am sure he knows I am one of his biggest rooters," he said. "I want to lead the baseball celebration when he hits 714 and 715."

Aaron skipped the official luncheon the next day. Almost all other players attended, as did the commissioner and participants in the 1933 All-Star Game. (That inaugural game took place at Comiskey Park in Chicago, and it starred a thirty-eight-year-old outfielder near the end of his career. Babe Ruth hit a home run that day.)

On Tuesday afternoon, Kansas City was gearing up for the

evening's game and hoping that the rain showers would stop before the 7:30 P.M. start. Unofficially, it was to be Hank Aaron's night. Though the torrent of mail had turned favorable in recent weeks, death threats continued to arrive in the postal bags around Carla Koplin's desk. One letter warned Aaron that should he be within twenty homers of Ruth by July 24, "you will be shot on site by one of my assassins" at the All-Star Game. He was within fourteen.

Morning and afternoon rains canceled batting practice. Groundskeepers needed time to prepare the drenched Astro-Turf. They vacuumed the green-carpet infield and employed special machines, Gamesavers, to press water from the outfield surface. The opening festivities began as scheduled, with the park jammed, the sky cloudy, and the temperature in the upper seventies. Kansas City showed off its state-of-the-art water fountain. A military band played, a chorus sang, and members of the first All-Star team—Bill Dickey, Charlie Gehringer, Lefty Grove, Carl Hubbell, Joe Cronin, Earl Averill, Wes and Rick Ferrell, and a dozen others—bowed to polite applause. As the starting lineups were introduced, players trotted to the baselines one by one. Royals fans cheered their own players— Amos Otis, Cookie Rojas, and John Mayberry—and booed the large Oakland contingent. (The A's had moved from Kansas City in 1968.)

But the 40,849 fans reserved their most resounding greeting for Hank Aaron. When his name was announced, they rose from their seats and gave him such a spirited ovation that it seemed obvious they felt impelled to show Aaron, on behalf of most of America, that he was appreciated. He tipped his cap twice.

Aaron contributed an RBI single to his team's 7–1 victory. Bobby Bonds stroked a home run and electrified the crowd by turning a single into a double through sheer hustle. He won the MVP award. It was a good night. When it was all over, players pressed toward the parking area. Fans grabbed and pushed and called for autographs. Aaron breezed past the group.

"Drop dead," one man yelled. "Who needs you?"

"We don't want no nigger breaking the Babe's record," added another.

Aaron walked off into the night.

12

A HERO RETURNS

ank Aaron's eyes blinked open around three in the morning, and he found himself stunned awake, as if someone had shocked him with a prod. Where was he, anyway? The Essex House in New York? The Marriott in Philadelphia? The Sheraton in San Francisco? The room was dark, save for a sliver of light seeping in from behind drawn curtains. He was on a hotel bed, in a room alone, the air conditioner droning its monotonous song. He needed sleep but his mind raced and his eyes were wide open.

He had never had trouble sleeping and now these spells were surfacing regularly. The change was disconcerting. What was it about? Had the pressure of the chase finally gotten to him? Was the media coverage too intense? Was he worrying for the safety of his children? Was it Babe Ruth? Was he pushing too hard to break the record in an effort to reclaim his life? "Maybe it's because you're constantly getting bugged," he said, talking again as if his problem were someone else's. "It's hard to say what it's due to. . . . If I could just relax a little bit. If I could just get away one day and go fishing . . ." The thought trailed off.

The home runs were no longer coming. Two weeks had passed since the All-Star Game, and Aaron had found the seats just once, leaving him stranded an unlucky thirteen short of Ruth. Even in batting practice, he couldn't drive the ball over the fence. His chances of passing Ruth in 1973 were dropping like a sharp sinker, and he knew it. "I don't really think that it's possible," he said.

Aaron desperately needed a jolt.

Hank Aaron played with good company. Throughout his career, he had been fortunate to be in a lineup with strong hitters. There had been Eddie Mathews, Joe Adcock, and Wes Covington, and later Rico Carty, Joe Torre, and Orlando Cepeda. With other capable sluggers providing a threat, pitchers could not easily work around Aaron. Their presence contributed to his success, to a lesser degree but in a similar way that Lou Gehrig and other Yankees contributed to Ruth's. Though there were no Gehrigs on the Braves, Aaron's teammates reminded opponents with startling consistency that the club's hitting didn't end with baseball's biggest name.

In early August, with a game tied in the ninth and two runners on base, Aaron moved into the on-deck circle swinging a weighted bat as if cutting weeds with a long-handled sickle. The sight of him charged the small, under-7,000 crowd. But as he settled in at the plate, the mood turned sour when San Diego catcher Fred Kendall motioned for an intentional walk. Boos rained onto the field. Manager Don Zimmer had decided to load the bases, remove Aaron's bat, and face twenty-six-year-old Darrell Evans. "If he had pitched to me," Aaron laughed later, "I'd probably have popped up or something." But Evans singled home the winning run.

It wasn't the only time such a move had backfired. Aaron usually batted fourth, succeeded by Dusty Baker or Davey Johnson or Evans. Like Aaron, roommates Johnson and Evans were competing with Willie Stargell for the lead in home runs. The three Braves motivated each other. Baker, having emerged from his slump, was putting up good numbers, too. "This is the best offensive club in baseball, and we hit more home runs than anybody," said Johnson, whose power surprised those who had watched him in Baltimore. He had never had the kind of season he was enjoying now. "Being around Hank Aaron and Darrell Evans and an explosive club, I guess it just rubbed off." Twice, Davey Johnson had hit home runs after pitchers intentionally walked Aaron.

In August, it looked as if Johnson, Evans, and Aaron might each be en route to 40 home runs. If it happened, it would be a first. No three teammates had ever achieved that feat. Despite their shining performances, Evans and Johnson found little opportunity to emerge from Aaron's shadow. They said they didn't mind; they were witnessing history. "He's the number-one story in baseball," said Evans. "The guy is finally getting what's due him. I'm excited over it, too. I'll be the first to congratulate him when he hits 715."

Nicknamed "Howdy" by teammates for his resemblance to TV puppet Howdy Doody, Evans admired Aaron. In 1969, when he came to spring training for the first time, Evans found his locker in an intimidating place, between veterans Clete Boyer and Bob Aspromonte and across from Hank Aaron. He was twenty-one, and at his parents' home near Pasadena, a Hank Aaron poster still hung on the wall of his former bedroom. "I had no friends when I first came here," Evans said. "Hank Aaron was the first to talk to me." Aaron told Evans he had heard a lot about him, wanted him to be able to relax, and felt he might be able to help the team. It was an Aaron story to which others could relate.

Aaron took pride in Darrell Evans and Dusty Baker. He had been watching them for years and had lobbied the team president to give them a full-time opportunity. "He promised me they would play," Aaron said. They did in 1972. "Let me tell you about these two kids," Aaron said after one game. "They have the potential to be two of the greatest ballplayers in the league.... Dusty had a fantastic year last year and you know what Darrell is doing now.... And because of all the attention I've been getting, they will have had the experience without being in the limelight. This could be a blessing in disguise for them, the lack of publicity."

The day after Evans' game-winning hit, Aaron once more appeared at the plate in the ninth inning. The Braves were down 4–3, and the bases were clear. Again, Atlanta fans sensed the potential for Aaron-induced drama, and again Zimmer deprived them of it. Because of lineup changes, pitcher Danny Frisella was due to bat after Aaron. Zimmer knew that Eddie Mathews had depleted his bench and that Chuck Goggin, a utility infielder, would be called to hit for Frisella. So he played the odds. He walked Aaron, which infuriated Atlanta fans. But the strategy worked. Goggin ended the game on a grounder. For three weeks, Zimmer got hate mail from people who interpreted the walks as evidence of bias. "People were saying I was prejudiced. The only thing I was prejudiced against was losing," he said.

S truggling at the plate, Aaron limped into Milwaukee for an exhibition in the city that had given him his start. August 6 was Hank Aaron Day in Wisconsin, and it had the feel of a hero's homecoming. Thirty-three thousand showed up at County Stadium to celebrate the man who had starred with the Braves in all but one of the team's thirteen local seasons. Though another franchise, the Brewers, had arrived in 1970, Milwaukeeans still harbored resentment over being jilted for Atlanta. But their sense of betrayal didn't taint the warmth they held for their heroes of yesteryear. For two of them, Monday marked a special day.

Nine hundred miles away in Cooperstown, Warren Spahn,

one of baseball's best left-handers, was being enshrined in the National Baseball Hall of Fame. He used the occasion to praise a former teammate. "Henry Aaron," he said, "is the greatest athlete I've ever seen in my life."

Aaron arrived at County Stadium hours before the game, accompanied by Bill Bartholomay. He greeted a parade of old friends and former associates: his first manager, banjo-strumming "Jolly Cholly" Grimm; teammate Felix Mantilla, who had played with him in Jacksonville; Del Crandall, catcher for the World Champion Braves of 1957 and now manager of the Brewers; and former Eau Claire president Ran Bezanson. "Say hello for me to the people of Eau Claire," Aaron told him. He also reconnected with Brewers chief Bud Selig, whom he had known since the early days when Selig's father, Ben, owned a Ford dealership that loaned cars to Milwaukee athletes. As a private citizen, Selig had battled to keep the Braves in the beer capital of America. Aaron and Selig used to go to Packers games together.

"This is where it all started eighteen years ago," Aaron told a crowd of reporters. "I want you to know that I'm happy to be back. . . . I've got so many memories here and so many friends. It is very easy to remember the Milwaukee days." It was in Milwaukee, he said, where he decided to become a power hitter. "I found that I could be a .350 hitter and be an 'ordinary' ballplayer. So I tried to change," he said. "I felt I could get more recognition by hitting home runs."

Aaron was in a glorious mood, putting a positive spin on every topic. He dismissed the notion that playing in Milwaukee prevented him from getting the acclaim he deserved. "That's a lot of bunk," he said. "It's not the town; it's the player. Johnny Bench plays in Cincinnati, and it hasn't seemed to hurt him. The press builds up a player, and a fellow who consistently hits home runs will get his share of publicity no matter where he lives. The trouble is that it took me a long time to realize that."

Aaron also rededicated his quest to young fans, "They are

the ones who are seeing me now, and I want them to remember Hank Aaron twenty years from now, just like the kids of yesterday remember Babe Ruth."

Later, dressing in the clubhouse, Aaron grinned as he fastened his belt. "Not too bad," he said, glancing at his waist. "I've gone up an inch or two . . . but you've got to expect that with age and maturity. I'm filled out now. When I came to Milwaukee at the age of eighteen, I couldn't look anything but lean. I had been eating hamburgers instead of steaks, like I do now." The cheery disposition camouflaged Aaron's back pain. He had sat out three of the previous five games, and if this contest had been anywhere other than Milwaukee he would have sat out again. But Aaron didn't want to disappoint the thousands who had bought tickets. Milwaukee fans had never blistered him with obscenities, and he knew he needed to be in the game. Half of the fans, maybe more, had come to see him.

Eddie Mathews insisted that he would allow Aaron to play only if he could be a designated hitter and spared the discomfort of covering the field. The controversial DH was new to the American League, and National League rules forbade teams from using the DH even in scrimmages. Braves officials scrambled before the game to get a waiver from league president Chub Feeney. But he was near Cooperstown, and they couldn't reach him. The Braves and Brewers prevailed upon umpire Bruce Froemming, who had grown up in Milwaukee rooting for Aaron, to ignore National League rules and allow Aaron to bat. Atlanta vowed to take the heat from the league office. Given the special circumstances, Roemming consented. (League officials ignored the infraction.)

Milwaukee honored Aaron prior to the game. In the ceremony, when Aaron was introduced, the response was long and thunderous. The roar swept over County Stadium and spilled into the neighborhood nearby. The place shook as it did in the 1950s when Aaron, Mathews, Spahn, and company made the city a winner. The affection flowed toward Aaron from all directions for two and a quarter minutes. The fans stayed standing as Aaron spoke. "I'm so happy to have played before so many wonderful fans."

Aaron got a half dozen standing ovations that evening.

By the sixth inning, he had appeared twice, grounding out and walking. With the Brewers ahead by three runs—and the fans having booed Bill Parsons for pitching around Aaron his previous time up—Parsons decided to challenge Aaron. "If I walk him again," he thought, "the fans will tar and feather me." He figured they had come to see Aaron take his swings, so he threw a fastball and Aaron put it in the seats.

Again, as Aaron circled the bases, as he touched home, as he shook the hands of other players, as he jogged into the dugout and reemerged to tip his cap, the crowd stood in respect and cheered. In the stands, Sharon Money, wife of Brewer Don Money, looked around and noticed that fans were crying. Above Aaron along the second deck hung a hand-painted sign. "Welcome Home, Hank!" it said. The emotion of the moment struck Aaron. His eyes were wet and red, too.

An hour after the game, hundreds waited outside the locker room for a glance at the future home-run champion. Police had to rope off a path so Aaron could leave, shortly after 11 P.M. But before he departed, Aaron said that he would like to return to Milwaukee—as a team executive. "I've got to eat," he said. "I've got to support my family and have a job." Then, he added, in words that sounded more like a plea than a pleasantry, "I promise to work as hard being in the front office as I did when I was a player. . . . If I had a choice, it would be Milwaukee."

Days later, Bowie Kuhn tried to smooth the dispute with Aaron and eradicate his public-relations problem. Kuhn made a trip to St. Louis to surprise the Braves star. Prior to a

Thursday evening game, he talked with Aaron at Busch Stadium and suggested that perhaps the flap over the telegram had been a media-fueled misunderstanding.

"No. No, it wasn't," Aaron said.

Kuhn stated his case, explaining that he rarely congratulated players on their achievements. "There are so many of them," he said, "that you're going to run the risk of offending someone you didn't remember." Kuhn repeated his pledge, though, that he would set aside his usual protocol "to lead the cheering section" when Aaron hit his 714th and 715th home runs. Aaron was content to let the commissioner's explanation stand on its own weak legs. Grinning, Aaron related later that Kuhn had told him that "if he started sending telegrams, he'd end up sending telegrams every time someone got three doubles." Kuhn's words weren't the only rubbish being tossed at Aaron that night. In the fourth inning, umpire Bob Engel stopped play after a commotion in the left-field stands, where a few fans were chucking crushed cups at Aaron.

By mid-August, Hank Aaron had gone sixteen days without a home run. He was choosing to sit out more frequently, having started barely half of the nineteen contests since July 21. Aaron skipped batting practice one afternoon. "What's the use?" he asked. "When I come out there, it's 'do this interview,' 'take this picture.'" Eddie Mathews worried that Aaron, despite his assurances, was not feeling well. "It's nothing you can put your finger on," he said. "It's just the reaction I get some nights when he decides not to play."

13

CHICAGO REVIVAL

Hundreds of *Little Leaguers* looked to the podium, where the Rev. Jesse Jackson addressed a Thursday morning prayer breakfast. With Aaron, head bowed, beside him, Jackson told the children, "Hank Aaron refused to defile his body, refused to have his mind defiled. Because he has overcome staggering odds, we look to him as a success model, as one who represents the very best to our people." The audience, almost entirely black, was comprised mostly of boys. They wore Scout uniforms and denim jackets and dress pants and sat at long tables in a high-ceilinged room on the south side of Chicago. Adults lined the walls, and everybody cheered as Aaron stood to speak. He shared one of the hate letters he had received.

"Why are they making such a big fuss about you hitting seven hundred home runs?" Aaron read. "Please remember you have been to bat 2,700 more times than Babe Ruth. . . . So, Hank, what are you breaking? . . . Hank, there are three things you can't give a nigger." Aaron paused and the quiet of the crowd was interrupted by a single child's voice.

"Uh-oh," the boy said.

Aaron continued: "A black eye, a puffed lip, or a job."

Aaron smiled, and the audience laughed.

"These are the kind of letters I receive. Things like this make me push harder."

"Yeah," a man answered. Applause erupted.

Aaron seemed to be changing as he spoke, his tone growing inspirational, as if he were becoming more convinced than ever that God had given him a mission. Somewhere along the way, he realized, this had evolved into something much greater than baseball.

"In Mobile, Alabama," Aaron said, "I realized as a black person I already had two strikes against me. And I certainly wasn't going to let them get the third strike." By one account, Aaron pledged to hit a home run for the children who had gathered. Most of them would be heading to the ballpark.

The Cubs led 2–0 by the eighth inning that afternoon and appeared on the verge of ending their ten-game losing streak. With one out, relief pitcher Bob Locker walked Aaron, drawing boos from Cubs fans who thought they had witnessed the star's last Chicago appearance of the season. Locker followed with another walk and then a double and a single and another single before Jack Aker replaced him on the mound. The Atlanta barrage continued with hits by Ralph Garr, Mike Lum, and Darrell Evans, which brought Hank Aaron back to the plate. Aaron took two strikes, a ball, and fouled one off before getting his pitch. The count at 2–2, Aker laid a fastball across the plate, eighteen inches too high. Aaron put the pitch out of the park and beyond Waveland Avenue, where a fifteen-year-old boy pounced on it. The ball traveled over 425 feet. "It was the hardest ball I hit in three weeks," Aaron said. The Chicagoans overwhelmed Aaron. "It gives you a little bit of a tickle around the heart when they give you those great ovations here," he said.

The home run, number 702, had come on August 16. On the same day in 1948, exactly twenty-five years earlier, newspapers ran special editions and radio stations broke into regular programming with this bulletin: "Babe Ruth is dead."

Aaron and the Braves headed to Jarry Park for a weekend series in Montreal, the place where Jackie Robinson had begun his drive to the major leagues. The year before he got promoted to the Brooklyn Dodgers, Robinson played with the Royals of the International League. He found the city more welcoming than most of America. For the rest of his life, he talked of the kind treatment he had received there. Aaron also enjoyed the city, though the park itself wasn't a favorite.

In 1972, shortly after Eddie Mathews had become manager, the Braves visited Montreal and quickly dropped two games. Playing miserably, they were desperate for a victory. Behind 1–0 in the final inning, Aaron knelt on one knee near the on-deck circle and watched as Darrell Evans flew out to right field. Bill Stoneman had been tough all afternoon, allowing just two hits. Aaron approached the plate, pulled his helmet onto his head, and proceeded to blast a ball to deep left. Everyone in the Braves dugout knew it was gone. They bolted from the bench. They celebrated. The game was tied, they thought. But a strong gust halted Aaron's long fly. The ball dropped in left field—into Ken Singleton's mitt. It was as if Mother Nature had stolen a home run from Aaron. Dusty Baker made the final out. Demoralized, the Braves showered in silence, dressed, and headed to the team bus for the ride back to the Queen Elizabeth Hotel.

Aaron and Paul Casanova took the backseats. It was their tradition, a bow to their separate tenures with the Indianapolis Clowns. Veteran Clown players used to make rookies like Aaron and Casanova ride in the backseats. Now, the two of them did it by choice, a reminder of how far they had come. But no one was laughing on that day.

Aaron was in a dark mood, and Casanova tried to get him to talk.

Aaron shook him off.

Casanova tried again.

"Ham, you okay?" he asked.

"Yeah, man," Aaron said finally. "You know, I think Babe Ruth was up there blowing that damn ball back."

The comment cracked up the other players, and laughter replaced the stony silence. The Braves went on to win five straight.

This time, the wind wouldn't deny Hank Aaron. In the sixth inning of the Friday opener, he drove a fastball to left-center for home run 703. It erased Montreal's lead, but 23,800 Expos roared their approval. The hit tied Aaron with Stan Musial for a record 1,377 extra-base hits. Afterward, Aaron announced, "I'd like to break it in Montreal this weekend."

He toppled Musial's mark the next day, contributing his third home run in three days. "This was very important to me," Aaron said. "It is a tremendous achievement for me." And then he added a startling footnote: "Getting that many extra-base hits means even more to me than 714 or 715 home runs."

The Braves returned home to play St. Louis, which had settled into first in the East Division. The Cardinals jumped to an early advantage Tuesday, but Atlanta responded. Aaron sparked a rally with a bases-loaded single. He singled again in the fifth and doubled in the sixth. Aaron's three hits, two runs scored, and three runs batted in helped the Braves to an 11–7 victory. Eddie Mathews commended his friend. "He won't sacrifice his value to the team by swinging for homers in any situation," he said.

Aaron clouted home run 705 off Reggie Cleveland the next day. It was his fourth home run in a week, and it fed speculation that the record would be within reach by late September. "Who knows? Maybe this will be the year," Aaron said. The *New York Times* had begun tracking his progress on the front of the sports section. Every time he hit one, the *Times* ran a story with a graphic showing Aaron's face in a baseball imprinted with his current total: 703, then 704, then 705, etc. The nightly news charted his progress, too. He appeared on the covers of *Newsweek* and *Ebony* and was featured in publications as varied as *TV Guide* and *Black Sports*. Businesses ran contests inviting customers to predict the historic date. Jimmy the Greek, the famed Vegas oddsmaker, put Aaron's 1973 chances at 3–1. Statistician Seymour Siwoff forecast that Aaron would hit 714 on September 30. Two professors at Georgia State University had been documenting the season and feeding pertinent information into a mainframe computer. After the recent barrage, the computer calculated that Aaron had a 42 percent chance of passing Ruth in September. "But the computer says the week of August 23 to 29 is a critical period," one paper reported. The computer's projections added a futuristic flavor to the story. Most people's exposure to computers, after all, had come secondhand from television, books, and movies like *2001: A Space Odyssey*.

The Pittsburgh Pirates followed the Cardinals into the Launching Pad, the nickname given to the Atlanta ballpark because of its earned reputation as a home-run park. (Its altitude, more than a thousand feet above sea level, helped the ball carry.) Aaron had been looking weary and was being overwhelmed with requests. "Aaron is too nice to say anything," said Eddie Mathews, who decided to do something about it. "We've had so many people trying to crash the clubhouse, I've ordered it stopped. Nobody comes in here after we've had fielding practice. That includes the news media." Days earlier, Mathews had confronted a writer from a national magazine. The guy had been monopolizing Aaron's time for three days. When the reporter turned up in front of Aaron's locker a fourth day—between games of a doubleheader, yet—Mathews lost his cool. Mathews had an intimidating physical presence and an explosive temper, and most who observed him felt that if so inclined he could kick the ass of almost anybody on his team. Mathews ejected the writer from the dressing room. Though known for his toughness, Mathews confessed that he could not handle the pressure Aaron had been under. "A guy has to be made of iron to stand it," he said.

Aaron resumed the chase against Chicago the last week of August. The series marked the first Atlanta appearance for Aaron's old teammate, and occasional nemesis, Rico Carty. He had been shipped to Texas, which in August sent him to Chicago. Carty saved his best for Atlanta. Like Aaron, he was playing left field and batting fourth. In his first try, he put the Cubs ahead with a two-run homer. A half inning later, with two runners on, Aaron responded by sending a ball 375 feet from home plate and over Carty's head, giving the Braves the lead. A message board, part of the outfield fence, lit with the number 706 and served as a backdrop as Aaron circled the bases. Carty tied the game by knocking in two more runs in the fifth and Aaron drove one home in the sixth, padding a Braves lead and giving each man four on the day.

Overall, August proved to be a dry month in the pursuit of Ruth. Aaron added a clump of five home runs to his total. But his average soared. He was hitting .382 in the heat of the summer— far better than he had in previous months. Aaron had even gotten a triple, a rarity at his age. Interest nationally guaranteed that when the Braves visited other cities attendance jumped. But turnout in Atlanta remained dismal. Local columnists tried to inspire admiration with heartfelt tributes to Aaron. "Sitting in the clubhouse of the Atlanta Braves," wrote Furman Bisher of the *Journal*, "I sometimes look at Aaron and try to get a feeling of the historic now. I ask for some unseen influence to overwhelm me with a proper realization of the immortality I'm seeing alive and moving, breathing and talking."

14

WHERE EVIL LURKS

With the season sweeping into its final month, Hank Aaron had more on his mind than baseball and Babe Ruth. He was thinking about the safety of his four children. They had returned to school: his youngest to a Montesorri elementary, his sons to a private high school, and his oldest to a university in Tennessee. They had all been threatened in one way or another, often in letters that urged Aaron to abandon his goal for the sake of his family. One writer sent a newspaper photo of Aaron and his daughter Dorinda, eleven, with a note that said, "Daddy, please think about us." But the threat judged most serious targeted his college-aged daughter.

Gaile Aaron attended Fisk University in Nashville. Founded in 1866 to teach freed slaves, Fisk had a rich history, marred by early confrontations with some who disliked the idea of an educational institution for African-Americans in their town. W. E. B. DuBois had graduated from Fisk, as had poet Nikki Giovanni eight decades later. The campus had been active during the civil rights movement.

While Gaile studied at Fisk, a ransom request had been sent to Aaron and turned over to the FBI. It threatened that one of his children would be abducted. The letter came from Nashville. A journalism student, Gaile had interned that summer at the *Nashville Tennessean,* where a young Al Gore worked as a reporter. She wrote a piece about her father that heightened her visibility. It was no secret that she attended Fisk.

At school, she had been receiving suspicious phone calls, and other students reported that a man had been inquiring about her routine. A crew of FBI agents swooped onto the campus and questioned friends, acquaintances, and others who came in contact with her. Disguised as maintenance workers, agents stayed at Fisk to watch over Aaron's daughter. They advised her that if kidnapped she should cooperate with her abductors. "And please know that we are right behind you," one said.

Aaron called Gaile frequently, and when the baseball schedule allowed, he flew to Nashville to check on her. Others did the same. Once, after a friend, Pete Titus, had been visiting in Atlanta, Aaron asked him to stop in Nashville on the drive home. He did, and found Gaile safe.

Meanwhile, Aaron kept his worries private and tried to shelter his children from publicity. He wanted to keep them out of the news. The less the public knew, the better. As school began, an Atlanta journalist, unaware that Aaron had taken special precautions, showed up at Marist High School, an all-boys Catholic school. He wanted to interview sixteen-year-old Hank, Jr., a talented football player. Instead, the reporter ended up talking to the Braves star, who announced that "Hankie," as the family called him, was off-limits to the press. "He has enough of a handicap as it is being the son of someone in the public eye," said Aaron. "I advised him not to talk for publication for a while, and I believe there are many valid reasons why we should play it this way." Aaron listed a bundle of them— none hinting of the danger he felt they faced. The threats also kept his sons from serving as batboys. Aaron worried they would be easy targets. "Hankie" did work at the park, though in a less visible role. He served on the grounds crew, earning back $1,500 to pay for repairs to a family car he had crashed.

Aaron was a protective, caring father, intent on not spoiling his children. His feelings for his kids affected Dusty Baker in a profound way. After Hank and Barbara Aaron's marriage fell apart, Baker helped Aaron move into an Atlanta apartment. He saw in the months that followed how the separation from his children pained him. Aaron became depressed. "The kids were always on my mind," he said. In some ways, Baker, at twenty-one, still viewed his mentor through worshipful eyes. Though he didn't always heed his advice—as when Aaron discouraged him from living with his girlfriend or from dating white, Asian, and Hispanic women while in the South—he respected him. Aaron was, as he had pledged to be, a father figure, and Baker saw him as somewhat invincible. It stunned him then when he realized how deeply Aaron's physical distance from his children hurt him, and it resonated for Baker, who began to see his own father in Aaron's pain.

"You don't think that your dad can hurt," he said.

For years, Baker had little or nothing to do with his father. He didn't call him, and he didn't include him in his life. As the oldest child, he would drive his siblings to his dad's place, drop them off outside, and drive away without acknowledging him. In those years, when the Braves came to San Francisco, Johnnie B. Baker, Sr., would be in the stands watching but there would be no aftergame dinners for the two of them. His court challenge of the Braves' contract had forced the creation of a trust into which a share of Dusty's earnings went until he turned twenty-one. Baker resented his father's interference.

But seeing how much Aaron missed his children helped open his eyes, and it was one factor among several that led him to reconnect with his own father. By the summer of 1973, the Bakers were close again.

The Braves started September in California, visiting San Francisco first, then San Diego, where before the series opener Aaron told the widening throng of reporters, "I hope I get the record this year. I'd like to do it as quickly as I can. I want to get this nightmare over with." Aaron hit two home runs that evening. The first came off Clay Kirby in the third inning. Aaron drove the ball toward the left-field bleachers. When a teenage vendor spotted it in flight, he tossed aside his cotton candy and went for the souvenir, which another boy caught and promptly sold to a third teen for $70. Aaron hit another in the fifth, popping a Vicente Romo fastball into the stands. It raised Aaron's total to 708, tying him with Ruth for most home runs in one league. Aaron got a shot at a third one later in the game. (He had achieved that feat only once in his career, on June 21, 1959, in Seals Stadium where the San Francisco Giants spent two seasons.) But fate—and pitcher Mike Caldwell—deprived Aaron, who watched a third strike sail past him. San Diego fans booed their pitcher, as well as umpire Bill Williams.

Aaron liked hitting in San Diego. He found it easy to follow the ball after pitchers released it. The clean, uncluttered background and the hot nights helped him hit five of his fifteen road home runs at the stadium. He almost hit a sixth during the September series. Rookie Rich Troedson, who had allowed Aaron's first of the season, elicited jeers when he walked him in the first. Later, Aaron lined a double to left. It thudded against the canvas, a foot beneath the home-run marker. Troedson took no chances in the eighth, walking Aaron again to more boos. But Troedson paid for it when Dusty Baker sent a ball over the center-field fence. The next night, though he had announced plans to start Aaron throughout the series, Eddie Mathews rested his star. San Diego fans were furious. In the final innings, a chant rose from the stands: "We! Want! Aaair-ronn! We!

Want! Aaair-ronn! We! Want! Aaair-ronn!" But Mathews kept him on the bench.

The first-place Cincinnati Reds waltzed into Atlanta Stadium September 7 on the sweet melody of a seven-game winning streak, anticipating the same easy dance that most teams enjoyed with the Braves.

"We're going to sweep this series," Aaron told Pete Rose during batting practice.

"Well, if you do," Rose replied, "I'll present you with ten thousand dollars cash at home plate after Sunday's doubleheader."

"What about three out of four?" Aaron joked.

Rose didn't like those odds.

Ron Schueler stymied Reds hitters, scattering five hits and allowing no runs, and Dusty Baker and Marty Perez socked the home runs that gave the Braves a 5–0 victory. For a change, Aaron, who walked twice, looked across the locker room at the crowd around Perez. He liked that the attention was diverted from him. "I'm tired of talking," he said. "Ain't got nothing else to say."

Rose and Aaron took the lineup cards to home plate before Saturday's game. They joked about Rose's waist size, Rose contending that he had dropped an inch working out. Chumminess aside, the Reds needed wins against the Braves. They wanted to put distance between themselves and the Dodgers, who were two-and-a-half games behind. Atlanta had been eliminated statistically from the playoffs but could alter the pennant race.

The game slid into the late innings scoreless until Hank Aaron unleashed home run 709 off Jack Billingham. Dusty Baker followed with his second in two days. Then the Reds responded. Rose drew a walk and Joe Morgan homered. In the ninth inning, Davey Johnson clubbed his 39th of the year, the best in the major leagues. The Braves won. The Reds swept the Sunday doubleheader and salvaged the series. Good thing Rose hadn't taken the bet.

Even in September, Aaron did not monopolize the sports news. There was Ali. And Billie Jean. And Secretariat. Muhammad Ali, thirty-one, had talked his way back into the spotlight, hyping a rematch with Ken Norton, who had broken his jaw in March. Ali trained vigorously. "If I lose this fight in the shape I'm in, it's time for me to quit," he said. In tennis, Billie Jean King walked off a Forest Hills court. She was close to fainting and had to forfeit her U.S. Open title. "I'm glad," said Bobby Riggs, who in seventeen days would face her in a much-hyped Battle of the Sexes. Meanwhile, Secretariat, the beloved racehorse, was preparing for a lucrative invitational, where he would race stable mate Riva Ridge. And somewhere in America motorcycle daredevil Evel Knievel wondered what he might do to further endear himself to a legion of adolescents after having jumped a stack of fifty cars in Los Angeles. Maybe soar over a canyon?

Before each game, equipment manager Bill Acree prepared the baseballs that would be used when Aaron came to bat. In transparent ink, he wrote code numbers on a few dozen balls. Visible only in infrared light, the numbers allowed the Braves to verify the authenticity of the home-run balls and to deter those who might scam the club, which was offering cash for the collectibles: $710 for home run 710, $711 for 711, and so on.

During play, Acree and batboy Gary Stensland sat on the field in chairs along the wall between the padded backstop and the first-base dugout. They had two supplies of balls, the usual ones that they kept in a leather bag and the special Aaron supply that they stored in a box under their seats.

The rewards had practical and promotional benefits. The cash value made it easier to reclaim the mementoes because the amount was substantial. (The average American's salary had yet to reach $12,000 a year.) The Braves also figured that the prizes would create interest and draw more people to the park. For two bucks, wouldn't it be worth a chance at such a payoff—and to see a legend make history?

Apparently not. Less than 2,900 people came on Monday, September 10, to see the Braves play the Giants. Four of the National League's five home-run leaders were on the same field: Johnson, Aaron, and Evans for the Braves and Bobby Bonds for the Giants.

The Braves touched Juan Marichal early. In the first inning, Mike Lum doubled and Darrell Evans drove him home with a single. When Aaron came to the plate, the flow of the game was disrupted. Stensland ran to umpire Ed Vargo to exchange the regular balls for the special Aaron variety. Vargo retrieved the game ball from Marichal and tossed him a new one. After Aaron singled, they repeated the routine, the batboy reclaiming the Aaron balls and giving the umpire a supply of the other ones. It had been happening that way since Aaron got his 699th home run, and it reminded pitchers that they might be part of history.

Don Carrithers relieved Marichal in the third inning. The Braves were ahead 3–0 when Darrell Evans drew a walk. Again, Stensland brought out the coded balls as the miniscule crowd recognized Aaron. Carrithers rubbed the new ball. Aaron looked toward him and plugged on his helmet. Time to go to work. Aaron got the count to two balls and one strike before he hammered the pitch 390 feet over the mesh metal fence in left-center and against the twenty-two-foot sign that had been illuminated with the number 709. The sign soon flashed 710. In the bullpen area, mascot Chief Noc-A-Homa ascended an extension ladder in moccasins and decorative garb and changed the digits on the "Atlanta Salutes Hank Aaron" billboard that had been erected by the chamber of commerce. Aaron had fifteen games in which to hit four home runs to tie Babe Ruth. The record was within reach.

In Cincinnati, Aaron often visited with Pete Titus, a postal carrier. Titus had come to know Aaron during his rookie season. They had mutual friends in baseball, and when Aaron broke his ankle near the end of 1954 and was being treated in an Ohio hospital, he and Titus grew closer. Aaron was twenty at the time and a long way from Mobile, Alabama. Titus brought him homecooked food, cheered him with conversation, and escorted a barber to his hospital room to give him haircuts. In the decades that followed, Titus rarely missed a game when the Braves came to Crosley Field and later Riverfront Stadium. By 1973, they were close friends who had been to each other's houses and knew one another's families well.

The two men, along with a third buddy who happened to be an FBI agent, often went for dinner after games. Titus noticed that every time someone entered the restaurant, Aaron would look up to gauge the person's intentions. Aaron had confided to them about the death threats. Despite dismissing them publicly as the work of cranks, he took them seriously. On one of their postgame outings, the agent brought a paper bag and set it on the table. It wasn't the first time. Titus thought it odd and finally asked his friend, "Paul, why do you keep bringing that brown bag with you?" The agent unfolded it and angled the opening at Titus and Aaron so they could take a peek. Inside was a pistol.

During the height of Aaron's ordeal, Titus and the agent regularly escorted him to the historic Sheraton-Gibson Hotel, where the Braves stayed. They accompanied him to one of his two hotel rooms, the one registered under a pseudonym: his mother's maiden name, Carla Koplin's last name, or another altogether. (Traveling secretary Donald Davidson considered using "Babe Ruth" as one of the aliases.) Before leaving Aaron at the hotel, Titus and the agent checked his room to ensure no one was lying in wait. You just never knew.

After Aaron had closed to within four home runs of Ruth, the Braves visited Cincinnati for a mid-September weekend series. Sparky Anderson's Reds were formidable, rolling toward the best record in either league. They had been on a torrid streak, winning twelve of their previous fourteen contests. Most of the season the Braves had proven an easy target for the Reds, and the second September series followed the trend. Reds fans already had pennant fever but Aaron's appearance pushed attendance figures even higher. More than 135,000 people came out that weekend, about the same amount Atlanta drew some months.

One Friday evening, the left-field section behind Pete Rose—they called it "The Rose Garden"—thickened with souvenir hunters an hour before the first pitch. They hoped Hank Aaron might deposit a batting-practice ball in the stands. The team's ticket office had been handling requests from as far away as New York and Iowa. Some were smuggling fishing nets into the park to claim game balls that might fetch thousands of dollars. One college athlete showed up wearing a Yankees helmet in anticipation of the knocks he might take should he recover a ball. "Somebody's going to get killed," said an attendant. "They're crazy." Aaron didn't hit a home run Friday but he singled in a run in the third and scored what appeared to be the game-winner in the ninth, sliding past Bench and nearly wrenching his ankle at home plate. But the Reds rallied and won.

All weekend, autograph seekers jammed the lobby of the Sheraton. In front of the hotel, a car nearly hit a woman who had chased Aaron across the street in pursuit of his signature. The phone rang continuously in the decoy room reserved under

Aaron's name, but no one was there to answer it. Even other players sought Aaron's signature. A photographer had snapped a picture of Aaron sliding into Bench, which Bench asked Aaron to autograph. "To John," he wrote jokingly. "Try to stay the hell out of my way."

Aaron went hitless Saturday evening and, true to his regimen, did not start the Sunday afternoon game. But with his team down 3–2 in the ninth inning, Eddie Mathews called on Aaron to pinch-hit, and the crowd of 50,000 responded, knowing it would be his last at-bat in Cincinnati that year. Aaron lined Dick Baney's pitch off the wall in left-center, eighteen inches short of a home run. "I thought it was gone," said outfielder Cesar Geronimo. "It surprised me when it bounced off the wall." Mathews removed Aaron for pinch-runner Chuck Goggin, and the crowd again gave Aaron a standing ovation as he left the field.

The season brought a mix of emotional highs and lows. The thrill of the big, supportive crowds and the huge applause at Riverfront Stadium could be offset quickly by something unforeseen and unexpected, something disturbing.

The media crew following Aaron ballooned in September. Reporters from across the country were trekking to Atlanta and pursuing Aaron on the road. NBC announced that it would interrupt its regular telecasts for home runs 712 to 715. Aaron had yet to reach 711. According to a Harris Sports Survey, most of the country was pulling for him. Though Americans loved to tune into Archie Bunker as he fumed about a minority couple moving in next door or some equally vexing "problem," the Harris survey showed that most of America— nearly seven in ten people—said they wanted Aaron to capture the record. Aaron's quest wasn't just changing him; it was changing the country.

Built along the Ohio River and opened in 1970, Riverfront Stadium was a modern stadium, carpeted with fake grass and shaped like a "concrete doughnut," according to one critic. Among its features were several levels of parking beneath the stadium. A wide concourse ran under the stands on the same level as the clubhouse. Given the concerns for Aaron's safety, the Reds allowed Pete Titus and his FBI friend to drive a vehicle into the tunnel to pick up Aaron beyond the clubhouse door.

After one game, Aaron settled into the sedan's backseat, where he preferred to sit. He rolled his window partly down. Titus sat in the front passenger seat, and the agent drove slowly through the concourse toward an exit, careful of the scattered pedestrians. The friends talked as the car crawled through the tunnel.

Suddenly, a hand shot through Aaron's window toward his body. It held what in a blur they thought to be a gun or a knife. Aaron jumped back. The intrusion startled Titus. He feared for Aaron's safety. In their years together, he had never seen such a look of terror on Aaron's face. The agent sped away. It had all happened so fast that it took a moment for the image to register, for them to look back and realize that it wasn't a gun or a knife being plunged toward Aaron. It was an ink pen. The intruder wanted an autograph.

That moment suffocated whatever joy had been in the car. They had all witnessed Aaron's vulnerability.

15

AARON'S DRAMA

utumn touched the Monday night air. It had rained earlier, and the ballpark felt damp and chilly, not ideal baseball weather. Two prominent visitors, Bowie Kuhn and Herbert Aaron, found themselves among a mere 1,362 fans watching the September 17 game, a new low for Atlanta Stadium. Aaron's father had driven up from Mobile. He regaled reporters who stopped by his seat with tales of Henry's childhood, of him hitting bottle caps with mop handles, of them watching Jackie Robinson play an exhibition.

The baseball commissioner, serving his penance and honoring his vow to "lead the cheering section" when Aaron got close to Ruth, came to Atlanta after home run 710 to start his vigil. He also brought a gift for the future king: an invitation for Aaron to throw out the first ball at the World Series—an honor given to presidents, dignitaries, and retired stars but never active players.

The night's pitiful attendance might have remained Atlanta's sad little secret—a forgettable footnote to the game story—had Aaron not hit number 711, an almost-foul, eighth-inning drive off San Diego's Gary Ross. But the countdown had begun, and newspapers and newscasts throughout America were recording Aaron's progress. The *New York Times* reported the latest home run on its front page. "A crowd of only 1,362 paying fans watched," the *Times* noted. The number itself made headlines. It was miniscule. High school football teams in Georgia drew better than 1,362. So did sweaty gymnasium wrestling matches between Pompero Firpo and Bobo Brazil. There weren't even enough people to represent each of Ruth's and Aaron's home runs. It was difficult to ignore the empty stands.

The *Los Angeles Times* described Atlanta as "strangely unemotional" about Aaron. *Newsweek* said he was performing in "isolation." *Time* described turnout as "woefully low." Aaron was playing in "relative secrecy," reported the *San Francisco Chronicle*. "Atlanta doesn't deserve Henry Aaron's drama," wrote a *New York Times* columnist. Across the nation, headlines indicted Aaron's host city:

"Atlanta Fans Just Don't Seem to Care"

"Atlanta Underwhelmed by Aaron"

"Home Fans Ignoring Hank"

Official Atlanta did cheer Aaron. The chamber of commerce had unveiled plans for a scholarship fund in his name. The airport erected a welcome sign featuring Aaron; a young entrepreneur, Ted Turner of Turner Communications, donated twenty billboards for a campaign; and the city was talking of naming a street in his honor. Regardless, the ticket-buyers didn't materialize.

Myriad explanations were proffered: it's dove-hunting season, the kids are back in school, no one wants to see a losing team, it's football time, crime's too high near the ballpark. But it was difficult to alibi the travesty of the situation.

What about race, some asked? The mayor's press secretary dismissed suggestions that it might be playing a role. "Listen, Henry Aaron is loved around here," she said. "Race is irrelevant." But many residents disagreed. "Hey man, there's some people here who don't want Hank to make it," said a black cab driver. "My wife and I go to a lot of games. We can hear them out there screaming 'nigger' at Hank." Another cabbie, this one white, concurred. "You outsiders don't realize it," he said, "but it will never be any different." Yet, if white Atlantans were avoiding the park, black residents weren't doing any better. African-Americans rarely comprised more than 5 percent of the audience in a city where blacks qualified as a majority.

Aaron admitted that he'd prefer to hit for 50,000 fans. On the field when he looked up around him, he couldn't help but see a vast ocean of vacant blue seats, three tiers' worth. "It's disappointing to see only thirteen hundred," he said. "But being a professional ballplayer, I feel like the thirteen hundred who came are entitled to see you play as hard as you can."

Added Eddie Mathews, "We need a winner."

After home run 711, Bowie Kuhn marched into the clubhouse to congratulate Aaron. "You're a showoff," he joshed. The man who hadn't wanted to set a precedent by congratulating Aaron for a momentous home run posed for a photo with Aaron and Davey Johnson, who had tied Rogers Hornsby's record for most home runs by a second baseman. "Dave's your man tonight," Aaron told reporters. "He's the one who caught a ghost."

Later, at his home in the high-rise Landmark Apartments, from which he could see the lights of Atlanta Stadium, Aaron got a phone call from daughter Gaile in Tennessee. She hadn't heard about the home run.

"What did you do in the game tonight?" she asked.

"Oh, nothing," he said.

"As usual," she teased.

"Yep, as usual," he said.

The Braves' fifth-place standing pleased no one. Though they had improved since the All-Star break, they were still floundering. Changes needed to be made. But the offense couldn't be blamed. It topped the league in hits, home runs, batting average, slugging percentage, and runs scored. The problems centered on the pitching staff. It was allowing more runs per game than any other National League team. Except for Carl Morton, the pitchers the Braves had obtained in trades had failed to blossom. As a first move, officials decided that Eddie Mathews should fire his pitching coach and close friend Lew Burdette. Mathews refused. "I'm not going to," he told vice president Eddie Robinson. If Robinson felt Burdette needed to be fired, he should do it himself, Mathews said. Robinson did.

Mathews and Burdette, guys reputed to be as hard as rocks, shared a few tears over the firing. As it turned out, Burdette wouldn't miss coaching. "You have to paint pretty pictures that don't exist for too many people," he said.

Mathews and the remaining coaches got contract extensions.

After splitting their series with the Padres, the Braves left Atlanta late Tuesday night, arriving in Los Angeles at 1:00 A.M.—4:00 A.M. Georgia time. Eight scheduled games remained, and Aaron needed three home runs to reach Ruth. The Dodgers had hyped Aaron's appearance, and 40,000 fans—and one baseball commissioner—had gathered at the ballpark. To their great disappointment, Aaron was not in the starting lineup. Some chanted his name; others booed Eddie Mathews, unaware that he allowed Aaron to decide which games he played. It was a unique arrangement, and it worked only because of their relationship. Mathews knew Aaron would never take advantage of the privilege. Before each game, coach Jim Busby would get a thumbs-up or thumbs-down sign from Aaron and relay it to Mathews, who would then make out the order.

In the ninth inning, with the Braves down 4–1 and pitcher

Joe Niekro due to bat third, fans scrambled toward the Braves dugout, certain Aaron would be called upon to pinch-hit. Chuck Goggin, replacing Sonny Jackson, struck out. As Paul Casanova headed to the plate, shortstop Marty Perez appeared in the on-deck circle, preparing to bat for Niekro. Nearby spectators grumbled. Casanova bunted his way to first, and the fans' discontent grew as Perez walked toward home. He paused en route, looked over his shoulder at Mathews in the dugout, and seeing that Aaron would not be relieving him continued to the batter's box. Fans let their displeasure be known. Perez grounded out, and so did Ralph Garr. Aaron didn't play. "If I had a couple of men on base, I would have used him, damn right," said Mathews.

Afterward, Bowie Kuhn visited the Atlanta dressing room. "Goodness gracious," he said. "Where were you, Henry? I was waiting for you all night long."

The cross-country flight had done in Aaron. "I hate to disappoint people," he said. "But by making decisions like this, I've been able to hit home runs and to keep my average up, too. I understand my physical problems better than anybody else. . . . You can't let one hit that means something to Hank Aaron get in the way of the ball club. It would only throw another log on the fire for the critics. I don't need that."

In his room at the Sheraton West Hotel, Aaron, like tens of millions of others, tuned his television to the colorful spectacle that had Americans talking, laughing, and arguing: The Battle of the Sexes.

For almost four months, Bobby Riggs, a 1939 Wimbledon champion, had been taunting Billie Jean King. Riggs, a fifty-five-year-old grandfather, had proclaimed himself the nation's foremost male chauvinist pig and had predicted he would trounce the twenty-nine-year-old King. "Tell the men not to worry," he said weeks before their match. "I'm back in training.

No booze. No living it up. . . . My biggest problem is overconfidence." Riggs was a gambler with a knack for publicity. He wore thick-rimmed glasses with a modified pageboy cut, his hair dyed improbably brown. He claimed to have discovered a fountain of youth through the 400-plus vitamins that he said he popped daily. He pledged to present King with a casket and funeral wreath during their competition. "I'll bury that libber once and for all," he said.

The $100,000 challenge match rivaled a Vegas production in its glitz. A harem of buxom women pulled Riggs to the Houston Astrodome court on a rickshaw. King arrived on a divan, held aloft by muscular, bare-chested beefcakes. She presented Riggs with a baby pig; he gave her a huge Sugar Daddy sucker. Boxer George Foreman, actress Claudine Longet, football player Jim Brown, and singer Andy Williams were among the celebrities watching the extravaganza in person as a tuxedo-clad Howard Cosell broadcast it to the nation. The Barnum quality of the event partly disguised the more serious gender issues underlying it. But King confronted the common belief that top female athletes were no match for men. King swept her challenger in three sets, deflating that misconception, derailing Riggs' hustle, and putting women's sports at the forefront.

Aaron must have shaken his head as he watched Billie Jean King. She seemed to be having fun. Aaron was not.

"Hank, are you really enjoying all this?" he was asked in late September.

"That question I'd rather not answer," he said.

Los Angeles, though accustomed to celebrities, lavished attention on Hank Aaron. After Wednesday's game, the Braves drove their bus onto the field and loaded in front of the dugout to escape the mob of fans. At a coffee shop, thirty people waited for Aaron to pay his bill before surrounding him for autographs. While walking outside the hotel, he was halted by a woman, who said, "I know you're the home-run king." "No," Aaron joked. "You're looking for Davey Johnson, and he's upstairs asleep." In the hotel, employees discovered a group of boys pounding their bats on the door of Aaron's decoy room. At the ballpark Thursday, the Dodgers brought in twenty extra guards and ushers to watch over the crowded left-field pavilion. Aaron met Greg Morris of TV's *Mission Impossible,* and posed for a photo with members of the Hollywood Boys Club, holding a 78-inch, 480-ounce bat carved from a pine log with a chainsaw.

Dodger fans demonstrated their affection for Aaron every time he strode toward the batter's box, and Aaron responded by doing everything other than hit a home run. The game went twelve innings, and Aaron played all of them. He contributed a single and two doubles, walked, scored a run, and drove in two of the Braves' three. But the Dodgers won their fourth straight, keeping them in contention with Cincinnati. After the loss, the Braves boarded a commercial flight to Houston. As Aaron settled into a seat, the pilot greeted his passengers, alerting everyone who didn't already know that he had a special guest. "I'd like to welcome Henry Aaron and the Atlanta Braves," he announced. A murmur fluttered through the plane.

Not far behind—perhaps the same day or maybe the next—a tall, sturdy gentleman with slicked-back hair also boarded a plane to Texas. He was following Hank Aaron. It was Bowie Kuhn, the commissioner, "a prisoner in his own baseball kingdom," observed one writer.

Houston, rousing from its Billie Jean King–Bobby Riggs hangover, found itself the focus of yet more attention with the Braves in town on Saturday. Many reporters remained in the city after the tennis match hoping to capture a bit more history. One prominent journalist, author George Plimpton of *Sports Illustrated,* was racing to the Astrodome in a taxi when Aaron faced Dave Roberts in the sixth inning. Aaron's arms were tired from the long season, and he selected a lighter bat from the rack. With Marty Perez on third base and his team one run behind, Aaron knew instinctively that he must drive the ball deep to allow Perez to score on a sacrifice. That was his goal, but he did better. Aaron slammed Roberts' first pitch 375 feet. Left fielder Bob Watson didn't bother to turn and watch it exit. The ball pelted the stands and ricocheted back onto the field. Aaron trotted the bases, his arms bent at the elbows, his head bobbing gently. It was just another home run, number 712.

Aaron needed two more to tie Ruth and three more to realize his quest. He had six games left. Though he hoped to accomplish it before the end of the season, Aaron didn't deviate from the pattern he had established. He sat out Sunday's game in Houston. With a persistence that bordered on superstitious, he abided by his practice of not playing a day game after a night game, making no exception with Monday being an off-day and the season at a close. In late July, the last time the Braves had been in Houston, Aaron strayed from his regimen and tried to get in an extra game. "It took me a week to recover," he said. "Certainly, I would like to get it over with, but I'm not going to go up there and press for home runs."

To Dusty Baker, Aaron exemplified patience and professionalism. "Anyone else might be swinging from the heels, but not him," he said. "He has unbelievable mental strength."

The year was proving to be spectacularly lucrative for the other sports stars of September '73. Ali, King, and Secretariat had all earned substantially more than Aaron. Ali, victorious over Norton, was guaranteed $275,000 for that fight alone. Secretariat, by defeating Riva Ridge and capturing the Marlboro Cup, had won $250,000, putting his year's purse at over $1 million. King also had enjoyed a prosperous year—and a bundle of endorsement deals. In the same late-summer issue of

Newsweek that featured Aaron on the cover, Billie Jean King appeared in a full-page ad for Colgate toothpaste. But the rich advertising contracts eluded Aaron. On the verge of ascending to baseball's throne, Aaron had parlayed his prominence into only a few minor deals. Johnny Bench, Mark Spitz, Tom Seaver—they were doing much better than Aaron in that respect.

While Aaron loved playing baseball, he approached it as a job. It was how he supported his family. It was his paycheck. Though he earned a high salary, he had never profited handsomely from the outside income that often flows through endorsements and advertisements.

Aaron had done commercials but they'd all been relatively minor. In Milwaukee, he hawked syrup, cigars, and lumber on radio—for the latter, speaking the tag line "And that ain't no Baltimore bloop." He had appeared in an ad for Gillette, touting razors while in his Braves uniform. It ended with an unseen narrator telling Aaron, "That's a really great ad lib—for an outfielder." A Wheaties commercial featured Aaron fumbling easy grounders after having skipped breakfast. "Hey, Aaron," taunted one fan. "Get your Wheaties!" For Brut cologne, Aaron declared, "On the field I let my bat do the talking. Off the field, I let my Brut do the talking." More recently Aaron had lent his lathered body to Lifebuoy soap and allowed game clips of him in action to be used for Oh Henry! candy bars. But still he awaited the big payoff that everyone told him would come with his growing celebrity.

This in mind, Berle Adams, president of William Morris Agency's sports division, flew to Atlanta from Beverly Hills to meet Aaron and discuss his prospects.

"How much do I have to give up?" Aaron asked.

"Give up?"

"In income—because I'm black."

Unflustered, Adams replied, "If you had asked me ten years ago, I would have said sixty percent. Five years ago, maybe forty percent. Today, maybe twenty or twenty-five percent."

Aaron proceeded cautiously. Maybe he would finally reap the reward of the chase.

Donald Davidson knew Aaron as well as any Braves employee did. He had been with the team as long as him, serving as publicity director and now traveling secretary and special assistant to the president. Davidson figured into the lore of Henry Aaron, too. He had witnessed all but one of his home runs, had assigned him number 44 in 1955 when Aaron requested double digits for his uniform (like Robinson and Mays), and had even tagged him with his first nickname, "Hammerin' Hank." (Sandy Koufax gets credit for the later one, "Bad Henry.")

What everyone noticed first about Davidson was his height. He was a dwarf, a fact alluded to repeatedly in press accounts, which described him as "the impresario," "the little giant," "the four-foot-short front-office dynamo," "the midget with the authoritarian strut," and the "much-loved little traveling secretary." A colorful storyteller with a fierce temper, Davidson could tap memories of his days in the 1930s as a clubhouse boy playing catch with Babe Ruth or of fishing with Ted Williams. He had been a reporter in Boston before becoming a baseball executive. He wore bright-striped sports coats, tinted shades, and rings on both hands. He counted Aaron and Mathews as close friends.

While in Houston, Davidson received an unsettling phone call from an Associated Press reporter in Pittsburgh wondering if the frightening rumors were true. Had Hank Aaron been shot? Davidson laughed it off. "I'm positive he'd have called me if he'd been shot," Davidson said. His flip response disguised a legitimate concern. The threats against Aaron were often specific. The Braves had been warned before one game that a man in a red jacket was going to shoot Aaron. Aaron had been alerted by team officials, who discouraged him from sitting on the dugout bench. He should stand out of sight in the club-house tunnel or hang out in the dressing room, they recommended. But Aaron would have no part of it.

"I'm not going anywhere," he said.

Dusty Baker and Ralph Garr were beside Aaron in the dugout, and he told them about the possibility of a brightly dressed gunman. He suggested that to be safe they might want to sit elsewhere. The threat appeared not to affect Aaron, but it bothered Baker and Garr. It made them jittery, and they continually scanned the stands for a would-be assassin. But neither would leave Aaron's side.

"Hank, we're down with you, man," said Baker. "We ain't going nowhere."

16

RAINY NIGHTS IN GEORGIA

he Hank Aaron Home Run Hero Tour and Media Circus Sideshow returned to Atlanta for the final performances of 1973. It had come down to five games, and Aaron felt he had a good chance of tying the record. From Pittsburgh, Willie Stargell offered words of encouragement. "If I can hit three homers in four games, you can hit three in five," he said. Aaron had been averaging a home run every nine at-bats. Against Los Angeles and Houston, he figured to get twenty or more plate appearances. But would he get pitches to hit?

The question was especially pertinent when playing the Dodgers and Astros, whose staffs tried to work around him. They walked Aaron more than other teams and, not coincidentally, had allowed him less home runs—two each—than all but the Pirates. "As I get closer, I'm getting fewer pitches to hit," Aaron said early in the campaign. "Pitchers seem more conscious of the home runs. I get pitches to hit off Tom Seaver, Bob Gibson, and Steve Carlton, men with a lot of pride. They challenge me. But the others are going to be very careful."

For months, pitchers had been repeating those words. Some lifted their brows at the comment, viewing it as Aaron's attempt at a "psyche job." Some saw it as a slight. Two Dodgers, Claude Osteen and Don Sutton, recalled his words when Los Angeles came to town. Osteen was due to face Aaron in the third game. "If Hank thinks I'm going to challenge him . . . he's full of mud," he said. Sutton, who would be going fishing with Aaron after the season, feigned hurt at being omitted. "You'll notice my name wasn't there," he said.

Monday brought an off-day for the Braves but Aaron performed no special rituals in preparation for the games. He went about his life, picking up a freezer's worth of four hundred pounds of beef that had been butchered for him. That evening, Aaron, a devout football fan, watched the Cowboys annihilate the Saints 40–3 as Howard Cosell, "Dandy" Don Meredith, and Frank Gifford offered their insights. Aaron had gone through most of the day without hearing Babe Ruth's name. But that would change before he drifted off to sleep. While switching channels, he came upon a panel discussion—about him and Ruth. "Uh-oh, here we go again," he thought.

Don Sutton, twenty-eight, broke into the majors in 1966 as the fourth man in a rotation that showcased Sandy Koufax, Don Drysdale, and Claude Osteen. By the early 1970s, Sutton, born and raised a few hours from Mobile, had become one of the league's dominant starters. "How will I pitch to him tonight?" he asked. "Reluctantly, that's how."

Game time saw 10,211 fans in the stadium. One of them posted a bull's-eye with the number 713 in the left-field stands. Visitors to the park were astonished that on the brink of history so few fans had bothered to come. Four times this year, Aaron had gotten two home runs in one game. If he did it again, he would tie Ruth—at a poorly attended game. "This is unbelievable," said a young man visiting from Ohio. Added a fan from Tennessee, "Some nights when I come here or listen to the games on the radio and see and hear the small crowds, it brings tears to my eyes."

Sutton proved nearly invincible, allowing one single before Aaron's seventh-inning appearance. As Aaron loosened in the on-deck circle, batboy Gary Stensland ran four coded baseballs to umpire Bill Williams. The ball exchange made Aaron feel "like a freak." It also had the unintended effect of reminding pitchers to be extra careful, because, after all, those special balls served their purpose only if driven out of the park.

Aaron had been seeing a lot of curveballs, sliders, and junk pitches from Sutton. When he detected a low fastball, he took a cut, hesitating imperceptibly, and lofted the ball 400 feet to deep center. The crowd reacted as if it were a home run. Sutton thought it was gone. "I was getting ready to express how it felt giving up his 713th homer." But it fell before the fence. Willie Davis caught it on the warning track. Aaron jogged toward the dugout, near which sat his fiancée, Billye; his secretary, Carla; his father, Herbert, in a striped sport coat, tie, and porkpie hat; and the commissioner of baseball. "I felt good," Aaron said. "But I just ran into somebody a little bit better than I was tonight."

"Hank, are you still going fishing with Don Sutton?" asked one reporter.

Aaron joked that his fishing trip would be canceled. Then he paused, and reconsidered. "Maybe," he added, "I'll take him up the river and drown him."

The Braves lost, not that it mattered.

Carla Koplin was in her office the next day amid piles, trays, bundles, and bags of letters. She felt skittish for her boss. "There's nobody else exactly like him," said the inscription under a poster on the wall. It was afternoon when Aaron dropped in to check with Koplin. She was nervous and excited all at once. It was the combination of things: the impossible torrent of mail, the throb of media attention, and the electric nature of the chase, which she hoped would end Sunday. She was feeling the strain that he claimed not to be noticing. Koplin and an assistant had responded to 50,000 letters so far, and multiples of that number still awaited. The Braves stored the surplus in a separate room. Some would never be answered. Though the warm, encouraging, uplifting notes poured in from throughout America, Japan, Canada, Australia, Israel, Africa, and elsewhere, the other kind still came, too. Koplin downplayed them, trying to focus on the positive as if she might be able to will away the worries.

"You're taking this worse than I am," Aaron told her. "I'm not coming up here anymore," he joked.

For all his assurances that he was not under pressure, Aaron did exhibit signs of it to those who knew him well. Eddie Mathews observed Aaron lighting more cigarettes during games, hiding in the clubhouse tunnel, away from the cameras, and stealing quick drags between innings. Dusty Baker noticed the loneliness that seemed to swallow Aaron, especially on the road. Billye Williams detected longer moments of silence.

Officer Cal Wardlaw was now following Aaron home after games, making sure he arrived safely. Aaron couldn't escape. Reminders of his predicament surfaced continually: a pregame bomb threat that had police checking under the team bench, a cup of urine dumped on his head from the stands, a glass of whiskey tossed in his face by a woman outside a park, and a terrifying few moments in Montreal when firecrackers echoed like gunshots while he stood motionless in the outfield, not wanting to give the culprit the satisfaction of seeing him flinch while mentally calculating whether he had been struck by a bullet. On occasion, Aaron would spend the night alone at Atlanta Stadium, seeking solitude in the trainer's room.

An Associated Press photographer captured a defining image of him during this time: a profile of him on the bench, a single figure in a statuesque pose similar to Rodin's *The Thinker*, his elbow propped on leg, chin on fist, eyes staring off at nothing—except that there was a ball cap on his head, slightly askew, which gave him a boyish appearance, and he was biting a fingernail.

Rain delayed the start of Wednesday's game by almost an hour. The grounds crew rolled a protective tarp over the infield. While getting dressed Aaron answered questions for ninety minutes, occasionally sipping from a cup of vegetable soup and stealing a drag on a cigarette when the television cameras weren't filming. His stomach was hurting. "Big-time tonight. You'd better get out there and get some hitting," said locker neighbor Davey Johnson, who was battling Willie Stargell for the league home-run title.

"You better get out there and catch Stargell, son," Aaron replied.

The Dodgers started Al Downing, a thirteen-year veteran who had begun his career in 1961 as a teammate of Roger Maris. In late June, "Gentleman Al," as teammates called him, had allowed Aaron's 693rd home run. Aaron almost got 713 off him in the opening inning, drilling a pitch to the wall in left where Von Joshua caught it. Aaron faced Downing once more, singling in the second before the Dodgers brought in a reliever. He got four more appearances but did no other damage. Darrell Evans, though, connected for his 40th home run. If Aaron could hit one more, he, Evans, and Johnson would make history.

The high-scoring game, 9–8—Atlanta pitchers gave away a late lead—finished in a drizzle near midnight, with Aaron clinking a foul pop to Steve Garvey. By then, the park had emptied of 5,571 damp patrons. "We should have won," Aaron said.

"When you stand around out there in the rain and think you have a victory, it's tough."

Thursday brought another rainy night in Georgia. The skies opened at dinnertime and drenched the Atlanta field for an hour and a half. Normally, the game would have been postponed with not a hint of hesitation. But there was nothing normal about this night. Everyone—umpires, managers, players, executives, fans, and Aaron himself—recognized that if the game were not played, Aaron's chances of breaking the record in 1973 would diminish. The Dodgers had a game scheduled for Friday in another city. There wouldn't be a makeup. Aaron would simply lose a game's worth of swings—against Claude Osteen, no less.

Umpires delayed the start time by an hour, and the grounds crew worked as fast as Watergate burglars. They spread dirt near the bases and home plate and brushed water toward the outfield drains. During the downpour, Los Angeles pitcher Doug Rau pointed out the futility of a cleanup effort by taking a headfirst, Pete Rose slide into a puddle in shallow left, where water reached to the ankle. Someone joked that the water was over Donald Davidson's head.

Aaron entertained a cramped clubhouse of more than a hundred journalists who had come from across the country and beyond: from Chicago, Detroit, Cincinnati, Cleveland, and Washington, from Texas and California, from Mexico and Japan. And New York. Always New York. Beat reporters in other cities often resented New York guys like Dick Young, whom they felt held too much sway with the commissioner. There were the Atlanta regulars, too, like Frank Hyland and Furman Bisher of the *Journal,* Wayne Minshew and Jesse Outlar of the *Constitution,* WXAP's Joe Walker, a blind, African-American radio reporter of whom Aaron was fond, and others. And there were magazine guys. Imagine the locker room contrast of

George Plimpton with his East Coast, Ivy League, aristocratic tone and manager Eddie Mathews with his rugged, guitar-strumming, country music–loving, hardass ways.

The questions flowed like Boone's Farm wine:

Seeing how close you are, do you wish you had played a few more games during the season? (No.)

If you were a sports reporter, what would you write about this? (Nothing. He'd be covering the Eastern Division race between the Mets, Cardinals, and Pirates.)

What are you going to do Friday on your day off? (Watch son Lary play football, spend time with fiancée Billye, maybe go fishing.)

Can you think of a question you've not been asked? (No.)

Aaron got a brief respite from the inquisition when governors Jimmy Carter of Georgia and Sherman Tribbitt of Delaware came to wish him well. Privately, Carter was pondering a run for president. Aaron's brother-in-law, David Scott, worked for the governor.

As the rescheduled start time approached, Aaron found himself at the center of a discussion over whether the game should be played. He was consulted by Braves chairman Bill Bartholomay, chief umpire Tom Gorman, and managers Alston and Mathews. It was a truly rare occurrence for a player to be asked whether a game should be canceled. But Aaron gave his approval, and Gorman called off the contest. The field was not playable, and Aaron didn't think it right for seventeen others to risk an injury so he could go for the record. "I feel kind of bad about all you guys who've come so far to see me hit that homer," Aaron told reporters.

Unbeknownst to almost everyone, manager Eddie Mathews had scratched Aaron's name from the lineup anyway. "I just couldn't have let him go out on that field," he said.

17

ATLANTA'S REDEMPTION

he marquee outside the Atlanta hotel carried a simple message in snap-on letters: "Henry, you are what's happening." Early Saturday, capitalizing on the massive congregation of reporters in town to watch Aaron, Berle Adams of the William Morris Agency held a press conference at the hotel. He announced that Aaron had signed with the agency, joining Secretariat and Olympian Mark Spitz. "We'll generate and earn more income for Henry Aaron than he earned in the last twenty years," pledged Adams. He projected that Aaron would make between $1.5 and $2 million over the next two years through endorsement deals, appearance fees, and other non-baseball activities.

"I've waited very patiently for this day," said Aaron.

The promised payout dwarfed any he had yet to receive. Whether because of his quiet disposition, his small-market career, or his relative lack of pizzazz, Hank Aaron had never been in demand as a spokesman. Race was a factor, Aaron believed, and a major 1973 marketing survey, commissioned by top national advertisers, supported his conclusion. Thousands of men across America were asked to rate sports celebrities in various categories. Willie Mays was cited as "most recognized." Aaron followed in twelfth place. But in the crucial category of "most trusted," no black athletes finished in the top twenty-five positions.

"I made very little compared to some ballplayers," Aaron said when his new deal was announced. "I just kept the faith, and played the game as it's supposed to be played."

Coincidentally, among the thousands of pieces of correspondence that had arrived in Carla Koplin's office earlier that week was one from the president of Magnavox, Alfred di Scipio. "On behalf of the Magnavox Company, I hereby extend to you a bona fide offer to acquire . . . each bat and each ball, if recoverable, that you use for each home run hit from here on for as long as you remain an active major league player."

Within weeks, while looking through Koplin's file, Berle Adams would discover the Magnavox telegram and hatch an idea that would produce the kind of payoff he had promised Aaron.

Herbert Aaron's wife, Estella, joined him in Atlanta for Saturday's game. She had been listening to the Braves on the radio in Mobile, Alabama, worried that her presence in Georgia might jinx her son. But it had been a week since his last home run. What could it hurt to watch the final two games in person? Much of her family would be there anyway, seated with Bowie Kuhn in a specially constructed section beside the Atlanta dugout. There would be Hank Aaron's four children, including Gaile, home from Fisk University; two sisters, Gloria from Mobile and Alfredia from Atlanta; an aunt and uncle from Detroit; Hank's parents; and Billye. None of his brothers would make it. Tommie's Savannah team had finished in second place, and he had been asked to manage in Mexico.

Hank Aaron had hit only two home runs against the Astros all season. One had come off Jerry Reuss in May, the other a week ago off Dave Roberts. Teammates had been calling

Roberts "712" ever since. Both men were scheduled to start in the weekend series, Reuss first. Neither was eager to talk.

But Leo "The Lip" Durocher had no qualms about doing so. Before the game, he told tales from his forty-one-year career. Known for his feistiness and occasional episodes of meanness, Durocher was in an uncharacteristically grand mood, enjoying what he realized might be his final games in baseball. Though the news wouldn't break for several days, Durocher, sixty-eight, would be leaving the Astros after Sunday's contest. He would never manage again. Durocher had spent most of his life in the sport, beginning as a player with the Yankees in the 1920s. He knew Babe Ruth. "If he walked into this room, the chandeliers would shake and the players' mouths would hang open," Durocher said. "There's never been anyone quite like him. He'd be headed for the clubhouse before a game and stop by the hot dog stand, eat six hot dogs, filled with mustard, then hit two homers. . . . And he never made a mistake. Everyone forgets he was a good fielder and he always threw to the right base."

Durocher rated Aaron as "the best right-handed hitter since Rogers Hornsby." But he conferred his highest praise on another man, whom he managed with the New York Giants. "Willie Mays is the best player I've ever seen," he said. "He can run, throw, and field better than Aaron. And Ruth hit the ball higher and harder. But if they wheeled Aaron up in a wheelchair, he'd still scare me."

Almost 18,000 fans came out for the Saturday night game—not nearly as many as came to the Billy Graham revival in June—but not bad for the Braves, not when silhouetted against the bar mitzvah–sized crowds that preceded it. Still, when Aaron's sister Gloria, an infrequent visitor to Atlanta Stadium, looked out into the park at the vacant right-field stands and the empty blue seats in the upper deck beyond third base, she couldn't believe it. Didn't Atlanta appreciate her brother? Didn't its residents care? She felt a cloud of bitterness settle over her.

At six-five, Jerry Reuss stood tall on the mound. The twenty-four-year-old lefty had sixteen victories and, regardless of what Aaron did, was ensured of a winning season. The first time Aaron batted, Reuss fed him slow curves, followed by a fastball, which Aaron hit for a single. The next time, Reuss lobbed him pitches softer than a Karen Carpenter ballad. Aaron walked. When he faced him in the fifth inning—after the special balls had been brought out to the umpire and after Mike Lum and Darrell Evans had singled and after the jubilant fans had rewarded Aaron with yet another of seven standing ovations—Aaron waited for Reuss' next curve. It came on the first pitch, and he was ready. Aaron drove the coded ball to deep left-center. A charge swept through the stands as the white blur streaked the sky.

Aaron didn't crook his neck to trace its trajectory. He didn't wish it over the wall with a wave of his hand. He didn't stutter-step his way to first base or pump his arms or contort his face or swirl, jump, hop, dance, yelp, or howl. When the ball passed the fence and pelted the scoreboard, Aaron trotted the bases with the nonchalance of a Methodist minister, just as he had hundreds of times before, his demeanor calm, his approach workman-like, his ambivalent expression hiding whatever joy or relief his heart harbored. While on the base path, he left the emotion to others. In front of him, Darrell Evans slapped his hands together, and then welcomed Aaron to home plate with a shake and swat. Beside the dugout, Billye Williams bobbed on her toes and let loose with an unfettered scream. Aaron's mother, Estella, held her hands in front of her body, palms open, fingers spread, as if praising in church. His father, Herbert, had his fists clenched and his arms thrust toward the heavens, the pose of champions.

As he headed toward the dugout, Aaron looked up and saw his ecstatic father, and he noticed that almost everybody was standing. The sustained cheers enveloped him and continued after he disappeared from sight. Moments later, the celebration still had not died. Aaron's teammates urged him back onto the field. He waved and tipped his hat. "That ovation was tremendous," he said. In the abating hum of the applause, Dusty Baker

also stroked a home run off the unnerved pitcher. Reuss retali-
ated against Davey Johnson, stinging a fastball into his back
and earning himself an instant $50 fine. By the next inning,
Reuss was gone, replaced by Larry Dierker—one of the pitchers who had drawn Bowie Kuhn's ire by saying that he would
serve Aaron a sweet one. But when given the opportunity,
Dierker did not do it. "It was different than I thought it would
be," he said. Aaron singled.

His three-hit performance had raised his average to .297.
Not only was he on the verge of tying Babe Ruth, he might also
hit for .300, a goal he had set for himself. The home run gave
Aaron 40 for the season, making Aaron, Johnson, and Evans
the first trio of teammates to reach that plateau together. In the
postgame press conference, Aaron tried to bring them into the
glare of the camera lights. After a cordial question or two, reporters focused again on Aaron. And finally, he mentioned the
P-word. "You can't imagine the pressure," Aaron said, "knowing that even if you get a single with the bases loaded, you've
disappointed the people. . . . Tomorrow is going to be the test
I've been waiting for all these years. If I get a pitch to hit, then
the world will know if I'm a good hitter. If I don't hit it tomorrow, it's going to be a long, cold winter."

Two decades into his sterling career, Aaron still wanted to
be tested.

After Aaron's home run Saturday evening, a surge of fans
rushed to the ticket booth to secure seats for Sunday's
game. Phone calls swamped the stadium switchboard. Within a
half hour, a line had formed. The sellers' windows remained
open until midnight and then reopened the next morning to another line. Business never slowed. The Braves sold as many tickets as physically possible. From a window at a hotel across from
the stadium, Aaron's sister Gloria looked out at the congested
streets and the mass of people converging on the ballpark. For

days, her father had been hoping the Atlanta region would "catch the fever" and support his son. It was happening, Gloria Robinson realized. "It suddenly dawned on me what was going on," she said. It was enough to erase her bitterness about the previous night's turnout. By the 2:15 start, 40,517 tickets had been bought—14,000 more than for any other 1973 home game.

Herbert Aaron had worried that Hank might not get enough sleep at his own place. "We have so many people at his apartment they keep bothering him all the time," he said. But Aaron felt fine. He ate breakfast at Billye's place, where he read newspaper coverage of his home run. He was more rested and less stressed than on Saturday, and he was determined to tie the record.

On Houston's team bus, ensnarled in traffic near Atlanta Stadium, Dave Roberts implored the other drivers to clear a path. "Let me through, people," he joked, trying to relieve his jitters. "They can't start without me. . . . They should've sent me a limousine and chauffeur. I'm the guy everyone's coming to see." His teammates had been razzing him since last night, calling him "714." In his hotel room, all he had thought about was Hank Aaron. To distract himself, Roberts had started to watch a movie, *The Poseidon Adventure*. But when he discovered that it was about a disaster at sea, he turned it off. In the clubhouse before the game, Roberts' teammates put the number 714 above his locker in place of his uniform number. He altered it to 17, the amount of victories he would have if he beat Aaron and the Braves. Don Wilson, a fellow pitcher, told Roberts that he expected to retrieve Aaron's home-run ball that night and would be waiting for it in the bullpen beyond the outfield fence when Roberts served the historic pitch. Roberts had given up 712 and wanted no further part of Aaron's record. "I thought what Henry said on TV was interesting, that he'd probably tie or break the record off some overpowering pitcher like Tom Seaver or Bob Gibson, someone who'll challenge him. Well, I'm not that kind of pitcher. I don't have overpowering stuff. I won't challenge him. . . . I'd rather be a nobody in baseball forever than to go down as immortal because I served up one of the big ones to Henry."

Eddie Mathews and his players could hardly move in the locker room. The place was thick with an invading army of TV cameramen jostling for close-ups, radio guys maneuvering microphones toward Aaron, reporters taking notes, photographers popping flashes. If Aaron made history today, every bit of it would be documented. The *Atlanta Journal* had a chunk of its staff at the ballpark. One writer was staking out a men's restroom to talk to visitors unlucky enough to be using the facilities when Aaron hit the home run. Another tried to hang out inside Chief Noc-a-Homa's teepee. Mathews evicted him. "They were mad at me the whole goddamn time," he later said of the media. "Hell, I didn't do anything right."

The sun shone, if only for a short while, when Aaron appeared for his first at bat. The Astros had given Roberts a quick 1–0 lead, and the Braves were threatening with Mike Lum on third. It was an ideal situation for an intentional walk. But given the circumstances—and the potential for a fan revolt—neither Roberts nor manager Leo Durocher wanted to go that route. As Aaron approached the plate, Roberts, with coded ball in glove, glanced toward the bullpen in center field. Don Wilson, continuing his joke, had positioned himself close to the fence in case Aaron hit one there. Roberts laughed and waved Wilson away. Aaron noticed Roberts chuckling but didn't know why. He expected Roberts to start him with a slow curve. But Roberts zinged a fastball past him for a strike. Aaron wouldn't see another strike the rest of the day. By the time Roberts had left the game with a stiff back, Aaron had three singles, all on slow curves. The prankster Wilson replaced Roberts.

Sometimes, for no tangible reason, a good pitcher will stifle a great hitter throughout their overlapping careers. A major leaguer since 1966, Wilson had that kind of fortune against Aaron. Wilson was decent enough, but his success against Aaron exceeded his success in general. If he could have pitched to everyone as well as he pitched to Aaron, he would have won twenty games several times. For whatever reason—the movement on a certain pitch, a psychological advantage, the angle of release— the Braves star never posed a problem. They had encountered one another dozens of times, but Aaron had hit only one home run off him. Further, Wilson remembered surrendering a mere four or five hits to Aaron over their careers.

The showdown came in the eighth inning in Aaron's last at bat of 1973. It had been raining hard that afternoon, and there had been thunder during the contest. Leo Durocher had never seen a game continued under such conditions, but he didn't object. The atmosphere at the park was festive, and the audience sober, beer being unavailable on Sundays. Banners and bull's-eyes marked the facing of the decks, fishnets dangled from the railing above the bullpen, and an occasional balloon drifted onto the field.

Aaron wanted desperately to get 714, to satisfy the 40,517 fans who had come. He wanted to complete at least part of his mission, to forever attach his name to a share of the record. Wilson figured that Aaron would be expecting a fastball outside, so he delivered one inside. He jammed him, and Aaron swung. The ball hit—and cracked—his bat, and blipped harmlessly up and into the mitt of second baseman Tommy Helms. Aaron's season-long pursuit ended with a blunt thud. Aaron appeared perturbed at himself for having swung at the pitch, for having failed, and for having disappointed Atlanta's only significant crowd.

It drizzled as Aaron took the lonely jog back to left field for the final inning. Water beaded on the back of his neck. His damp uniform clung to his skin. As he trampled onto the wet outfield grass, bracing for whatever words might be hurled, the fans before him stood and applauded. He continued toward them, and the ovation grew louder. It spread from there in both directions, over all three tiers, like cascading dominoes, until 40,000 fans were on their feet. All season Aaron had been hitting home runs in Atlanta before sparse gatherings of 3,000 and

5,000 and 9,000. Now, before this enormous crowd, he had failed to hit one—and still they cheered him. The applause flowed from all sides, unabated for a full three minutes. Several times, Aaron waved. Once, he crouched into position, his glove cupped over his knee, as if the sight of him ready to play might quell the noise. It didn't. He waved again, a singular figure set against the grassy green expanse of the outfield.

In the press box, jaded journalists watched in silence, their throats constricted with emotion. Braves announcer Ernie Johnson, one of Aaron's teammates in the 1950s, had never witnessed anything comparable. "It was the most touching thing I've ever seen in baseball," he said. Even Houston players felt the moment melt their enemy armor. The ovation gave Astro Doug Rader goose bumps. Beside the dugout, Herbert Aaron stood straight and proud, his shoulders pulled back, his tie in place. If the reaction had come after a home run, it wouldn't have meant nearly as much. Fans applauded home runs everywhere, and momentous home runs always drew significant applause. But, of course, this wasn't about home runs. It was about something else. It was an embrace, an affectionate pat on the back, a way of telling Aaron that those hecklers and letter writers and furious little bigots didn't represent them, that he was appreciated, not just for his record pursuit, but for everything: his remarkable consistency, his superior talent, his dignified behavior, his contributions over the years. They wanted him to know that Atlanta did care.

"That moment," as many participants referred to it, emboldened city boosters who had bristled over national reports about poor ticket sales. *Journal* columnist Furman Bisher, who had pushed hard to bring a major league team to Georgia, used it as ammunition to rebut critics. "A newspaperman travels across the country to write about an event and he feels the crowds should justify his being there," Bisher stated. "Don't try to convince me Atlanta isn't a baseball town. It was a baseball town when Anaheim was a joke on the Jack Benny show.

When Kansas City was a cow town. And Arlington, Texas, was a traffic light between Dallas and Fort Worth. You give Atlanta something to cheer for, it'll be there wearing the skin off its palms."

Atlanta had redeemed itself in Aaron's eyes, too.

After the game, Aaron didn't mope like a man defeated. He strode into the press conference room in his stocking feet, his stirrups dangling at the back of his ankles. Aaron perched himself on a wooden folding chair behind a garden of microphones and beamed as he answered questions.

Sure, he was disappointed.

Yes, he had been swinging for home runs all day.

Nah, he hadn't gotten good pitches, just one.

Yep, next season would be his last.

Of course, he felt pleased about his year.

It had been an excellent season for anyone and a spectacular one for a man of thirty-nine. At that age, Mickey Mantle and Joe DiMaggio had been retired two years and Ty Cobb had scored just 48 times and Stan Musial had gotten only 91 hits. At thirty-nine, Willie Mays had poked a respectable 28 home runs and Babe Ruth, 22. But Hank Aaron had recorded 40 in 392 at bats. No one else had ever done that at age thirty-nine. Plus, with 6 hits in the final two games, he had raised his embarrassing early-season average to above .300, best on the team. "I have all winter to rest up and try to make next year just as good a season," he said.

One interviewer pointed out that Babe Ruth had reinvigorated baseball, literally saved the sport, after the Black Sox scandal. "What have you done for the game of baseball?" he was asked.

The question struck some as an insult. Taken aback initially, Aaron paused before answering. "Maybe what I've done is create some new fans," he said finally. "At first, there was a lot of that mail from people, older people, who didn't want me to break Babe Ruth's record. The younger generation took notice of that and supported me. I think they want me to relate to, to see me have a record, not someone their granddads saw play."

The record would have to wait until next year when the Braves would open their season on the road, possibly in San Francisco or Los Angeles, maybe in Cincinnati. "I'm hoping I can hit it here, in Atlanta Stadium," Aaron said. Bill Bartholomay hoped that as well. So did Eddie Mathews. "I'm not going to hold him out, but I wouldn't be surprised if he gets an upset stomach," Mathews said. And that was the last thing Bowie Kuhn wanted to hear.

Hank Aaron celebrated the end of the season that afternoon and evening, first privately at his apartment with his parents, then at a Braves' dinner, and finally with a clambake at sister Alfredia's home, where card games unfolded, music played, and Herbert Aaron danced a few happy steps.

One home run. Aaron had fallen short by one home run. For the superstitious, it must have felt like an omen. He had just missed a guaranteed share of the all-time title by a single home run. Not an acceptable three or a disappointing two but a gaping, miserable, torturous one. How could the baseball gods have allowed him to journey so far, only to halt his pilgrimage at the gates and force him to wait a half year? So much could happen in a half year.

Aaron downplayed his disappointment. "All I have to do," he said, "is live."

It sounded like a Greek tragedy in the making. Aaron confronted the unspeakable, emboldened by a sense of destiny. "I could have an automobile crash or get in an airplane and have it drop," he allowed. "Whatever will be, will be. I can't change it."

Baseball's history brims with stories of tragedies, of careers quashed and lives ended prematurely. Meningitis halted

Addie Joss' heart—and stellar record—in 1911, two days after he turned thirty-one. Austin McHenry was a young .300 hitter when a brain tumor claimed him. Willard Hershberger slit his throat midseason after a Cincinnati loss. A crash on an icy road in January 1958 paralyzed catcher Roy Campanella. White Sox pitcher Paul Edmondson died in a 1970 mishap on the way to spring training. Brewers pitching prospect Mickey Fuentes was shot in a fight outside a bar. Herman Hill drowned in the off-season.

But it wasn't those tragedies that Aaron's words evoked.

Roberto Clemente—that's what fans were thinking. His death throbbed yet. Nine months later and the disbelief lingered. The end had come on New Year's Eve 1972. Clemente, the National League's other great right-fielder, had been on a humanitarian mission to Nicaragua, taking food and supplies to victims of an earthquake that had devastated Managua. Thousands had died, and the disaster had inflicted immense damage, leaving almost a third of a million people homeless. Aboard an old DC-7 plane overloaded with 16,000 pounds of cargo, Clemente vanished with four other men off the coast of San Juan, Puerto Rico. The plane had taken off in darkness and disappeared in the night, swallowed by the sea. Months earlier, Clemente, thirty-eight, had gotten his 3,000th hit, a double against the New York Mets. It was the last regular-season hit of his career, and it came on September 30. One year later, Aaron finished his 1973 season, one home run short—on the exact date, September 30.

"Whatever will be, will be," said Aaron.

18

KING HENRY

utumn and winter looked like a Hank Aaron coronation. With the country mired in turmoil—President Richard Nixon battling to keep incriminating tapes from being released to investigators; Vice President Spiro Agnew resigning amid charges of tax fraud; and an oil embargo by Arab nations threatening to cripple the American economy— Aaron found himself widely celebrated as a national hero.

The honors started in October, when he threw out the ceremonial first pitch to open the World Series. The championship provided a sweet diversion. The flamboyant Oakland A's, with their bold green uniforms, long-haired stars, and domineering owner Charlie O. Finley, defended their championship against the New York Mets, who had risen from the depths of their division to defeat the favored Cincinnati Reds in the National League playoffs. Oakland featured a troupe of colorful performers, among them a bright, egotistical slugger, Reggie Jackson; a countrified pitcher, Jim "Catfish" Hunter; and Rollie Fingers, who with a handlebar mustache looked like he belonged to another century. The Mets were led by the impeccable Tom Seaver, who enjoyed *New York Times* crossword puzzles; urbane Rusty Staub, a lover of fine wines and gourmet food; and Willie Mays, hoping for one last burst of glory. But all of them had to briefly share the fans' adulation with Hank Aaron, whose presence thrilled the crowd. On Saturday afternoon in the bright California sun, Aaron delivered the pregame pitch. The invitation to do so was Bowie Kuhn's peace offering. "I finally made another World Series," Aaron cracked.

Since the end of the regular season, Aaron had been enjoying some semblance of a normal life. He had been spending time with family. He had been fishing in Alabama, and he had been watching his sons play high school football. Still, "anytime a crowd gathers, it gets to Babe Ruth," he said.

Aaron, who had predicted New York would prevail, witnessed the first two games, both in Oakland. The A's took the opener, and the Mets came from behind to win the second. But the lasting image wasn't of the New Yorkers rallying in the ninth inning. It was of Willie Mays enduring what he described as "the toughest day I can ever remember." Inserted as a pinch runner for Staub, Mays stumbled and fell rounding second. He had to scramble desperately to get back to the base. In the outfield, he lost sight of a ball and tumbled clumsily into the turf. No one watching—not Aaron, not Kuhn, not the owner of the A's—could have helped but feel a twinge of sadness for Willie Mays and a sense that he had stayed a season too long. But maybe not. Maybe Mays had brought something intangible to the locker room, something beyond his statistics, that helped the Mets secure first place.

While in California, Hank Aaron spent a week preparing for the *Flip Wilson Show*. Television producers had flooded him with off-season opportunities. From talk shows to variety hours, Aaron had his pick. He had agreed to appear on Wilson's show with actress Lee Grant and Atlanta natives Gladys Knight and the Pips, whose "Midnight Train to Georgia" was chugging to the top of the charts. In one skit, Aaron tried to purchase a baseball bat from Wilson but found he lacked enough cash for the asking price of $7.14—as in 714 home runs, get it? "I only have $7.13," he said. "Would you settle for that?"

"Would you?" Wilson wondered.

"No way," said Aaron.

The *Flip Wilson Show* aired a month later, in mid-November. By then, Aaron (and Billye) had already appeared on *Dinah's Place,* singing and cooking with Dinah Shore. He also had been the focus of an NBC documentary, *The Long Winter of Henry Aaron.* It was telecast days after Atlanta made history by electing an African-American mayor, Maynard Jackson, a first for a major Southern city.

Between TV appearances and interviews, Hank Aaron and Billye Williams slipped off to Kingston, Jamaica, to be married. They figured the Caribbean capital—with its tropical climate, sandy beaches, soothing breezes, and stunning Blue Mountains—would provide the perfect escape. An alluring paradise, Kingston had hosted the George Foreman–Joe Frazier championship fight earlier in the year, and had drawn the world's premiere rock acts, the Rolling Stones and Elton John, for recording sessions. But for Aaron and Williams, its appeal lay partly in its location, a distance far enough from the American shore to deter photographers and reporters. Releasing few details in advance, they married on November 12 in a small, private affair attended by two of their children and a few other witnesses, including a Jamaican government official and some cameramen. The Rev. Dr. Horace Russell, a leading black minister, performed the ceremony at the University of the West Indies chapel. The bride wore a yellow-and-brown silk chiffon dress; the groom, a black tuxedo with bowtie. They savored the picturesque setting and relative peacefulness for several days before returning to their very public lives.

The tranquillity didn't last long. Within months, Aaron would find himself plunged into controversy. A hint of it surfaced in December when he mentioned that he and Eddie Mathews had talked about the Braves' 1974 schedule. "We agreed that if I hit a homer to tie the record on the road, he'll sit me down until we go home. That way," he said, "I'll have a chance to set a new record in our own park."

Such talk pricked Bowie Kuhn.

Aaron stayed in shape through the off-season by jogging, working out at a YMCA, playing handball with Mathews, and continuing the karate lessons he had been taking for several years. Meanwhile, an abundance of honors and invitations came his way. Governor Jimmy Carter named Aaron a ceremonial admiral in the Georgia navy. The state assembly also paid tribute to him. Aaron accepted the recognition in person, sitting beside wife Billye and saggy-eyed segregationist Lester Maddox, who delivered a surprise by suggesting that a portrait of Aaron be hung in the state capitol. (He had earlier railed against a painting of Martin Luther King, Jr.) "I hit numbers five hundred, six hundred, and seven hundred here," Aaron told the lawmakers, "and I'd like to break the record here, too, where all my friends can see it." Legislators crowded around him for autographs and photos.

The Red Cross asked Aaron to head up a winter blood drive, and the Easter Seals named him national sports chairman. Entertainer Sammy Davis, Jr., hosted him at his Los Angeles–area home. He proposed a movie be made about Aaron's life and inquired about purchasing the record-breaking ball for $25,000. Aaron disliked the Hollywood lifestyle. "That is another world out there," he said. "It's not for me. It's too fast."

In Chicago, a black business group gave Aaron its Par Excellence Award. In Rhode Island, he dined with former Governor John Chafee at a benefit for aged African-American women. Milwaukee baseball writers bestowed their Super Star Award upon Aaron, drawing city and state officials, as well as Brewers president Bud Selig. Judge Robert Cannon, who had once represented the players' association, heaped hyperbolic praise upon Aaron. "Because of conduct like yours, a black man today sits on the United States Supreme Court and another in the Senate of the United States," he said. "Men and women are holding office who couldn't do so if you hadn't helped create this atmosphere in baseball."

At the annual star-packed Boston baseball writers' dinner, Aaron received the Emil Fuchs Award, named for the late owner of the Boston Braves. Aaron drew the "greatest reception" that emcee Curt Gowdy had heard in twenty-three years of attending the event. He even gave autographs to fellow major leaguers. "He signed mine in pencil," said Carlton Fisk, "and Rick Wise's in a huge black magic marker. He was thanking Wise for his contributions to the record."

Aaron flew to Las Vegas, Nevada, in late 1973 to tape the *Dean Martin Celebrity Roast* in a chandeliered ballroom at the MGM Grand Hotel. Aaron sat next to the rostrum, fingering a cigarette, occasionally wiping his forehead with a handkerchief, and laughing at the digs of his celebrated critics: host Dean Martin, who hadn't rehearsed his lines and consequently tripped over some of them; actress Audrey Meadows, who chastised Aaron for scratching himself while at the plate; friend Eddie Mathews; pitcher Dizzy Dean; Jack in the Box's tiny spokeschild, Rodney Allen Rippy; and singers Lynn Anderson and Lou Rawls.

Foster Brooks, in character as a bumbling drunk, mistook the ballplayer for Raquel Welch. "That's a wild tan she's got there," he said. "I think you might have roasted her too long." Joey Bishop suggested to Aaron that when he hit his 715th home run he should walk around the bases, tip his hat at home plate, drop his pants, and sing "Black Bottom." Norm Crosby joked that the Braves had found a way to correct Aaron's fielding problems. "Next year, they're going to paint the ball green. You never saw one of those guys," he said, nodding toward Aaron, "drop a watermelon." And Nipsey Russell offered a poem: "If the baseball fan at the candy stand wants some chocolate for his sweet tooth, he got to call out O'Henry now and not just Baby Ruth." Aaron addressed his roasters with a smile. "If I had known I was going to be insulted like this," he said, "I would have stayed home and read my hate mail."

Aaron could have gone to a banquet almost every night had he chosen, and the payoff would have been handsome for the time—$2,500 to $4,000 per event. But money was no longer as pressing an issue. In January, he signed a five-year, $1 million deal to promote Magnavox. A month later in frigid Atlanta Stadium, he filmed his first commercial for the television manufacturer.

Still, Aaron made about a dozen banquet speeches over the winter.

In Modesto, California, at a place along Highway 99, where a portrait of him decorated the wall behind the podium, Aaron charmed the mostly white, working-class crowd. "Many people think I'm after the record of a white man, which isn't true at all," he said. "I don't want people to forget about Babe Ruth. I just want to make sure they don't forget about Henry Aaron." The banquet attendees embraced Aaron with their applause. In speaking out more frequently on racial issues—particularly the lack of minority executives and managers—Aaron didn't come across as caustic or divisive. But he persisted in making his point. "Black men have proven themselves as super giants on the playing field," he said. "It's time one of them was named to manage."

Aaron was asked whether his record would serve as an inspiration. "I'm hoping someday that some kid, black or white, will hit more home runs than myself," he said. "Whoever it is, I'd be pulling for him." Aaron was appearing, incidentally, about eighty miles southeast of San Francisco, home of Bobby Bonds and the Giants.

Hundreds of students packed into the gymnasium at Atlanta's Frederick Douglass High on February 5. When Hank Aaron walked through the doors, the teenagers exploded with applause and the school band played "Happy Birthday." Banners and oversized cards greeted Aaron on the occasion of his fortieth. Standing before the students on the varnished floor of a basketball court, Aaron told them that he was reminded of a long-ago event in his adolescence. "I remember sitting in a school assembly at Central High in Mobile and listening to one of my idols, Jackie Robinson, tell us that we ought not to want anything less than to be at the top of our professions," he said. "I thought then that I someday wanted to be as good a baseball player as I was capable. No matter what your profession, always try to do your best. Please continue your education, finish high school and go on to college. Do it for my sake. We need you."

As Aaron marked his birthday, a frightening news story broke out of Berkeley, California, riveting the nation's attention. Patty Hearst, a nineteen-year-old heiress to a newspaper fortune, had been kidnapped from her apartment, dragged out the door screaming, and tossed into the trunk of a stolen getaway car. A group calling itself the Symbionese Liberation Army soon claimed responsibility. Aaron hardly needed another reminder of his and his family's vulnerability, but Hearst's abduction provided one. The presence of Cal Wardlaw provided another.

Aaron and the officer had stayed in touch after the season and become friends. Aaron invited him to his place to shoot pool, a pastime he had taken up as a teen in Mobile when he'd skip class to hang out in a Davis Avenue joint and listen to radio broadcasts of Dodger games. Wardlaw learned that Aaron's silent competitiveness extended well beyond the baseball diamond. "Sometimes you have to know when to lose," he said. As they played, they would chat about family, football, and fishing. Wardlaw knew that he would be watching over Aaron when the season began. But Aaron sprung a surprise on him. Training camp would begin soon, and Aaron asked him if he would be willing to provide security in West Palm Beach. Thrilled, Wardlaw agreed. The okay came from high up, from Atlanta's new mayor, Maynard Jackson.

Two weeks before Aaron headed to Florida for camp, he went home to Alabama to be honored by the city where he was raised. Mobile had proclaimed Friday, February 15, as Henry the Great Day, and the entire community—black and white—celebrated. "It looks like we could have sold three or four hundred more tickets to the banquet," said Shelby Sutton of the Mobile Chamber of Commerce. "The requests have been pouring in. I wish we could accommodate everybody, but we're limited to only three hundred fifty seats."

The black-owned *Mobile Beacon* declared it an historic moment: "There will be no color line. . . . That is the way it should be not only in this instance but three hundred sixty-five days a year with all of us whether the hero or heroine is black or white. . . . It seems rather ironic," the paper continued, "that more progress toward better race relations has been made in sports than through the Christian church."

Hank and Billye Aaron's flight arrived at Bates Field around noon, and hundreds waited to greet them at the gate. A parade of fans, friends, and dignitaries followed the Aarons through the airport. "We want Hank," some chanted. Aaron met with reporters, including those from high school newspapers, before introducing Billye to Mobile. The trip marked her first to Aaron's hometown and the sites of his early life: the house on Edwards Street, Central High School, Davis Avenue.

At a candlelight banquet that evening in the municipal auditorium, a who's who of Mobile—business and community leaders, elected officials, fellow major leaguers like Cleon Jones and Tommie Agee, faces from his past—showered Aaron with accolades and gifts. "Welcome Home" said a banner above the dais. The chamber of commerce pledged to raise $75,000 to seed a Hank Aaron scholarship fund. The mayor presented him with a painted portrait. The city renamed a new stretch of downtown roadway as the Henry Aaron Loop. A state legislator awarded him a personal license plate that read "H.A. 715." Nearby Prichard heralded him as honorary mayor, the Mobile Youth Baseball program inducted him into its hall of fame, and the Gulf City Order of Elks made him a life member. A representative of Governor George Wallace, who in the 1960s had vowed to "stand at the schoolhouse door" to prevent blacks from integrating the University of Alabama, awarded Aaron cuff links and a tie tack. Bowie Kuhn sent a telegram, as did President Richard Nixon. In turning down an invitation, a Nixon assistant had noted in a January letter that the commander-in-chief would be unable to attend. "Regrettably, too, a representative of the President cannot join you . . . due to the heavy demands on all those working here with him now," the letter stated.

Hank Aaron introduced his family: his parents, his wife, his daughters Gaile and Dorinda, and his sisters and his brothers, including Tommie. He described Mobile as "one of the greatest cities in the world . . . my home," and vowed that he would never forget the honor given him. "Tonight," he said, "I feel like everything is just great."

While Hank Aaron was deep-sea fishing off the Alabama coast, Braves president Bill Bartholomay announced that his star would not start the team's first three games in Cincinnati. Aaron might pinch-hit against the Reds, but the Braves wanted him to tie and surpass Babe Ruth during their eleven-game stand in Atlanta. "It is unprecedented to speculate on an opening lineup at this early date, but Braves' fans deserve to know our plans," said Bartholomay in a declaration designed to boost ticket sales. Eddie Mathews concurred with the decision, saying Aaron "more or less belongs to the people of the Southeast."

Those were fighting words.

Partly in answer to concerns raised by baseball writers, Kuhn phoned Bartholomay to register his disappointment and urge him to reconsider. Afterward, Kuhn's office issued a press release stating that the Braves had assured him they "will do their very best to win the opening three games in Cincinnati." That might have been the end of it, except that Kuhn's response did not satisfy New York's influential sports columnists. Dick Young of the *Daily News* decreed, "Baseball has gone crooked. . . . Eddie Mathews is a good man. So is Henry Aaron. And yet they have been swept up in this pernicious thing, until they cannot tell right from wrong." Dave Anderson of the *Times* accused the Braves of being in "brazen defiance of baseball's integrity." Larry Merchant of the *Post* described it as an "insidious fix." The *Times'* Red Smith, having spoken to Kuhn, assured, "If Henry Aaron is fit on April 4, he will be in the Atlanta Braves' outfield." Days later, Dick Young weighed in again. "The audacity of Bowie Kuhn offends me," he said. "He thinks all people are gullible fools. . . . When a situation cries out for strong action, he invariably comes out with weak words."

The New York contingent drew support from writers in Boston, Chicago, and Detroit. Joe Falls of the *Detroit Free Press* made an emotional appeal: "A small boy wrote a letter to Henry Aaron last year. He said his class in school was going to celebrate his birthday and they were going to do it even though they were Mets fans. He said they were going to celebrate with cupcakes and lollipops. He said to Henry Aaron, 'Thank you for being born.' Please don't let this boy down," Falls implored.

The dispute divided Atlanta's sports reporters. But almost unanimously they resented what they saw as the heavy-handedness of the New York writers. Aaron stuck by the team's decision. "The people of Atlanta are the ones I have to please," he told a local gathering. "I believe they want to see it. I feel I owe it to them. Besides, this ballpark has been pretty good to me." But his word wouldn't be the last on the matter. The controversy festered as Aaron prepared to head to training camp.

Meanwhile, Reg Murphy, editor of the *Atlanta Constitution*, left his home Wednesday evening, February 21, to meet a man who said he wanted to donate 300,000 gallons of heating oil to help needy residents. But it turned out to be a ruse. The man pulled a gun and abducted Murphy, who in September had touted Aaron for his role in easing racial prejudice. The abductor, identifying himself as a colonel in the American Revolutionary Army, complained to Murphy about the "leftist, liberal" media. Forty-nine hours later, after the *Constitution* delivered the $700,000 ransom, Murphy was released. Soon, a Gwinnett County couple was arrested. In California, meanwhile, Patty Hearst remained missing.

19

THE HIDEAWAY

Hank Aaron reported early to sunny West Palm Beach, intent on getting himself in shape. Eddie Mathews was there, along with most of the pitchers and catchers. Ralph Garr was there, too. But Dusty Baker would be days tardy, as would Paul Casanova, who remained in Caracas, Venezuela, where he had purchased a discotheque.

Aaron looked bulky in his Braves uniform, partly because of his age and partly because of the rubber shirt and pants he wore beneath his uniform to induce sweating. "I want all the uninterrupted practice I can get," he said. "Last spring, I wasn't ready. I loafed too much, I guess." To help Aaron concentrate on the task, Donald Davidson instituted new rules. The major one dictated that there would be no on-field interviews. "We'll have press conferences, of course, but Hank will name the times and places," he said. "They certainly won't be on the ball field."

"I want to cooperate," Aaron reiterated, "but not on the ball field."

For purposes of privacy, the Braves moved him out of the players' dressing room and into a clubhouse area with Eddie

Mathews and the coaching staff. Away from the park, Aaron stayed separate from the club. His teammates roomed at the Ramada Inn; Aaron lived nearby in a private condominium with Billye and her daughter, Ceci. The location was a secret, and Aaron used an alias, Diefendorfer. "Even if you knew Aaron's address, you couldn't get very close to him," said Davidson. "There'll be an Atlanta detective on the premises and at his elbow every second. The detective is . . . licensed to carry a gun and knows how to use it."

Davidson overstated Calvin Wardlaw's presence, perhaps as a deterrent. The officer actually lived at the Ramada Inn. He did shadow Aaron, but not around the clock. He drove him to and from Municipal Stadium, watched over him from the dugout, escorted him through crowds, and sometimes accompanied him about town. He also socialized with the Aarons.

On the last day of February, Aaron and other Braves took a break from training camp to shoot a few rounds at West Palm Beach Country Club. Aaron golfed for relaxation. He invited Wardlaw, who knew nothing of the sport, to chauffeur the electric cart. Looking stylish in a white sweater and two-tone shoes, Aaron drove a good ball. The first time he landed one near the hole, Aaron watched in stunned disbelief as Wardlaw committed one of the sins of the course. He drove the cart onto the pampered putting green. Wardlaw felt its wheels sink on the soft surface, and he knew immediately from the yelps of his party and other golfers watching that he had done something wrong. They laughed about it later. "I don't consider him a bodyguard," said Aaron. "He's a friend, that's all."

Donald Davidson was more candid about the dangers. "Frankly, I'm concerned," he said. "I read about the Hearst girl's kidnapping. I read of Reg Murphy's kidnapping. So why shouldn't I worry about Henry Aaron?"

"He's being guarded like a threatened heiress," one observer noted.

Bill Bartholomay flew to New York on Monday, March 4, to meet with Bowie Kuhn about the lineup controversy. Kuhn pressed him to start Aaron in Cincinnati. Bartholomay insisted that it was his prerogative as owner to make those decisions. He argued that there was precedent for altering lineups to increase gates. It wasn't mere coincidence, after all, that some famous pitching duels were enacted in one town on one weekend and then reenacted in the other team's town on the next weekend. And in 1958 with Stan Musial one hit short of 3,000, the Cardinals had benched their star in an attempt to save the feat for a St. Louis crowd. (Musial, as it turned out, was forced into action as a pinch hitter and reached the plateau on the road.) Kuhn warned Bartholomay that if necessary he would write the lineup for the Braves.

The next week, Kuhn announced that Aaron, unless injured, would be expected to play two of three Cincinnati games. "If the commissioner says I play, then I guess I'll have to play," Aaron said. "I really don't have that much to say on the matter. Besides, anything the commissioner might do doesn't really surprise me anymore."

Kuhn's action provoked more sniping between columnists Furman Bisher in Atlanta and Dick Young in New York. Bisher blamed New York writers for Kuhn's tougher stance and described Young as "a dishwater-gray little man with a voice that soothes like a pile-driver." Responded Young, "Some brilliant Atlanta newspaperman, who never got over covering the Civil War, warned that those insidious Northern sportswriters were trying to dictate who shall play and who shall not play for the glorious Confederacy and, by Gawd, we're not going to stand for it, are we, Rhett, suh!"

Kuhn followed his oral directive with a letter to Bartholomay threatening penalties if the Braves disobeyed. "The reputation of the game is in your hands," Kuhn stated. But if he thought that would end the matter, he was mistaken.

Heads snapped when bowlegged Sammy Davis, Jr., strode into the locker room on Saturday, March 9, before the Braves' first spring game.

"Hey, man," he said to Aaron. "I was in Miami and I saw in the paper where you cats were playing and I thought I'd come over and watch. I just bought a ninety-footer [a yacht], so why not? . . . You're about to do it, man," he added, his left glass eye visible through tinted lenses.

"Yeah," said Aaron. "You going to be there?"

"No. I'll be in Australia. You'll be way past Babe Ruth when I get back."

Davis, Aaron, and Ralph Garr settled around a table littered with newspapers, dirty ashtrays, and empty Coca-Cola bottles. Other Braves lingered not so discreetly to watch the Rat Pack hipster. It seemed as if someone famous was always coming to visit Aaron. If not a civil rights leader like Jesse Jackson or Andrew Young, then a political figure like Jimmy Carter or Maynard Jackson or entertainers like the Staple Singers or a media personality like Harry Reasoner. "You name them, we met them through Hank," Dusty Baker said.

It wasn't only celebrities who wanted to greet Hank Aaron. After games, fans waited for him to emerge from the clubhouse. Often, he would be the last player to leave the dressing room, giving the crowd time to dissipate. Fans were becoming bolder, too. Before a Miami exhibition against the Orioles, Aaron was chatting with other players when a man abruptly leaped over the fence and onto the field and headed toward him. Alarmed, Wardlaw darted in that direction to intercede. Ushers rushed there, as well. They cut off the intruder before he reached Aaron. The man meant Aaron no harm. He merely wanted a signature, he said. But the startle he created awoke Wardlaw's sense of danger.

Hank Aaron's presence dominated spring training. He was the story, the reason area hotels, filled with journalists, had to light their no-vacancy signs. Five games into the spring season, Hank Aaron slapped his first home run off a tall, wild Houston Astro, James Rodney Richard, who was two years old when Aaron first wore a Braves uniform.

On the other side of Florida in St. Petersburg, Willie Mays worked with young New York Mets hitters. He said he imagined Hank Aaron was feeling miserable. "The pressure must be hell," he said. "I remember when I was going for Mel Ott's National League record of 511. I couldn't eat. I couldn't sleep. I was so tight when I got within a couple of home runs of the mark that for a couple of weeks I never got close to the ball. I'm sure it must be the same for Hank. Every day, there'll be a crowd around him asking him questions about hitting number 714 to tie and then it will be the same until he hits number 715 to break the record. He'll do it, of course, but it may be two or three weeks before he does it. Once it's done, it will be like a ton of bricks removed from his head."

Aaron admitted as much. "When I break the record, when the chase is over, it will be fun again," he said.

Police in West Palm Beach rushed to Aaron's condominium one day with potentially horrific news: Billye and her daughter were missing. Aaron and Wardlaw were assured that patrols were scouring the region for them at that very moment. Aaron was frantic. His worry, however, consumed just minutes before Billye and Ceci burst into the condominium after a day of shopping.

Sports Illustrated hit newsstands in mid-March with Babe Ruth on the cover. "The Legend Comes to Life," it stated. Over the next three issues, the magazine excerpted chapters from senior editor Robert Creamer's insightful biography of Ruth. Oddly, though on the verge of overtaking the Bambino, Aaron had not been featured on a *Sports Illustrated* front in three and a half years. Not that anyone noticed. His face was everywhere else.

Aaron lined his second spring training home run on Monday, March 25. "Call the commissioner," he said, "and see if these down here won't be enough. I wish they were. It would mean it would be all over."

Rumors swirled in camp that Marty Perez or Ralph Garr might be offered in a trade for a right-handed hitter or a relief pitcher. The Braves had earlier obtained shortstop Craig Robinson, making Perez expendable, and with young outfielder Rowland Office hitting above .400, Atlanta officials thought they might be able to do without Garr—for a significant price. "There is nothing really concrete right now, but we have been looking and we have been talking," said Eddie Mathews. "Something could happen later on this week."

Amid the distractions, some things didn't change. One morning at camp, Garr went to his favorite teacher and asked for base-running advice. Garr was the fastest man on the Braves and an established hitter, but he found in Aaron an infinite source of knowledge. So they went behind the ball field to an area with a sliding pit, and Garr practiced his lead, his break for the base, and his slide as Aaron watched and commented. He told Garr that he was doing it the right way, running straight, sliding straight, and returning to his feet quickly, like Bobby Bonds. "He has helped me ever since I got here," said Garr, noting that Aaron's advice hadn't been limited to baseball. "He has told me at times I talk too much. He said I shouldn't be so easy to criticize. Constructive criticism is good, he told me. Just talking to be talking is no good. . . . You never know who's listening."

Marvin Miller, director of the players association, met with Braves players on a Friday morning in March, seeking their views on the new compulsory arbitration plan. He was asked whether Bowie Kuhn had overstepped his rights by ordering Aaron to play in Cincinnati. No, he said. "I think this is a matter that falls into the prerogative of management. The tragic part of the whole thing is that Aaron is involved. The issue puts added pressure on him at a time when he should be completely free of such pressure." Eddie Mathews concurred, saying the debate had soured Aaron's time in West Palm Beach. "This was supposed to be a pleasant spring for Hank," he said. "He was supposed to get ready at his own pace. Instead it's been heavy with pressure and very difficult for him." Aaron also offered a hint of strain while commenting on the likelihood that someone would eventually challenge his record. "Believe me, I'll be pulling for him," he said. "And I hope they give him as much hell as they have me."

With the opener against Cincinnati less than a week away, the Braves had a game-free day on Friday, March 29, and stayed in West Palm Beach to practice. A group of hitters had gathered around the batting cage, waiting for their swings. Davey Johnson was at the plate taking his cuts. Aaron was watching, leaning too close to the netting, when Johnson deflected a pitch into the mesh, striking Aaron on the forehead and creating a knot. Two inches lower, the ball would have been driven into Aaron's left eye—and his career might have been over.

The Braves concluded their spring season with scrimmages against the Orioles in Louisiana and Alabama. Before the final game in Birmingham, Eddie Mathews stewed in the locker room over the Bowie Kuhn matter. The more he thought about it, the madder he got. He was the manager, not Kuhn. He should have the right to choose his lineup. He should be allowed to determine who bats and in which games. No one outside of his bosses should be able to tell him that Aaron must play in Cincinnati. "What if it's thirty degrees up there? Does he still have to play?" Mathews asked. "He didn't last year in weather like that. What if he hurts himself? Has anyone taken that into consideration? Everyone has jumped on the band-wagon, saying what a hell of a story Hank is. But at the same time, they've failed to recognize Hank and his feelings. That goes from the commissioner on down."

Aaron had wanted to meet with Kuhn but had been re-buked. "Since I was the one involved, I think that maybe he should have talked to me," said Aaron. "He didn't."

More than 9,000 fans turned out for the Birmingham exhi-bition and cheered Hank Aaron, who went hitless. The Braves won their third straight game. That night back at the team ho-tel, Paul Casanova suggested to Aaron that they go out for soul food. As they were about to leave, they encountered two Al-abama officers guarding Aaron's door. The police wanted Aaron to stay inside. His life had been threatened, they said. He might be in danger if he left. Tired of hiding out, Aaron ignored their warnings and departed with Casanova. They took the stairs instead of the elevator.

The story of Hank Aaron's life, as told by his friends, is filled with prophetic moments in which Aaron announces to them—as if fated—that he intends to hit a home run in a spe-cific at-bat or at a given time. Sometimes, he would just know it. He'd be heading up to the plate and he could feel what was coming. "It's kind of eerie," he once admitted. "You wonder why you're blessed..." Dusty Baker witnessed such pro-nouncements. So did Ralph Garr. And on that night in Birm-ingham, after they had returned to the hotel, Aaron revealed another one of them to Paul Casanova. Aaron told him that he would tie Babe Ruth in Ohio and surpass him in the first game in Georgia. Casanova didn't doubt him.

The flight to Greater Cincinnati Airport left Wednesday morning.

20

AMID A STORM

Hank Aaron peered out a window at the Cincinnati airport, his eyes nervously tracking the ghoulish, narrow finger of a funnel cloud twitching across the darkened sky. It was late afternoon on Wednesday, April 3, 1974. Aaron and his teammates had arrived at Riverfront Stadium in the morning to find their practice rained out, and now Aaron was back at the airport awaiting the flight that carried Billye, his father, brother Herbert, Jr., and secretary Carla. He was worried.

Journalist Jerry Green, relieved to have landed after a bumpy ride from Detroit, noticed him in the terminal.

"Hank, nice of you to come out and meet me," he joked.

"Good to see you again," Aaron said.

"Do me a favor. Get the two [home runs] right away so I can go home."

"I hope I can," said Aaron.

In the distance, the tail of a twister loomed ominously above the landscape, a fitting symbol of the storm that had been following Aaron for more than a year as he pursued the record. Threats against him and his family, racial abuse in the mail and from the stands, a frustrating slump, an uninterrupted stream of criticism, disputes with the Hall of Fame and the commissioner of baseball, reporters and photographers everywhere, phones ringing continuously, fans knocking at his hotel door, police officers shadowing him—Aaron found no peace. Even with the chase almost over, he felt like a stalked man.

Aaron did not yet know whether he would be playing tomorrow in the National League opener against the Reds. Earlier in the day, Eddie Mathews, riled by what he viewed as Bowie Kuhn's meddling, said he hadn't made up his mind about Thursday's lineup. His bosses had directed him not to comment. But Mathews, a self-described "blabbermouth," said he couldn't keep silent about Kuhn. "As far as I'm concerned he still hasn't ordered me to do anything, and I won't take an order from him." Across the field in the Reds' clubhouse, manager Sparky Anderson sided with the Braves. "Atlanta has been made to look like a villain in this thing," he said. "I don't think that's fair. I think Atlanta had integrity in announcing what it planned to do. This is going to be the greatest sporting event in my time and I don't want to see it tarnished. . . . Many people are questioning Aaron's integrity, but I wonder how you can question a man like this. I don't think he should have to take all this crap he's getting."

Buffeted by winds, a plane from Georgia rolled to an uneasy stop and Aaron's group disembarked. Aaron hugged Billye as she came safely through the gate, her jacket folded over her arm.

The tornado was one of 148 that would touch down by morning, ravaging a path through thirteen states, Alabama to Michigan, claiming more than three hundred lives and injuring thousands. Not fifty miles from Cincinnati, the massive storm nearly demolished the town of Xenia, Ohio. "It looks like a battlefield, like bombs hit—only bombs don't do that much damage," said a deputy at daylight.

A cleansing, mid-morning breeze washed over Cincinnati Thursday as a bright spring sun soothed the damp, scarred landscape of southern Ohio. In their suite near the top of the Netherland Hilton, Hank Aaron shared breakfast with Billye and steeled himself for the hectic day ahead. By 11:20 A.M., he was at the ballpark getting ready for a press conference about his scholarship fund.

Back in Atlanta, Aaron's children went to school as they would any other weekday. The local papers carried news of the tragedy from the storm that had also churned parts of Georgia. Tucked inside the *Journal* was a special forty-page section saluting Hank Aaron. On the front of the tribute appeared a piece by Aaron in which he said he enjoyed the competitive challenge of going for the record. "But it hasn't been all that good, chasing a record like this," he said. "It's changed my life and my family's life and I really didn't have anything to do with it. There was nothing I could do as long as I kept hitting home runs. Now everything's changed. It's mostly in the attitudes, I guess, both among my teammates and the fans."

Jammed alongside the articles were ads from merchants. A Ford dealer promised $714 in savings on a Grand Torino. A jeweler unveiled the "Star of Georgia" gem, named for Hank Aaron, "King of the Diamonds." Coca-Cola saluted a fellow Atlanta institution, and Magnavox hyped a $388 "nineteen-inch diagonal solid state color TV" that had Aaron's face pictured on the screen. The ads honored Aaron. But that wasn't the case everywhere. In the current issue of *Newsweek,* Jim Beam bought a page for its bourbon. The Kentucky distiller showed a shot of Babe Ruth swinging, with this tag line: "You can't improve on the original."

At Riverfront Stadium, Bill Bartholomay and general manager Eddie Robinson pulled Eddie Mathews into a meeting early Thursday to talk about the battle with Bowie Kuhn. Bartholomay's viewpoint was well known. He wanted to save Aaron for Atlanta. They all did. But Kuhn had kept the pressure on the Braves. He expected Aaron to play in two of three games. Bartholomay asked Mathews whether under normal circumstances—in other words, with the home-run record not on the verge of being eclipsed—he would start Aaron.

"Yeah," said Mathews.

"Okay, then play him," he said.

While taking questions at a press conference, Aaron learned that he would be in the lineup. He admitted that he wanted to save number 715 for Atlanta. But, he said, "To be very frank with you, I hope I hit a home run here." Aaron had made history before in Cincinnati. The city saw him play his first major league game and collect his 3,000th hit. He recorded the first home run ever at Riverfront and hit more round-trippers off the Reds than off any other team. He even broke his ankle in the town. There were worse places to be.

In the Reds dressing room, slender Jack Billingham took his pregame regimen of protein pills, vitamins, and wheat-germ capsules. Billingham hadn't slept well. He and his family had spent the night camped out on mattresses scattered across the basement floor, fearful that more tornadoes would materialize. "They scared the devil out of me," he said. "I wasn't thinking of pitching against Aaron. I was thinking about the safety of my family." Billingham, coming off his best season, 19–10, said he would try to pitch Aaron outside. If he were to surrender number 714, he noted, "It will just be another home run. Nobody will remember it a month later."

Aaron, in the other clubhouse, stripped out of his sport coat, slacks, and off-white turtleneck shirt and dressed in his uniform. Reporters milled about, cautious of asking something bothersome. Aaron smiled and answered questions politely but with as few words as possible. He sipped a soda and smoked a cigarette and read a Cincinnati sports section as others wished him well.

"Supe," joked Dusty Baker, "you playing today, brother?"

The Rev. Jesse Jackson reached Hank Aaron by phone in the clubhouse. Jackson called from Memphis, Tennessee, where he was leading a memorial service honoring Martin Luther King, Jr. Six years earlier on the same day, April 4, King had been shot outside a motel in Memphis. Jackson suggested that Aaron and the other black Braves ask that Dr. King be recognized before the start of the baseball game. Aaron, Ralph Garr, Dusty Baker, and others embraced the idea. On behalf of all of them, Aaron requested that the Reds offer a moment of silence for King. An Atlanta publicist took the request to a Cincinnati official, who took it to his bosses.

Meanwhile, en route to Ohio from Andrews military base in Maryland, Air Force Two detoured from its path to fly low over Xenia so Vice President Gerald Ford could survey the tornado's damage. Bowie Kuhn and wife Luisa were also aboard the plane. Kuhn had invited Ford to the Cincinnati opener, which marked the start of the season. (Ford's wife, Betty, could not come; she was preparing for a Friday visit to promote the Artrain in Georgia, where she would spend the night at the governor's mansion with Jimmy and Rosalyn Carter.) A former University of Michigan football star, Gerald Ford had accepted Kuhn's invitation. In a memo, one of his assistants recommended that Ford "be certain to talk with Hank Aaron of the Braves."

In flight, Ford and Kuhn chatted about Aaron, martinis, and baseball arbitration. Over Xenia, both men got "an appalling view of the damage wrought by the tornado," Kuhn said. "The problems of baseball fell into proper perspective."

The Reds' first game always sold out, and this one was no exception. The city loved its team, and the Aaron saga added to demand for tickets. Cincinnati had been hawking standing room only admissions for several weeks. Attendance topped 52,150, a record for the Reds.

With 283 journalists credentialed to cover the game, no detail escaped notice—not Aaron's 33.5-inch, 34.75-ounce white-ash bat, not coach Jim Busby's role of physically putting Aaron's name on the lineup card, not the 600 sandwiches and 700 cans of beer and soda that the 283 journalists consumed, not the temperature of sixty-three degrees, nor the fact that Aaron clipped his toenails in the locker room at 11:50 A.M.

After driving a few balls over the fence during batting practice, Hank Aaron chatted with family near the Braves dugout. His mother had stayed in Mobile, too worried to make the trip to Ohio. She planned to watch her son on television. "I've been praying a lot for that kid, for him to overcome all that hate," she said. "It's bad when you've got to be guarded, so many security around. I've really been feeling bad about all that. Why do they want to hurt him? . . . Like Martin Luther King, he wasn't hurting anyone."

In the pregame ceremony, Cincinnati fans greeted Aaron warmly. Backed by a high school marching band, a local performer sung the National Anthem, and Vice President Ford, who as a child had seen Babe Ruth play, threw out the opening pitch to Johnny Bench. But there was no moment of silence for Martin Luther King, Jr. Aaron had been told the program was already set. Reds official Dick Wagner announced later, "As a policy, our club has never gotten into religious things. We don't get into politics. We don't get into race."

Jack Billingham threw his final warm-ups as Ralph Garr loosened. Billingham had said days earlier that he expected that facing Aaron on the precipice of history would get his stomach rumbling. Billingham looked jittery. He walked Garr to start the game. Mike Lum followed with a single to left.

With Hank Aaron on-deck, Billingham got Darrell Evans to fly out to Pete Rose, which brought Aaron toward the batter's box and the Cincinnati crowd to its feet.

Umpire Ed Vargo switched baseballs with Billingham, giving him one specially coded with "14-1" for the occasion. The game's two most popular players, Aaron and Bench, stood near the plate. "Good luck," Bench said.

Aaron watched Billingham's first four pitches, working the count to three balls, one strike—his favorite. With two runners on and Dusty Baker coming up next, Billingham needed to throw a strike. Pitching from the set, the tall right-hander tried to drop a fastball over the outside corner. But he hung it, and Aaron lined the pitch to left-center. "Holy shit, there it goes," said someone in the Atlanta dugout. Pete Rose turned to his left and sped toward the wall. The ball flew over the fence at the 375-foot mark. Billingham swiped at the dirt.

Aaron's teammates charged toward home. Aaron circled the bases slowly, his poker face intact. Paul Casanova, in the clubhouse changing his shirt after warming up Carl Morton, heard the roar and realized he had missed his friend's home run. In Mobile, Estella Aaron bolted from her rocking chair and dashed through the house yelling. Aaron's wife Billye, her head wrapped in a traditional African gele, beamed as tears trickled upon her cheeks. In the dugout, crusty bullpen coach Ken "Hatch" Silvestri bit his lip and veteran pitcher Jack Aker felt goose bumps just as he had at Mickey Mantle Day in Yankee Stadium. Aaron allowed himself a slight smile and a light skip as he planted both feet on home and was swallowed in a crowd of blue-and-white jerseys. Garr, Baker, Lum, Evans, Johnson—they were all there. The Braves closed in around him, slapping his back, jostling his shoulders, thumping his helmet.

Hank Aaron had tied Babe Ruth on his first swing of the season.

Bowie Kuhn, perhaps remembering the dispute that flared

when he failed to acknowledge Aaron's 700th home run, insisted on halting the game to recognize the moment. Reds executive Wagner balked, saying he didn't want to interrupt the contest. But Wagner relented when from the bunting-draped front row Kuhn threatened to immediately suspend him. On the field, Vice President Ford congratulated Aaron. Kuhn gave Aaron a trophy and described him as "one of the great gentlemen." Bill Bartholomay announced that the celebration would continue "Monday night in Atlanta, Georgia." Jack Billingham, perturbed that the game had been stopped mid-inning, threw warm-up pitches to Johnny Bench as the ceremony took place.

Aaron kept his comments brief. "Thank you very much," he said, "and I'm just glad it's almost over with." He got no other hits that afternoon, and the Braves blew a 6–1 lead, losing in the eleventh inning when Rose charged home on a wild pitch.

The defeat, combined with the Reds' refusal to honor Martin Luther King, soured the day for Aaron. "It's just another home run now," he said afterward. "If we had won, I'd probably be over there in our clubhouse drinking champagne." His words soft, Aaron said he and his black teammates "were all very disappointed" that Martin Luther King was ignored on the anniversary of his assassination. Seated beside him, wife Billye interjected: "It should not have been necessary to ask. The stature of the man demanded it."

Given the dispute with Bowie Kuhn, everyone wondered whether Aaron would play in the next game. "Yes, I'm going to play Saturday," he said. But Eddie Mathews wasn't so sure. That evening, Aaron celebrated his momentous home run over a quiet dinner with family and friends at Cincinnati's most exclusive restaurant, the five-star Maisonette. He also called his mother in Mobile. "I'm going to save the next one for you," he said.

Two hours after midnight, the phone rang in Koplin's room at the Hilton. It was Donald Davidson, the traveling secretary, and he was frantic.

"Carla, I can't find the ball," he stammered.

The home-run ball was missing. Davidson said he had hid it in his room to deter would-be thieves. But he couldn't remember where he put it and he couldn't find it. He wanted Koplin to help him search for it. He called Eddie Mathews, too. The three of them met in the hotel lobby, and Davidson recounted how he had carefully hid the ball before going out to celebrate. When he returned, tipsy, he couldn't locate it.

The three of them proceeded to Davidson's room and scoured the unit. They looked under the pillows and bed, they tore through the closet, checked the bathroom and behind the curtains, and they rifled Davidson's sport coats and suitcases. They all knew this was serious business. The ball was an important (and valuable) part of baseball history, and it was missing. They considered calling police, but the room didn't appear ransacked.

"Donald," Koplin asked finally, "did you put the ball in the hotel safe?"

He paused and then remembered.

"Of course," he said. "The safe."

Koplin and Mathews left Davidson in the room, their anger at him muted by a sense of relief and the comedy of the affair.

President Richard Nixon, somewhere over the Atlantic Ocean aboard Air Force One, called Hank Aaron Friday morning at the Hilton to congratulate him. Nixon was en route to Paris to attend a memorial service for French leader Georges

Pompidou. He asked Aaron about the home run. Nixon told Aaron that he hoped his record-breaking home run would come quickly.

The Braves had no game Friday, and practice had been called off because of the weather. It was cold and rainy. Aaron had been out of sight most of the day, making a luncheon appearance on behalf of Magnavox. When he returned to the hotel, twenty-some reporters desperate for fresh copy pinned him down in the lobby. Aaron, in a jovial mood, conducted an impromptu press conference standing on a staircase in an overcoat.

He told about Nixon's phone call and said that he had received a hundred or so telegrams, from Willie Mays, Roy Campanella, and others. "No," he said, "I haven't heard from Mrs. Ruth." He revealed that he ate trout for dinner and that, depending on the weather, he intended to play Saturday. He said that his 1957 pennant-winning home run remained his favorite. "But the 715th probably will mean more," he added. "Then you're standing out there alone, you're not sharing it [the record] with anybody."

Indeed, Aaron had only a piece of the title as of that afternoon. But more than three-fourths of America was pulling for him to break the record, according to a new survey. His support had leaped by almost ten points since August. The *Atlanta Daily World*, the city's black newspaper, praised Aaron in an editorial. "Hammering Hank's 714th home run was a thing of beauty. . . . Hank, destined to surpass the feats of Babe Ruth, an American baseball legend, might well be on the threshold of creating new bridges in race relations and achieving much more than the stroke of his bat seems to be doing on the baseball diamond." In New York, the *Daily News* ran a large Bill Gallo cartoon of Babe Ruth in pinstripes, holding his cap in his right hand and three bats on his shoulder. Gallo had Ruth speaking. "Welcome to the club, Henry," he said.

That evening, Eddie Mathews went for a walk in Cincinnati. The temperature was near freezing. Aaron didn't typically play in cold weather. Mathews decided that if it were anything like this on Saturday, he would not start Aaron. With NBC planning to televise the contest as *Game of the Week*—and with its ace crew of Curt Gowdy, Joe Garagiola, and Tony Kubek in town—he knew he would be blistered if he sat Hank Aaron. But he felt it his prerogative as manager. No matter what Bowie Kuhn said, Mathews intended to make out his own lineup.

Don Gullett was scheduled to pitch for the Reds. Aaron owned a searing .478 average against him. Proclaimed as the next Sandy Koufax by Sparky Anderson, Gullett had allowed Aaron seven home runs in four seasons. He threw hard, and Aaron enjoyed batting against him—usually.

S aturday at the ballpark, Mathews announced his decision. He went further than planned. "Hank Aaron will not play either today or tomorrow," he said. "His next game will be Monday night in Atlanta. We've been more than fair about this but my thinking has changed since he hit the home run. Right or wrong, I'm the manager and that's my decision. . . . I won't use him except as a pinch hitter in a game-deciding situation."

Kuhn had already left Cincinnati, abandoning his pledge to be present and lead the cheering section for Aaron. He had seen enough and would no longer be part of the entourage following Aaron. But one of his assistants remained, and when he heard Mathews' defiant words he phoned his boss. Kuhn was livid.

The Braves dismissed Gullett early, and Mathews went through four pinch hitters. Aaron stayed on the bench, passed over in the seventh inning with the game tied 5–5 and a runner on first. Mathews used left-handed Frank Tepedino against right-handed Pedro Borbon. The Reds won 7–5.

Afterward, in a telephone conversation, Kuhn ordered Mathews and Bill Bartholomay to play Aaron on Sunday. He threatened unspecified "very serious consequences" if the

Braves ignored his wishes. Fines and suspensions were likely. Concerned that the Braves might sideline Aaron with a last-minute "injury," Kuhn said he would have to be notified in advance—and approve—should Aaron be unable to play. Kuhn's actions were unprecedented in baseball history. "Because of this order and the threatened penalties, I intend to start Hank Aaron tomorrow," a defeated Mathews said.

Cincinnati celebrated Bat Day on Sunday, and about 2,500 children received Hank Aaron models. They probably had better luck with theirs than Aaron did with his. Clay Kirby stifled him in three at-bats, feeding him nothing but sliders. "Two kinds," said Kirby. "A big one and a small one." Sparky Anderson had directed Kirby to throw no fastballs to Aaron. "You got to make him supply his own power," Anderson said. The strategy worked. Kirby struck him out on three straight pitches in two consecutive appearances. Aaron took called-third strikes—and argued with umpire John McSherry—on both occasions. In his final attempt before being replaced defensively, Aaron dribbled the ball weakly to third baseman Dan Driessen.

"I did the best I could," Aaron said.

But not everyone thought it true. "Some people will think you deliberately didn't try to hit number 715 today," someone suggested delicately. Nearby, first baseman Mike Lum muttered an impolite word about journalists.

"I can't help what people think," Aaron replied. "It's not the easiest thing in the world to hit the ball out of the park. . . . I was just guessing wrong. The first two times, I guessed fastball and he threw sliders."

Kirby said he felt Aaron had been overswinging. He also said that the umpire had helped him out on a low third strike. "I just happened to make good pitches to him today," he said. Joe Morgan cited the fact that Aaron had argued with McSherry as evidence that Aaron made an honest attempt. "I've never seen

Hank so mad," he said. "I guess that proves he cared." Noted Ted Kluszewski, a Reds coach, "A certain percentage of fans will say he wasn't trying. That's ridiculous."

But not everyone agreed. Wrote Dick Young, "The Braves didn't want Hank Aaron to play today, and for all intents and purposes he didn't."

Atlanta won, incidentally.

The Braves' charter flight arrived in Atlanta Sunday night. A crowd of four hundred, including his mother, greeted Aaron at the airport. "I'm glad to be home, and going for 715 here will be my aim," he said. "I said all along we gave Cincinnati enough and now it's Atlanta's turn."

21

715

tlanta buzzed on Monday. The city had finally caught the spirit. Radios played "Move Over, Babe." Bartenders mixed "Hammerin' Hanks" and "Home Runs." Restaurants served sandwiches named in Hank Aaron's honor. Tour buses stopped on his street. Media celebrities boasted of his accomplishments. On WSB-TV, Bob Hope, Arnold Palmer, Monty Hall, the family of Martin Luther King, Jr., and numerous others praised Aaron in promotional spots. Throughout the region, two hundred billboards saluted a new American hero, greeting visitors from across the country and beyond. Hank Aaron needed only one more home run, and he had come home to Atlanta to hit it. Old-timers said the city had seen nothing like it since Clark Gable and Vivian Leigh graced the town for the 1939 premiere of *Gone With the Wind.*

It was game day. Yet, 10,000 seats remained unsold at Atlanta Stadium. Throughout February, the Braves had been steadily promoting ticket sales. Manager Eddie Mathews, pitcher Phil Niekro, and teammates had toured the South to encourage attendance. "See Hank Aaron become baseball's all-time home-run champion," urged newspaper advertisements in winter. The opening game, it had been announced, would be a "spectacular" tribute to the star. But despite the long buildup, despite the fact that Aaron had tied the record four days earlier and that the team had been in a public brawl with the commissioner to save the historic moment for Atlanta, the game still had not sold out as of Monday. By Major League Baseball rules, NBC's national broadcast should have been blacked out in the Atlanta area. But hours before the scheduled start, a last-minute swell swallowed the remaining tickets. Thousands had to be turned away, and Bill Bartholomay finagled a waiver to the blackout rule, allowing the game to be shown locally.

Security had been increased at the ballpark. During football season, parking lot robberies had plagued the area. In the most publicized crime, one assailant had shot and injured Jesse Outlar, sports editor of the *Constitution*. To relieve crime anxieties, city police had pledged a hundred officers in and around the stadium for baseball season. Of course, there was the other matter, too, of Hank Aaron's safety. Threats had continued to surface, warning that Aaron would not cross home plate alive, promising that he would be shot before he completed his 715th trip around the bases. No one worried more than Aaron's mother, Estella. "I've been uneasy about 'Man' because that record couldn't bring him back to me, fill his spot in my heart," she said.

Pitcher Al Downing and the Dodgers arrived in Georgia in the early-morning hours Monday after a late flight from Los Angeles. Due to start, Downing hadn't fallen asleep until 3 A.M. Though the Dodgers were undefeated after sweeping the San Diego Padres, their mood had been dampened by the death Saturday of Bobbi McMullen, wife of third baseman Ken McMullen. She had died of cancer after postponing treatment while pregnant. The Dodgers wore black armbands in her memory.

"Gentleman Al" Downing, an African-American, was the kind of guy who, in columnist Jim Murray's words, made "you feel nice just to be around him." Wrote Murray, "You like him the minute you see him walk. . . . He goes around like he's not terribly impressed to be Al Downing."

Downing approached his latest assignment with his usual good nature. He joked that perhaps Bowie Kuhn would order Aaron not to play. He acknowledged that he had given up two home runs to Aaron in 1973, but pointed out that he had won both games and that his record stood at a perfect 5–0 against the Braves. Like Jack Billingham, he believed that fans would remember the pitcher who delivered Aaron's last home run, not the men who released the record-tying or record-breaking pitches. The final home run, after all, would be the one that set the mark for future ballplayers. In his early years, Downing was a formidable fastball pitcher, leading the league in strikeouts in 1964 before coming to the National League, where he won twenty for Los Angeles. He debuted with the Yankees in 1961 as Roger Maris pursued Babe Ruth. "I'll pitch Aaron as I've always pitched him," Downing said. "I won't walk him unless the situation demands it. I won't throw four balls over his head. I won't get defensive with him. He's tough enough let alone when you fall behind on the count."

Though it was cold and damp Monday evening, the mood around the park was festive and expectant. Most fans had come to see history and to honor Hank Aaron. Some had also come to recover the home-run ball. A handsome bounty had been placed on it. Sammy Davis, Jr., was offering $25,000, and business investors had upped the payoff to $36,000. And, of course, Magnavox wanted it as part of its $1 million contract with Aaron. The deal required that Aaron loan the prize memento (if retrieved) to the company for five years.

A six-foot cyclone fence, padded along the top, marked the outfield at Atlanta Stadium. Anything hit over it qualified as a home run. About fifteen feet behind it in left field stood a twenty-two-foot wall that held scoreboards and advertising panels for Cotton States Insurance and First National Bank. During batting practice, fans sitting above the bullpen dangled fishing nets over the wall hoping to snag a souvenir. Los Angeles left-fielder Bill Buckner, who had gotten Aaron to autograph three balls for him, practiced leaping over the fence, figuring that if Aaron hit a home run he'd have as good a shot at claiming it as the Braves relief pitchers.

There was no guarantee anyone would hit a home run. It wasn't easy to do. Aaron averaged one every four games or so. Sometimes he hit two in a game or one in three straight games. Other times he went three weeks without.

With the baseball universe centered on Atlanta, commissioner Bowie Kuhn and American League president Lee MacPhail flew to Cleveland, Ohio, on the eve of the Indians' scheduled opener. Snow was forecast for Tuesday, but Kuhn accepted an invitation to a meeting of the Wahoo Club, a group of Cleveland boosters. He asked assistant Monte Irvin, a former Negro leaguer, to go to Atlanta on his behalf. Known for his easygoing personality, Irvin disagreed with Kuhn. He thought baseball's top official belonged in Georgia with Aaron. "Bowie figured that if he attended the game, he would not get a cordial reception," Irwin said. "I don't think he wanted to hear the boos of the Atlanta fans and decided to send me. Naturally, he's the boss and he can do what he wants. . . . Since this was almost like a sacred record, the commissioner of baseball should have been there."

Kuhn was right. Atlanta fans were upset with him. A Georgia lawmaker, fuming that Aaron had been ordered to play on Sunday, suggested Congress look into organized baseball. "I can't imagine one man having that much authority," said Rep.

Dawson Mathis. Aaron loyalist Donald Davidson, upon learning that Kuhn wouldn't be in Atlanta, asked snidely, "Who's hitting number 715 in Cleveland?"

The game would go on without the commissioner.

Dodger coach Jim "Junior" Gilliam, another Negro league veteran, watched his friend Aaron during batting practice. "Seven-hundred-fourteen home runs," he sighed. "Well, I didn't figure they'd ever put a man on the moon, either."

Much of the media contingent of more than three hundred had crowded onto the ball field. Dozens of cameras were pointed at Aaron as he stood near the cage with Dusty Baker and Ralph Garr.

"Lord Almighty, we'll sure be glad when it's all over with," said Garr.

Aaron quietly assured his friends, "I'll get it over with tonight."

Garr and Baker, catching each other's discreet glances, didn't doubt him.

Scattered throughout the stands in Atlanta, held aloft by spectators in coats and warm hats and rain ponchos, were homemade signs that testified to this audience's allegiance: "Phooey on Bowie." "Slam It, Hank!" "Send Kuhn to the Moon." "Hammer On!" Some fans wore buttons that urged, "C'mon Hank. 715." Attendance would reach a record 53,775, the seats filling while the pregame ceremony began. No one would be yelling obscenities or insults at Aaron tonight.

The Braves staged a version of "This Is Your Life," with family members, scouts, and friends occupying spots on an American flag that had been painted on the center-field turf in the shape of the continental United States. Beyond it in crisp formation stood the Jonesboro High School Marching Band. There were girls holding balloons near second base, a military color guard at first, and Dodgers and Braves players along the base lines. The stands were draped with bunting. "Atlanta Salutes Hank Aaron" stated an official sign on the outfield fence.

In front of home plate, special guests—Governor Jimmy Carter, Mayor Maynard Jackson, Congressman Andrew Young—waited to greet Aaron. Announcer Milo Hamilton called him onto the field, and Aaron emerged from the Braves dugout, smiling, ushered forth by a deafening roar. He walked through a friendly gauntlet of forty young ladies, all of them white, all in hot pants and Aaron jerseys and Braves caps and with bats on their shoulders that they swiped to the ground as he passed, like some perky version of the ghost-occupied suits of armor that in old movies dropped their battle-axes as Lou Costello walked through shadowy museums.

The ceremony combined the garish and gaudy with the solemn and serious. There were speeches and presentations. Billye Aaron received a bouquet of roses. At times, when words touched him, Aaron patted his eyes with a handkerchief. At other moments, he looked embarrassed. Aaron had made one special request, that a black choir perform "Lift Every Voice." Written in 1900, the hymn had the feel of a Negro spiritual. It had inspired at civil rights rallies and been named the Black National Anthem. And now its soaring words, sung out in unison beyond the pitcher's mound by the Morris Brown College choir, rolled over the audience, the lyrics resonating with the moment:

> *We have come over a way that with tears had been*
> *watered*
> *We have come, treading our path through the blood*
> *of the slaughtered*
> *Out of the gloomy past til now we stand at last*
> *Where the white gleam of our bright star is cast.*

In acknowledging the festivities, Aaron spoke concisely. "I'd like to thank my teammates and all my friends in Atlanta," he said. "I just hope this thing will get over with tonight."

Herbert Aaron, Sr., threw out the first pitch, and Pearl Bailey stepped forward to sing the National Anthem. "If humanity could do just a little more of what we're doing here tonight—do a little bit more—we'd have it made," she said. "We're here out of love. . . . Why not tomorrow, too?" Bailey performed, and a flock of helium balloons carried a sign into the gray heavens. "Go, Hank," it said.

Batboy Gary Stensland had noticed Hank Aaron in the clubhouse before the game. The place pulsed with electricity, and Aaron was at the center of it. While a nervous energy swirled around him, Aaron himself seemed oddly at peace amid the chaos. Watching him, the batboy sensed that it would be a historic night. Aaron "looked like he knew this was his moment," he said.

By game time, Atlanta Stadium was packed. All seats were gone, and the Braves had stopped selling standing room only tickets. "The commissioner of baseball is not here tonight for the biggest night in baseball," Milo Hamilton told his radio listeners. "He couldn't find time to honor Hank Aaron, and he won't be here tomorrow either. . . . With all apologies to Cleveland, I don't know of any dinner that could be big enough to keep him there instead of here."

Rain fell in the second inning when Hank Aaron appeared at the plate. The fans stood as he faced Al Downing. They booed Downing when he threw a ball. They booed umpire Satch Davidson when Downing pitched a strike. They booed louder when Downing bounced the next one and louder yet when the one after that found dirt. The fourth ball exasperated them. Aaron took first and scored when Baker followed with a double. The run secured him another honor. He surpassed Willie Mays as the all-time runs-scored leader in the National League.

In Jacksonville, where Aaron had finished his minor league days, a fifty-seven-year-old taxi driver played hooky from work, parking his cab outside his Campanella Street apartment, to watch the Braves-Dodgers game. He settled in front of the television, hoping to see Aaron capture the home-run crown. His wife wanted him to get back to his job. They argued, and the cab driver pulled a pistol and shot her. She fled their home with minor injuries. He took his own life. Elsewhere in the Florida city, Aaron's ex-wife Barbara and three of their children, Hank, Jr., Lary, and Dorinda, viewed the game on NBC. They were in Jacksonville for her grandfather's funeral.

The misty air glistened in the lights of Atlanta Stadium and cast a magical sparkle over the diamond, onto which an occasional damp wind swept napkins and concession refuse. One gust sent umpire Satch Davidson chasing after a hot dog wrapper that had blown into play. The crowd cheered when he snagged it. The fans were more celebratory than usual. This was a spectacle, after all. They had come to see Hank Aaron. Everything else—from the other Braves to the Dodgers to the beer vendors to the new calliope organ to the sporadic rain to the score—merely embellished the atmosphere.

In left field, the crowd whistled and hooted when two young fans hurdled over a guardrail and charged toward Hank Aaron to shake his hand, succeeding before police removed them. Despite their increased presence, officers couldn't plug all avenues to the field. Someone determined to bolt over the fence and interrupt play would have a good chance of succeeding. At events across the country, nude streakers were the rage.

By the fourth inning, flowering umbrellas dotted the stands. Aaron was due up second, after Darrell Evans. Evans came out of the dugout first and loosened in the on-deck circle. Then Aaron appeared, and the murmur of the crowd grew louder. People hustled back from restrooms and concession stands. Aaron told Evans that he was going to tag Downing for a home run. He had said something similar before hitting 714 off Billingham. When play resumed, Evans slapped a ball to Bill Russell at short. Russell bobbled it, and Evans took first on the error.

Off to the side, gripping his helmet in one hand, his thumb hooked over his belt, Aaron swung his bats like golf clubs. Before his name had been announced, fans began to rise, collapsing their umbrellas, pulling out their cameras, and shedding the plastic see-through sheets under which they had taken cover. Dusty Baker headed toward Aaron in the on-deck circle. He looked more nervous than his mentor. Aaron turned to him and confided that he was tired of the whole ordeal. He said he wanted to end it now. With those words, Hank Aaron walked to home plate, looked out at the other number 44, Al Downing, and pushed on his helmet with both hands. Almost everyone in the park was standing and cheering.

Had Aaron studied the crowd, he would have recognized many faces. In the special box beside the dugout sat his parents, Herbert and Estella Aaron, with Braves president Bill Bartholomay between them. There was his wife, Billye, and officer Cal Wardlaw beside her, the strap of his binoculars case in his hands, his eyes alert. "This might be it," Wardlaw said to Billye. There were his sisters Alfredia and Gloria, the latter having led a caravan from Mobile, and his secretary Carla Koplin, and his brother Herbert. Elsewhere sat Redd Foxx, star of *Sanford and Son,* in tam and bowtie and Ed Scott, who had discovered Aaron in Mobile but had never seen him hit a major league home run, and Donald Davidson, who had seen 713 of his home runs, and John Mullen, who signed him for the Braves, and Charlie Grimm, who managed him that first season, and Pete Titus, his Cincinnati friend, and Johnnie Baker, Sr., proud father of Dusty.

Downing's first pitch bounced into Joe Ferguson's mitt, provoking an impatient rumble of boos. With his team ahead and Evans already on first base, Downing did not want to walk Aaron and put the tying run on base. Aaron knew this, and he knew if he waited long enough Downing would throw a fastball. In six pitches over two at-bats, Downing had put three in the dirt. He seemed nervous, and he needed to come in with a strike to even the count.

Across America, nearly one in four homes with televisions had tuned to the game.

In Washington, D.C., President Richard Nixon—suffering through growing scandals and smarting from surveys that showed most of his countrymen retained little confidence in him—savored his favorite sport. He was watching Aaron.

Separately, Vice President Gerald Ford was watching, too.

In West Palm Beach, Tommie Aaron, at spring training with his Savannah team, sat in his hotel room, listening to Curt Gowdy and company.

In Jacksonville, Hank's three youngest children did the same.

In Nashville, alone in a dorm room at Fisk University, daughter Gaile, having turned down tickets to a Herbie Hancock concert, watched as well, an FBI agent not far away.

In Milwaukee, Bud Selig worked late in his office at County Stadium, the broadcasters' chatter keeping him company.

In Baltimore, former teammate Earl Williams wished he were still with the Braves, wished he were at Atlanta Stadium that very second, in the lineup, rather than in the American League, looking at the developing scene on a color screen.

Only three games had been scheduled for Monday, and the other two had finished by the time Atlanta began. Consequently, hundreds of major leaguers got to see Aaron face Al Downing in the fourth inning.

Across the world, 35 to 40 million people—from octogenarians born before Babe Ruth to young fans like ten-year-old Mark McGwire of Claremont, California—watched Hank Aaron cock his bat as Downing delivered the second pitch. Downing had wanted it to be low and outside but it sailed toward the center of the plate. Aaron uncoiled and connected. The ball rose toward left-center. A symphony of voices rose with it. Bill Buckner and Jimmy Wynn dashed toward the fence, Buckner vaulting up it as the ball flew over the 385-foot mark and into the glove of reliever

Tom House. Outside the ballpark, ticket-less fans huddling in the damp night air knew instantly from the thunderous explosion that Hank Aaron had broken the record.

Billye Aaron clasped Cal Wardlaw's head and screamed. She was ecstatic. Suddenly, Wardlaw was jolted from his jubilance by the sight of two young men racing across the field toward Aaron as shortstop Bill Russell shook his hand. Wardlaw grabbed his binoculars case and slid his hand inside and around the grip of his gun. A thousand questions flitted through his mind. Should he show his revolver? Should he charge onto the field? Did the young men present a danger? Should he risk spoiling the moment? What if he were to shoot and accidently strike Aaron? Wardlaw paused. The young men slapped Aaron's back and congratulated him. Wardlaw sighed. They meant Aaron no harm. The pair, Britt Gaston and Cliff Courtney, broke from Aaron's trot as they neared the third-base umpire, leaving the last stretch for Aaron alone.

"Pop-pop-pop-pop."

The noise pierced the night. Chief Noc-A-Homa had fired a small cannon near his tepee. Louder booms followed as the opening rounds of a fireworks display lit the sky. Estella Aaron thought someone was shooting at her son. She ran onto the field. Aaron's teammates swarmed around him as he neared the plate, Darrell Evans gripping Aaron's shoulders and shaking him, Ralph Garr grabbing Aaron's leg and planting it on home plate. They patted his helmet and back, they laid skin on his hand. They tried to lift him upon their shoulders as photographers in raincoats encircled the mob.

"He's mine, he's mine," yelled his father, Herbert Aaron, nearly losing his hat in the excitement.

Mrs. Aaron threw her arms around her son's neck and clung to him as if her body could shield him from the shots she imagined whizzing toward him.

In the frenzy, a reporter asked, "How you feeling, Mrs. Aaron?"

"I don't know. I don't know." She hollered the words over and over. "I don't know. I don't know."

Horns, whistles, cheers, applause, yelps of joy, fireworks—it was a cacophony of noise. Tom House had run in from the bullpen with the home-run ball. There were tears in Aaron's eyes as he peered over his mother's shoulder. "Hammer, I told you I'd give it to you," House said, handing him the ball. "Thanks, kid," Aaron replied.

Aaron lifted the ball and waved it. His hat was crooked, his eyes glazed. The sight tugged at thousands of hearts. Charlie Grimm wiped tears from his cheeks. James "Cool Papa" Bell, a Negro league legend who was too old to integrate the majors, fought the urge to cry. In the broadcasting booth, Ernie Johnson was quiet. It seemed as if minutes had passed—and as if an era had passed with it. It seemed as if some things would never be the same.

Umpire Satch Davidson paused the game for the celebration, and Al Downing went to the dugout to sit.

Cal Wardlaw felt Sammy Davis, Jr., tug on his shoulder.

"I'll buy it right now," Davis said. "I'll buy the ball right now."

Wardlaw was holding the baseball for Aaron.

"I can't sell it," he said.

Monte Irvin presented Aaron with a diamond-encrusted watch on behalf of Commissioner Bowie Kuhn, whose name incited a riot of boos. Aaron grinned. Governor Carter gave him a license plate marked with his initials and the crucial number, "HLA 715." Finally, Aaron stepped to the microphone, and the crowd calmed. There was no Lou Gehrig speech about feeling like the luckiest man on the face of the earth.

"I'd just like to thank God it's over with," he said.

Aaron took phone calls from his children in Florida and Tennessee. He got one from President Richard Nixon and one from Bowie Kuhn, too. Immediately after the game, Eddie Mathews closed his locker room to reporters, invited in family members, and toasted Aaron with champagne. Later that evening, freed of his burden, Aaron would celebrate until the next morning. But first, upon returning home after the game, Aaron escaped for a private moment. As he wrote in his autobiography *I Had a Hammer,* "I got down on my knees and closed my eyes and thanked God for pulling me through."

Aaron's home run drew attention across the world. Even *Pravda,* the official mouthpiece of the Soviet Union, acknowledged his achievement. But the kindest words came from fellow Americans. Twenty thousand sent telegrams. On the floor of the U.S. Senate, Hubert Humphrey praised Aaron. In Los Angeles, the *Times* said that Aaron proved "that nothing is impossible." A *Pittsburgh Courier* columnist, Louis Martin, said Aaron did more than break a baseball record. "Some of our society's ice was cracking, too," he wrote. George Coleman, whose poetry ran on the pages of the *Atlanta Daily World,* asked, "What now the notes of hate that came to me? What for them who will not accept equality? What for our nation so divided, black and white? This bat of mine, can its soft spoken message grant that which should be?"

Mrs. Babe Ruth had returned home from a day of shopping when Hank Aaron hit the home run at 9:07 P.M. She did not watch the game. Reporters called when it happened. "The Babe loved baseball so very much," she said. "I know he was pulling for Hank Aaron to break his record. I sent Henry a wire that covers everything. I'm just wishing him very good luck."

Within twenty-four hours of Aaron's historic feat, the speculation had already begun. Who will break Hank Aaron's record? Reggie? Bench? Cedeno? Luzinski? Kingman? "I don't think that there is any ballplayer right now who will make it," said Bobby Bonds. "For now, Henry Aaron is safe."

EPILOGUE:
THE LEGACY

hirty years have passed since Hank Aaron captured the record. He is seventy now, his hair more gray than black, and he says his life is good. He has his health and family. His children are approaching middle age, older than he was when the record fell, and they have blessed him and Billye with grandchildren. He has no worries financially. A BMW dealership carries his name, and he owns some franchises and other enterprises, as well.

Aaron is cherished and respected in Georgia, known for the good works of his Chasing the Dream Foundation. An end-of-the-century survey of *Atlanta Journal-Constitution* readers rated him among the ten most influential Southerners, with Martin Luther King, Jr., Jimmy Carter, and Billy Graham. (Aaron finished just ahead of Elvis Presley.) *Ebony* magazine chose him as the Greatest Black Athlete of the 20th Century, and Aaron finished third in voting for baseball's All-Century Team. In Mobile, they've opened a ballpark in his honor, and for several years, Major League Baseball has bestowed the Hank Aaron Award to each league's best hitter. Recently, fans named his 715th home run as the game's second most memorable moment. The acclaim has finally come, and some of the scars have begun to fade.

For a while, it was different. "What he went through, that would bruise any human being," said friend Bud Selig, now baseball's commissioner. "The guy was breaking the world's greatest sports record, doing it honestly and decently, and taking abuse for it. It was very sad."

Aaron must have watched and wondered as the country seemed to unanimously cheer Pete Rose in 1978 as he tracked Joe DiMaggio's fifty-six-game hitting streak and again in 1985 when he eclipsed Ty Cobb's career hit total. Rose did not stand before the crowd in Cincinnati and sigh with relief, "I'd just like to thank God it's over with." Rose treasured the moment. Aaron must have felt a twinge of envy at how warmly—and universally—America embraced Cal Ripken, Jr., when he toppled Lou Gehrig's consecutive-game mark. Even the President came to watch. And what of Mark McGwire's glorious 1998 season? Would it not have been human for Hank Aaron to have silently shaken his head and contrasted McGwire's experience with his own?

Much has changed since 1974. Atlanta Stadium is gone, demolished after the 1996 Olympics. Chief Noc-A-Homa has retired, and the Braves have become a dominant franchise, a perennial division winner averaging 40,000 fans a game. Aaron has shared in that achievement as one of the club's top executives.

After his historic season, Aaron left Atlanta, acquired in a trade by Brewers owner Bud Selig, who wanted to bring him back to Milwaukee. The fans sung "Hello, Henry" to the tune of "Hello, Dolly" at the team's first home game: "It's so nice to have you back where you belong . . ." Aaron finished his playing career there in 1976, and when he was done he owned a slew of records. He had played in more games, gotten more at-bats, knocked in more runs, collected more total bases, recorded more extra-base hits, and hit more home runs—755—than any other ballplayer. At the time, his 3,771 hits were second only to Ty Cobb's, and his 2,174 runs had placed him in an eternal tie with Babe Ruth. The baseball records are part of Hank Aaron's legacy.

Afterward, Ted Turner, who had bought the Braves, lured Aaron back to Georgia. He has been with the team in some capacity ever since. For years, he was the sport's highest-ranking African-American executive.

Most of the men who played with Hank Aaron in 1973 and 1974 are in their fifties and sixties. Many remain in baseball, Ralph Garr scouting for the Braves, Paul Casanova working with prospects in Florida, Darrell Evans coaching and running a fantasy camp. His secretary, Carla Koplin, followed Aaron to Milwaukee for a year and later married and moved to Connecticut, where she owns a business, Sweet Celebrations. Cal Wardlaw, now retired from the Atlanta Police Department, works security at the city airport. All of them remain friends with Hank Aaron.

Some have passed. Eddie Mathews, fired three months after Aaron broke the record (his drinking contributing to the dismissal), died in February 2001 at age sixty-nine. Donald Davidson preceded him in 1990. Hank Aaron's father, Herbert Aaron, Sr., a sister, and two brothers, including Tommie, have also passed.

But some things have not changed since April 8, 1974.

The old homestead still stands on Edwards Street in Mobile, and Aaron's mother, Estella, still lives there with family.

Hank Aaron still follows Jackie Robinson's long-ago advice, speaking out on issues that bother him, even if his principled stances cost him popularity. His own success and security have not lulled him into quiet complacency. Since Robinson's death, Aaron has been the sport's most consistent and prominent voice on issues of racial justice.

And Aaron still reigns as the all-time home-run king. Challengers have come and gone. Reggie Jackson, Mike Schmidt, Mark McGwire—none got closer than 172 home runs. A few years ago, a young Ken Griffey, Jr., seemed the most likely candidate to unseat him. "That Griffey kid in Seattle could break my record," Aaron said. But three straight injury-plagued seasons checked those possibilities. The one immediate threat to Aaron's record has risen on the West Coast, where Bobby Bonds' son Barry plays for the San Francisco Giants. When Bonds found an unparalleled burst of power in 2001 and clocked an amazing 73 home runs, he instantly made himself the number-one contender. The next year, he cracked the 600 home-run mark, and then he took sight of his godfather, Willie Mays.

Babe Ruth will be next. "In the baseball world, Babe Ruth is everything, right?" Bonds said at the 2003 All-Star Game. "I've got his slugging percentage, on-base percentage, walks, and I'll take his home runs. And that's it. Don't talk about him no more." And then Aaron's 755 will be all that remains. Bonds could be approaching it by the end of the 2005 season. His chase, should it materialize, will undoubtedly be a more pleasant experience than Aaron's, even given Bonds' prickly relationship with the media.

A year or two ago, Charles Schwab & Co. ran a commercial that featured Bonds. Maybe you've seen it. The scene: a moonlit night, an empty ballpark, and Barry Bonds standing alone on the field, taking practice swings at home plate. A voice, like the ethereal one in the movie *Field of Dreams*, interrupts him. "Barry Bonds, it's time," it whispers. "It's time to walk into retirement. . . . Why hang around just to break the all-time home-run record?" Bonds pauses and glances toward the announcer's booth. "Hank, will you cut it out already?" he says. The camera shows Hank Aaron, seated behind the microphone. "Hank?" Aaron asks incredulously. "Hank who?"

Aaron and Bonds filmed the advertisement on a weekend in

a recent off-season. It marked the first time they had spent significant time together, and Aaron astonished Bonds by encouraging him to go for his 755 mark. "Records are meant to be broken," he said. "If you have a chance to do it, then do it." It was a telling moment, and likely a harbinger for the years ahead. Since his playing days, Aaron has vowed that he will support the man who surpasses his record. "It's been mine long enough," he has said. "I believe in sharing." It's not difficult to imagine Hank Aaron at Pacific Bell Stadium in the middle of this decade, a smile gleaming on his face as he limps onto the diamond to publicly congratulate Barry Bonds, who has just hit home run 756.

How different would Hank Aaron's experience have been had Babe Ruth been alive in 1974—if at age seventy-nine the Yankee legend had been appearing at ballparks with Aaron and shaking his hand for photographers and grinning widely and anointing his successor with kind words? Throughout Aaron's chase, those who knew Babe Ruth said he would have been gracious about the matter. But would it have changed anything?

A wave of nostalgia was sweeping the country as Aaron neared the record. Troubled by the times, Americans turned to entertainment that evoked other eras. They escaped to the Roaring Twenties through *The Great Gatsby*. They revisited the 1930s with *The Sting* and *Paper Moon* and *The Waltons*. They cried for Robert Redford and Barbra Streisand in *The Way We Were*, a romance rooted in World War II, and returned to the Big Band sound with Bette Midler's remake of "Boogie Woogie Bugle Boy," a 1941 hit for the Andrews Sisters. They celebrated the 1950s with *American Graffiti* and *Happy Days* and *M*A*S*H.* and by bopping to Elton John's "Crocodile Rock" and by making Elvis Presley's "Aloha to Hawaii" the year's most watched concert. And they elevated to the level of a household name that of Archie Bunker, a television character from Queens, a bigot unwilling to change with the country, a man who began each show yearning in song for the days of

Glenn Miller, Herbert Hoover, and an old LaSalle that ran great. "Those were the days," he sang.

Babe Ruth was nostalgia, and Hank Aaron wasn't.

But perhaps it's *The Exorcist,* the period's biggest movie, that provides a better metaphor for Hank Aaron's trial. Anyone who thought that an African-American man pursuing the national pastime's most treasured record—held by the country's most mythologized white sports icon—would be greeted with overwhelming warmth saw those illusions shattered. Hank Aaron lured America's ugly demons into the light, revealing them to those who imagined them a thing of the past, and in doing so helped exorcise some of them. His ordeal provided a vivid, personal lesson for a generation of children: Racism is wrong. Through his impact on those children of the early 1970s and, indirectly, on their children of the 1980s and 1990s, Hank Aaron cleared a path for the Michael Jordans and Tiger Woodses of the sporting world. That is part of his legacy, too.

The May 1974 issue of *Playboy* was on newsstands when Aaron passed Ruth. "It's been decades since Jackie Robinson broke into baseball, since the black player proved he's super on the field," Aaron said in the featured interview. "Now, it's time for the owners to give him a job that's equal to his character. And baseball, as much good as it's done for a lot of people, has dragged its foot on this situation much too long, much longer than any other sport." That October, Frank Robinson broke the barrier, becoming baseball's first black manager. But change came slowly. By 1987, only three African-Americans— Robinson, Maury Wills, and Larry Doby—had been given the opportunity to manage. More have come and gone in the years since.

Any list of the top twenty managers of the past fifteen seasons would likely include Felipe Alou, Cito Gaston, and Dusty Baker. Alou has enjoyed success with the Montreal Expos and

San Francisco Giants; Gaston won two world championships with the Toronto Blue Jays; and Dusty Baker has been named manager of the year three times. All are minorities, and—by coincidence?—all three were with the Braves and Hank Aaron at spring training 1968 in West Palm Beach, weeks before Martin Luther King, Jr., died. (Joe Torre also was there.)

But it is Baker, more than the others, who absorbed Aaron's lessons: from his advice that very first day at Dodger Stadium, where Aaron told him to pursue baseball with his whole heart, to the talks about Jackie Robinson, to the way Aaron handled adversity when it seemed much of the world wanted him to surrender.

It's almost poetic, the flow of these lives: Robinson inspiring Aaron; Aaron carrying the torch of his deceased hero as he ascends to the sport's throne; Baker, his protégé, absorbing from him the wisdom of both men to become one of the game's premier managers and coach of the two players, Barry Bonds and Sammy Sosa, most likely to displace his own idol.

In his years as manager, Dusty Baker has been startled at times to hear himself at team meetings in the locker room, quoting his mentor. "My players tell me I can't give a speech without mentioning Hank Aaron," he said. "That says it all. There are not enough words to show my appreciation for the impact Hank Aaron has had on me."

At Cypress Hills Cemetery, not far from where Ebbets Field once stood, rests a grave marker with this inscription: "A life is not important except in the impact it has on other lives." It is Jackie Robinson's epitaph, but it speaks to Hank Aaron's legacy, as well.

BIBLIOGRAPHY: SELECTED BOOKS, ARTICLES, AND OTHER SOURCES

Aaron, Gaile. "Daddy," *Atlanta Constitution*, September 29, 1973.

Aaron, Hank. "Aaron on Robinson," *Milwaukee Journal*, April 15, 1997.

Aaron, Hank. *Home Run: My Life in Pictures* (Total Sports, 1999).

Aaron, Hank, with Furman Bisher. *Aaron* (Crowell, 1974).

Aaron, Hank, with Jerome Holtzman. "Are You Ready for a Negro Manager?" *Sport*, October 1965.

Aaron, Hank, with Lonnie Wheeler. *I Had a Hammer* (HarperCollins, 1991).

Aaron, Henry. "Journey to the Brink," *Atlanta Journal*, April 4, 1974.

Allen, Maury. *Roger Maris: A Man for All Seasons* (Donald I. Fine, 1986).

Anderson, Dave. "Baseball's Queen Widow," *New York Times*, August 12, 1973.

Anderson, Dave. "The Manager in the Middle," *New York Times*, April 4, 1974.

Anderson, Dave. "A Peek at Henry Aaron's Mail," *New York Times*, September 29, 1973.

Andrews, Sam. "Atlanta: A Bitter Pill," *Black Sports*, September 1973.

Angell, Roger. "The Long March," *The New Yorker*, November 19, 1973.

Baldwin, Stan, and Jerry Jenkins. *Bad Henry* (Chilton, 1974).

Belinfante, Geoff, executive producer. *Jackie Robinson: Breaking Barriers* (Orion, 1997).

Bisher, Furman. "For the Love of Henry," *Atlanta Journal*, October 1, 1973.

Bisher, Furman. *The Furman Bisher Collection* (Taylor, 1989).

Bisher, Furman. "A Sacrificial Substitute for a Winner," *Atlanta Journal*, May 9, 1973.

Buckley, Tom. "All Eyes on Aaron's Assault on Ruth Home-Run Record," *New York Times*, July 26, 1973.

Buckley, Tom. "The Packaging of a Home Run," *New York Times Magazine*, March 31, 1974.

Cady, Steve. "Jackie Goes Home to Brooklyn," *New York Times*, October 28, 1972.

Caldwell, Earl. "San Francisco's Blue-Chip Bonds," *Black Sports*, May 1974.

Capuzzo, Mike. "A Prisoner of Memory," *Sports Illustrated*, November 1992.

Caruso, Gary. *The Braves Encyclopedia* (Temple University Press, 1995).

"Chasing the Babe," *Newsweek*, June 4, 1973.

"Chasing the Babe," *Newsweek*, August 13, 1973.

Claflin, Larry. "Aaron Will Not Diminish Ruth's Image," *Boston Herald-American*, August 17, 1973.

Collins, Bob. "Hank Aaron: Record-Breaking Year?" *Saturday Evening Post*, Summer 1972.

Conroy, Pat. "715: Henry Aaron and the Magic Number," *Sport*, May 1974.

Creamer, Robert. *Babe* (Simon & Schuster, 1974).

Daley, Arthur. "In Pursuit of Ghosts," *New York Times,* September 9, 1973.

Davidson, Donald, with Jesse Outlar. *Caught Short* (Atheneum, 1972).

Davis-Horton, Paulette. *Avenue: The Place, the People, the Memories* (Horton, 1991).

Ethier, Bryan. "Hank Aaron Remembers," *American History,* June 1999.

Falkner, David. Great Time Coming: *The Life of Jackie Robinson, from Baseball to Birmingham* (Simon & Schuster, 1995).

Fandell, Todd E. "Unsung Slugger," *Wall Street Journal,* April 5, 1971.

Foley, Red. "They All Remembered Something of His Greatness," *Daily News,* October 28, 1972.

Frady, Marshall. *Jesse: The Life and Pilgrimage of Jesse Jackson* (Random House, 1996).

Garrow, David J. *Bearing the Cross* (William Morrow, 1986).

Gergen, Joe. "Atlanta Is Underwhelmed by Aaron," *Newsday,* September 25, 1973.

Gilman, Kay. "Billye Aaron: A Victim of Travel Fatigue," *Sunday News,* November 10, 1974.

Gilman, Kay. "Billye Williams? She's Apple of Hank's Eye," *Sunday News,* September 30, 1973.

Green, Jerry. "Dodging a Tornado," *Detroit News,* April 4, 1974.

Grimsley, Will. "The Fearless Pioneer," *Atlanta Constitution,* October 25, 1972.

Gulliver, Hal. "The Women Behind Hank Aaron's Smashing Success," *Today's Health,* April 1974.

"Henry Aaron: A Candid Conversation with Baseball's Record-Breaking Slugger," *Playboy,* May 1974.

"Henry Aaron's Great Autumn," *Time,* September 24, 1973.

Hertzel, Bob. "Will Aaron Play?" *Cincinnati Enquirer,* April 4, 1974.

Hoffman, Roy. *Back Home: Journeys Through Mobile* (University of Alabama Press, 2001).

Holway, John B. *Black Diamonds* (Meckler, 1990).

Honig, Donald. "The Power Hitters," *Sporting News,* 1992.

Hope, Bob. *We Could've Finished Last Without You* (Longstreet Press, 1991).

Hudspeth, Ron. "For Once, Winning Didn't Matter," *Atlanta Journal,* October 1, 1973.

Hyland, Frank. "The Forgotten Man," *Atlanta Journal,* April 3, 1974.

Hyland, Frank. "Hatred at Home Plate," *Atlanta Journal,* May 7, 1973.

Hyland, Frank. "Mad Henry," *Atlanta Journal,* March 9, 1973.

Irwin, Monte. *Nice Guys Finish First* (Carroll & Graf, 1996).

Johnson, Chuck. "Aaron Paid a Price for Beating Ruth," *USA Today,* April 8, 1974.

Koppett, Leonard. "Self-Righteous Guardians of Morals," *Sporting News,* July 14, 1973.

Kuhn, Bowie. *Hardball* (Times Books, 1987).

"The Last of the Big Bats," *Ebony,* June 1971.

Leggett, William. "A Tortured Road to 715," *Sports Illustrated,* May 28, 1973.

Lewis, John, with Michael D'Orso. *Walking With the Wind* (Harcourt Brace, 1998).

Maher, Charles. "Aaron vs. Ruth: The Argument Rages," *Los Angeles Times,* June 18, 1973.

Mathews, Eddie, with Bob Buege. *Eddie Mathews and the National Pastime* (Douglas American Sports, 1994).

"Maybe I'll Cry Tomorrow," *New York Times,* September 21, 1973.

Mays, Willie, with Lou Sahadi. *Say Hey* (Simon & Schuster, 1988).

McCullough, Carolyn. "Hank Aaron's Secretary a Great Fan of Her Boss," *Atlanta Constitution*, May 25, 1973.

McGraw, Tug, and Joseph Durso. *Screwball* (Houghton Mifflin, 1974).

McKenzie, Mike. "Family Man," *Atlanta Journal*, April 4, 1974.

McKenzie, Mike. "The House Where Henry Lived," *Atlanta Journal*, April 4, 1974.

McKenzie, Mike. "I've Been Uneasy," *Atlanta Journal*, April 4, 1974.

Minshew, Wayne. "Aaron: I've Earned Respect," *Atlanta Constitution*, May 8, 1973.

Minshew, Wayne. "Maris Pulling for Aaron to Top Ruth," *Sporting News*, August 4, 1973.

Minshew, Wayne. "Everyone Wants to Shake Hands With Aaron," *Sporting News*, April 20, 1974.

Murray, Jim. "Bad Henry He Isn't," *Los Angeles Times*, August 19, 1973.

Newhan, Ross. "Henry Aaron: A Quiet Man Pursues a Legend," *Los Angeles Times*, September 25, 1973.

Newhouse, Dave. "Handball, Karate, Roadwork Keep Aaron Busy," *Sporting News*, January 5, 1974.

Nipson, Herb. "Hank Aaron: Catching Up With the Babe," *Ebony*, September 1973.

"The Penalties of Fame," *Sporting News*, August 11, 1973.

O'Brien, Jim. "What It's Like to Be a Neglected Superstar," *Sport*, July 1968.

Outlar, Jesse. "The Memorable Summer," *Atlanta Constitution*, August 24, 1973.

Outlar, Jesse. "Sutton's Dilemma," *Atlanta Constitution*, September 26, 1973.

Pepe, Phil. "Babe Would Be Rooting for Hank," *Daily News*, July 13, 1973.

Pepe, Phil. "Center of Spring's Raging Controversy," *Daily News,* March 12, 1974.

Pepe, Phil. *Talkin' Baseball: An Oral History of Baseball in the 1970s* (Ballantine, 1998).

Pirone, Dorothy Ruth, with Chris Martens. *My Dad, The Babe* (Quinlan Press, 1988).

Plimpton, George. *One for the Record* (Harper & Row, 1974).

Poinsett, Alex. "The Hank Aaron Nobody Knows," *Ebony,* July 1974.

"The Quest for No. 715," *Time,* July 9, 1973.

"The Racial Taunts of Texas," *San Francisco Chronicle,* June 30, 1973.

"Rap with Jackie Robinson," *Black Sports,* March 1972.

Ritter, Lawrence S. *The Babe* (Total Sports, 1997).

Ritter, Lawrence S. *East Side West Side* (Total Sports, 1998).

Robinson, Jackie, edited by Charles Dexter. *Baseball Has Done It* (Lippincott, 1964).

Robinson, Rachel. *Jackie Robinson: An Intimate Portrait* (Harry N. Abrams, 1996).

Robinson, Sharon. *Stealing Home* (HarperCollins, 1996).

Rust, Art. *Get That Nigger Off the Field* (Book Mail Services, 1992).

Schlossberg, Dan. "Hank Aaron's Untold Brave Role," *Super Sports,* September 1972.

Seaver, Tom, with Norman Lewis Smith. *How I Would Pitch to Babe Ruth* (Playboy, 1975).

Smith, Red. *Strawberries in the Wintertime* (Quadrangle, 1974).

Smith, Red. "When Bowie Chooses the Line-Up," *New York Times,* February 20, 1974.

Smitherman, Dennis. "Hometown Honors Hammering 'Henry the Great'," *Mobile Register,* February 16, 1974.

Snyder, Deron. "Maestro of Managers," *USA Today Baseball Weekly,* October 12–18, 1994.

Sobol, Ken. *Babe Ruth and the American Dream* (Random House, 1974).

Strauss, Joe. "Where Have You Gone Eddie Mathews?" *Atlanta Journal-Constitution*, December 23, 1989.

Stump, Al. "Hank Aaron: Public Image vs. Private Reality," *Sport*, August 1964.

Thomason, Michael, editor. *Mobile* (University of Alabama Press, 2001).

Toback, James. "Henry Aaron: The Finest Hours of a Quiet Legend," *Sport*, August 1970.

Tolan, Sandy. *Me and Hank* (Free Press, 2000).

Tuite, James, editor. *Sports of the Times: The Arthur Daley Years* (Quadrangle, 1975).

Tygiel, Jules. *Baseball's Great Experiment* (Oxford University Press, 1983).

Unger, Norman O. "Cubs, PUSH host Aaron, 'friend'," *Chicago Defender*, August 14, 1973.

Waddell, Genevieve. "Gaile Aaron Has Own Identity," *Black Sports*, September 1973.

Washington, Denzel, and Debra Martin Chase, Brian Robbins, Mike Tollin, David Houle, Jack Myers, and Pat Mitchell, executive producers. *Hank Aaron: Chasing the Dream* (TBS Productions, 1995).

Wheeler, Lonnie. "Hammerin' into History," *Cincinnati Post*, April 3, 1999.

Yarbrough, Cathy. "Hank's Swing: It's Music to Their Ears," *Atlanta Constitution*, August 25, 1973.

Young, Dick. "Bowie's Big Boo-Boo," *Daily News*, April 11, 1974.

Young, Dick. "Hank Aaron . . . What's Going On?" *Sunday News*, February 24, 1974.

Young, Dick. "Racists and Ruth's Record Haunting Aaron," *Daily News*, May 2, 1973.

ACKNOWLEDGMENTS

n ways large and small, hundreds of people contributed to this book. I am particularly indebted to Mauro DiPreta, executive editor of William Morrow at HarperCollins, for his perceptive insights, welcome suggestions, and strong support; to Philip Spitzer, my astute agent, who helped this project find a good home; to Hank Aaron, who cleared the way for interviews with friends and close associates; and to Mike Varney, who shaped the book and assisted with research.

The recollections of Dusty Baker, Paul Casanova, Ralph Garr, Cleon Jones, Carla Koplin Cohn, Bud Selig, Cal Wardlaw, and Earl Williams proved invaluable in capturing a portrait of the era, their friend, and his achievement. All were generous with their time, as were Lew Burdette, Dr. Edwin L. Mathews, Ferguson Jenkins, Jerry Koosman, Dick Baney, Jim Barr, Bill Bonham, Nelson Briles, Clay Carroll, Darrel Chaney, Dave Cheadle, Jim Crawford, George Culver, Adrian Devine, Ken Forsch, Ernie Harwell, Bob Hertzel, Frank Hyland, Whitey Lockman, Jim Panther, David Pursley, Pete Titus, Ed Scott, and Gary Stensland. Along the way, these individuals also proved helpful: Rob Edelman, Steve Ferenchick, Mark Jacob, Maxwell Kates, Betsy Kavetas, Kathi Kretzer, Rich Levin, Sarah Mack, Bruce Markusen, Jeffrey Miller, Todd Miller, Scot Mondore, Rod Nelson, Bobby Plapinger, Howard Rosenthal, Michael Rudi, Mike

Shannon, Lisa Steinman, Stew Thornley, Jim Turano, Donnie Wagner, Tim Wendel, Wyatt Young, Joelle Yudin, David Brown, and Bob Zimring.

A great deal of research was conducted at the National Baseball Hall of Fame Library, where Tim Wiles, Gabriel Schechter, Claudette Burke, Jim Gates, Russell Wolinsky, Jeremy Jones, Rachael Crossman-Kepner, and W. C. Burdick shared their expertise. In addition, for their assistance I thank Ron Sodano, Nixon Presidential Materials, National Archives; Stacy Davis, Gerald R. Ford Library; Rosemary Hanes, Moving Image Section, Library of Congress; Sherry Schmidli and Stan Lisica, Macomb County Library; Elisa Baldwin, University of South Alabama Archives; Joann Hoffmeyer, MacDonald Public Library; Christina Coxe and Wilma Spanyer, Mobile Public Library; David Poremba, Burton Historical Collection, Detroit Public Library; Raymond Doswell, Negro Leagues Museum; Keith Schuler, Georgia Archives; Celeste Tibbets, Atlanta-Fulton Public Library; Patti Graziano, *Cleveland Plain Dealer;* Maryann Sterzel, *Florida Times-Union;* Charles Torrey, Museum of Mobile; Jo LaVerde, Nielsen Media; Michael Brubaker, Atlanta History Center; Gene Owens, *Mobile Register;* Adline Clarke, Black Classics Books; Louis Burden, a Mobile historian; members of the Society for American Baseball Research; and organizers of retrosheet.org. Further, the reporting of journalists who covered National League teams in 1973 and 1974—particularly Frank Hyland, Wayne Minshew, Jesse Outlar, and Furman Bisher of the Atlanta newspapers—provided a rich base from which to explore.

In writing of the influence that Jackie Robinson had on Hank Aaron and that Aaron had on Dusty Baker and others, I found myself reflecting on those who mentored me. I am especially grateful to journalists Jane Briggs-Bunting, Neal Shine, and the late Warren Stromberg, none of whom realize the degree to which they have impacted my life; to two uncles, Clem Stone and Edward Stanton, who always provided encouragement; and to my parents, Betty and Joe Stanton, who provided that and much more.

Writing a book consumes a significant chunk of one's life and affects everyone dear to the author. I am blessed and thankful to have such a supportive and loving family as my wife, Beth Bagley-Stanton, and our sons, Zachary, William, and Taylor.

INDEX

Aaron, Alfredia (sister), see Scott, Alfredia

Aaron, Barbara (ex-wife), see Lucas, Barbara

Aaron, Billye (wife), see Williams, Billye

Aaron, Dorinda (daughter), 23, 24, 139, 188, 219

Aaron, Estella (mother), 8, 12, 21, 113, 169, 171, 204, 205, 206, 211, 213, 220, 222–223, 227

Aaron, Gaile (daughter), 23, 24, 42, 139–140, 152, 169, 188, 221

Aaron, Gary (son), 23

Aaron, Gloria (sister), see Robinson, Gloria

Aaron, Hank, Jr. (son), 23, 24, 139, 140–141, 219

Aaron, Henry Louis "Hank"
  and Atlanta, 47–52, 56–57, 66, 150–152, 170, 175–177
  awards, honors and tributes, 23, 32, 50, 116, 117, 151, 175–176, 180, 183–188, 201, 206, 212–213, 216–218, 225–226
  batting slump, 36, 37, 39, 44–45, 132
  batting style and routine, 11, 44, 53, 54, 129
  and black community, 76, 80, 133–134

career highlights and achievements, 17–18, 32, 105, 106, 113, 136, 172, 208, 218, 226–227
controversies, (Hall of Fame pamphlet) 32–33, 122; (grooved-pitched story) 86–92; (lack of telegram) 119, 121–122, 131–132; (lineup dispute) 182–183, 189–190, 193, 197–198, 200, 202, 208–211
early years, 7–12, 16, 21, 113–114, 150
endorsements, 158, 168–169, 185
fan encounters, 34, 100–101, 124, 149, 155–156, 164, 187, 194, 219, 222
fan mail, 1–2, 59, 62–63, 85, 123, 163–164
as a father, 23, 24–25, 139–141, 169, 181, 225
fielding, 28–29, 32, 57–58, 72
hate mail, heckling and threats, 52, 54, 55–56, 58–59, 64–65, 66, 68, 71, 73, 76, 91–92, 93, 102, 123, 124, 133, 139–140, 149, 159–160, 164, 198, 213
health and injuries, 97–100, 101–102, 125, 130, 132, 154, 157, 165
impact of, 187, 208, 224, 230–231
and Indianapolis Clowns, 12, 101, 114

inspired by children, 85, 129–130, 133–134, 177–178, 185
knowledge of pitchers, 53–54
and media, 30–31, 78, 97, 114–115, 121, 132, 137, 166–167, 174, 177
in minor leagues, 12, 22, 23, 49, 55
and money, 29, 36, 55, 157–158, 168–169
nicknames, 113, 159
personality, 20, 33, 44, 49–50, 61, 64, 78, 93–94, 97, 101–102, 108, 115
popularity, 1, 34, 120–121, 147–148, 175–176, 208, 227
post-playing goals, 80, 131
pressure, 36, 93–97, 102, 125, 164, 172, 195, 197
on racial justice, 78–80, 109, 185
reception on the road, 51–52, 71, 77–78, 123, 128–132, 142–143, 147, 153, 156, 205
recreational interests, 68, 112, 114–115, 163, 181, 183
retirement considered, 63–64, 69–70
safety precautions and security, 66, 67, 68, 140–141, 146–147, 149, 159–160, 164, 186–187, 192, 194, 195, 198, 213, 222
uniform number, 38, 159
walks to, 71, 72, 126, 128, 142, 143, 161
wives, see Lucas, Barbara, and Williams, Billye
wrists, 53, 67, 117
Aaron, Herbert (father), 7, 8, 10, 16, 21, 45, 102, 114, 150, 163, 169, 171, 173, 176, 178, 199, 218, 220, 222, 227
Aaron, Herbert, Jr. (brother), 16, 114, 199, 220
Aaron, Lary (son), 23, 24, 139, 140–141, 167, 219
Aaron, Tommie (brother), 10, 30, 42, 69, 81–82, 169, 188, 221, 227
Aaron's Sports Page, 113
Acree, Bill, 144
Adams, Berle, 158, 168–169
Adcock, Joe, 126
Agee, Tommie, 38, 69, 188
Agnew, Spiro, 180
Aker, Jack, 134, 205
Ali, Muhammad, 49, 66–67, 144, 157
All-Star Games, 17, 97, 105, 119–124, 126
Allen, Dick "Richie," 29, 55

Allen, Ivan, 47, 49
Alou, Felipe, 42, 230–231
Alston, Walt, 36, 71–72, 167
Anderson, Dave, 189
Anderson, Lynn, 184
Anderson, Sparky, 121, 147, 200, 209, 210
Andrews, John, 99
Angell, Roger, 107
Arlin, Steve, 89
Armstrong, Neil, 2
Aspromonte, Bob, 127
Astrodome, 70–71, 155, 156
Atlanta, 47–49, 57, 58, 59, 66–67, 151–152, 176
Atlanta Braves, 48–49, 68, 120, 153
    attendance, 47–48, 50–51, 52, 138, 145, 150–152, 170, 172–173, 175–176, 212–213, 216, 218
    and race, 48–49
Atlanta Constitution, 190, 213
Atlanta Crackers, 66
Atlanta Daily World, 208, 224
Atlanta Journal, 174, 176, 201
Atlanta Journal-Constitution, 225
Atlanta Stadium, 62, 66, 137, 152, 164, 178, 214–215, 218, 226
Averill, Earl, 123

Baby Ruth, 15, 185
Bailey, Pearl, 218
Baker, Christine, 42
Baker, Dusty, 6, 29–30, 39, 41–42, 47, 72, 90, 120, 126, 191, 230
    and Aaron, 40, 42, 43–44, 80, 98, 101, 119, 127–128, 141, 157, 160, 164, 194, 198, 203, 216, 220, 231
    in games, 46, 57, 89, 135, 142, 143, 171, 205, 218
    and father, 30, 39, 41–42, 141, 220
Baker, Frank "Home Run," 14
Baker, John, Sr., 41, 141, 220
Baney, Dick, 148
Banks, Ernie, 4, 10, 17, 110
Bartholomay, Bill, 50, 57, 129, 167, 178, 188–189, 193, 201–202, 206, 209, 213, 220
Baseball Digest, 17
Baseball Has Done It, 108
Bavasi, Buzzie, 19
Bell, James "Cool Papa," 223
Bench, Johnny, 46, 120–121, 129, 147–148, 158, 204–206, 224
Berra, Yogi, 109

Bezanson, Ran, 129
Billingham, Jack, 86, 143, 202, 204–206, 214, 219
Bisher, Furman, 138, 166, 176–177, 193
Bishop, Joey, 184
Black Athletes Foundation, 75–76
Black, Joe, 4, 5
black managers (lack of), 5–6, 13, 76–77, 78–80, 108, 185, 230–231
Black Sox, 87, 177
Black Sports magazine, 137
Blefary, Curt, 26
Blue, Vida, 6
Blunt, Theodore, 114
Bonds, Barry, 39, 228–229, 231
Bonds, Bobby, 38–39, 48, 121, 123, 145, 185, 196, 224, 228
Boone, Bob, 118
Borbon, Pedro, 209
Boston Red Sox, 21, 91
Boswell, Tom, 18
Boyer, Clete, 127
Branca, Ralph, 4
Brando, Marlon, 83
Breazeale, Jim, 120
Brett, George, 117
Brett, Ken, 117–118
Briles, Nellie, 75
Brock, Lou, 99
Brokaw, Tom, 94
Brooklyn Dodgers, 4, 8, 9, 10, 12, 16, 135
Brooks, Foster, 184
Brown, James, 90
Buckner, Bill, 215, 221
Burdette, Lew, 36, 100, 153
Burkhart, Ken, 118
Busby, Jim, 118, 153, 204
Busch Stadium, 132
Bush, Guy, 90

Caldwell, Mike, 89, 142
Campanella, Roy, 4, 10, 12, 179, 208
Candlestick Park, 16, 37–38, 104, 111
Cannon, Robert, 183
Carew, Rod, 84
Carlos, John, 49
Carlton, Steve, 70, 161
Carrithers, Don, 145
Carter, Jimmy, 167, 183, 194, 203, 217, 223, 225
Carter, Royalyn, 203
Carty, Rico, 33, 42, 48, 84, 126, 138

Casanova, Paul, 29, 39–40, 42–43, 64–65, 101, 135–136, 154, 191, 198, 205, 227
Cedeno, Cesar, 121, 224
Cepeda, Orlando, 28, 48, 126
Chafee, John, 183
Chamberlain, Wilt, 50
Chicago, 51–52
Chicago Crusader, 23
Chicago Cubs, 52, 69, 77, 134, 138
Chicago Tribune, 52
Chicago White Sox, 15
Chief Noc-a-Homa, 145, 174, 222, 226
Cincinnati Reds, 46–47, 143, 147–148, 180, 202–206, 209–211
Clay, Cassius, see Ali, Muhammad
Clemente, Roberto, 179
Cleveland, Reggie, 86, 136
Cleveland, Ruth, 15
Cobb, Ty, 14, 15, 22, 32, 177, 226, 227
Coleman, Albert, 116
Coleman, George, 224
Coleman, Joseph, 114
Collins, Eddie, 14
Comiskey Park, 122
Connor, Roger, 14, 15
Cosell, Howard, 80, 155, 162
County Stadium, 128, 129, 130, 221
Court, Margaret, 83
Courtney, Cliff, 222
Courtney, Clint, 81
Covington, Wes, 126
Crandall, Del, 129
Creamer, Robert, 196
Cronin, Joe, 123
Crosby, Norm, 184
Crosley Field, 146
Culver, George, 72

Davidson, Donald, 147, 159, 166, 191–192, 207, 216, 220, 227
Davidson, Satch, 219, 223
Davis, Anthony, 76
Davis, Sammy, Jr., 183, 194, 214, 223
Davis, Willie, 163
Dean, Dizzy, 184
Detroit Free Press, 189
di Scipio, Alfred, 169
Dickey, Bill, 123
Dierker, Larry, 86, 172
Dietz, Dick, 98
DiMaggio, Joe, 57, 110, 177, 226
Dobson, Pat, 29, 30, 35, 59
Doby, Larry, 4, 5, 10, 79, 230

Dodger Stadium, 41
Downing, Al, 37, 165, 213–214, 218–221, 223
Driessen, Dan, 210
Drysdale, Don, 37, 162
Durocher, Leo, 19, 170, 174, 175

Ebbets Field, 231
Ebony, 115, 137, 225
Edmondson, Paul, 179
Ellis, Dock, 83–84
Ellis, Elmo, 116
Engel, Bob, 132
Evans, Darrell, 28, 29, 39, 120, 227
    and Aaron, 118, 127–128, 171–172, 219, 222
    in games, 54, 72, 89, 117, 126, 134, 135, 145, 165, 205, 220, 222

Falcon, Evans, 116
Falls, Joe, 189
FBI, 64, 66, 69, 139–140, 146, 149, 221
Feeney, Chub, 130
Ferguson, Joe, 72, 220
Ferrell, Rick, 123
Ferrell, Wes, 123
Fingers, Rollie, 180
Finley, Charlie, 180
Fisk, Carlton, 184
Flack, Roberta, 4
Ford, Betty, 203
Ford, Gerald, 203, 204, 206, 221
Foreman, George, 155, 182
Forsch, Ken, 71
Foster, Warren, 113
Foxx, Jimmie, 15, 27, 96
Foxx, Redd, 220
Frazier, Joe, 49, 182
Frazier, Walt, 77
Frick, Ford, 96
Frisella, Danny, 30, 35
Froemming, Bruce, 130
Fuentes, Mickey, 179

Gable, Clark, 212
Gallo, Bill, 208
Garagiola, Joe, 209
Garner, Horace, 22
Garr, Ralph, 29, 30, 34, 47, 48, 80, 90, 120, 191, 227
    and Aaron, 39–40, 42, 43–44, 70, 99, 101, 119, 160, 194, 196, 198, 203, 205, 216
    in games, 53, 57, 70, 72, 89, 107, 110, 134, 154, 204, 222

Garvey, Steve, 165
Gaston, Britt, 222
Gaston, Cito, 230–231
Gehrig, Lou, 25, 57, 126, 223, 226
Gehrig, "Ma," 20
Gehringer, Charlie, 123
Gentry, Gary, 30, 74–75, 120
Geronimo, Cesar, 148
Gibson, Bob, 161, 173
Gibson, Josh, 111
Gilbreath, Rod, 28
Gilliam, Jim "Junior," 4, 216
Goggin, Chuck, 128, 148, 154
Gone With the Wind, 116, 212
Gore, Al, 140
Gorman, Tom, 167
Gowdy, Curt, 184, 209, 221
Graham, Billy, 170, 225
Granger, Wayne, 99
Grant, Lee, 181
Gray, Pete, 43
Green, Jerry, 199
Greenberg, Hank, 15, 16, 96–97
Griffey, Ken, Jr., 228
Grimm, Charlie, 129, 220, 223
Groat, Dick, 17
Grove, Lefty, 123
Gullett, Don, 47, 209

Hahn, Don, 107
Hall, Monty, 212
Hamilton, Milo, 117, 217, 218
Hancock, Herbie, 221
Hank Aaron Award, 225
Hank Aaron Day, 128
Harris, Lamar, 67
Harris, Lum, 27, 120
Harrison, Roric, 30
Hartwell Field, 8, 9
Harwell, Ernie, 116
Hearst, Patty, 186, 190, 192
Hebner, Richie, 75
Helms, Tommy, 175
Hennigan, Phil, 86, 88
Henry the Great Day, 187–188
Hershberger, Willard, 179
Hill, Herman, 179
Hodgson, Claire, see Ruth, Claire
Hoerner, Joe, 75
Hooper, Harry, 21
Hope, Bob (Braves employee), 100–101
Hope, Bob (comedian), 212
Hornsby, Roger, 96, 152, 170
House, Tom, 222–223

Houston Astros, 70–71, 157, 169–171, 173–176
Howard, Elston, 4
Hoyt, Waite, 19
Hubbell, Carl, 123
Humphrey, Hubert, 224
Hunter, Jim "Catfish," 180
Hyland, Frank, 166

I Had a Hammer, 224
Indianapolis Clowns, 10, 12, 43, 101, 104, 114
Irvin, Monte, 4, 79, 215, 223
Israel, Al, 22

Jackson, Jesse (the Rev.), 4, 6, 13, 76–78, 85, 119, 133, 194, 203
Jackson, Maynard, 80, 182, 187, 194, 217
Jackson, Reggie, 76, 180, 224, 228
Jackson, Sonny, 154
Jarry Park, 135
Jarvis, Pat, 119
John, Tommy, 37
Johnson, Davey, 30, 43, 101, 119, 120, 126–127, 143, 145, 152, 156, 165, 172, 197, 205
Johnson, Ernie, 176, 223
Johnson, Lyndon, 70
Jones, Cleon, 38, 68–69, 110, 187
Jones, Deacon, 82
Jones, Randy, 88
Jordan, Michael, 230
Joshua, Von, 165
Joss, Addie, 179

Kaline, Al, 55
Kansas City, 120–121
Kansas City Royals, 123
Kauffman, Ewing, 121
Kendall, Fred, 126
Kennedy, John, 2
Kennedy, Robert, 18
Kibler, John, 70
Killebrew, Harmon, 17, 65
Kiner, Ralph, 16, 107, 109
King, Billie Jean, 83, 144, 154–155, 156, 157–158
King, Martin Luther, 3, 13, 18, 48, 60, 64, 66, 73, 78, 183, 203, 204, 206, 212, 225, 231
Kingman, Dave, 224
Kirby, Clay, 142, 210
Kluszewski, Ted, 211

Knievel, Evel, 144
Knight, Gladys, 181
Koplin, Carla, 59–61, 62–63, 64, 66, 85, 123, 146, 163–164, 169, 199, 207, 220, 227
Koufax, Sandy, 41, 104, 159, 209
Kranepool, Ed, 43
Kubek, Tony, 209
Kuhn, Bowie, 150, 152, 154, 156, 169, 181, 203, 205–206, 214, 218, 223–224
  lineup dispute, 178, 183, 189, 193–194, 197–198, 200–202, 206, 209–210, 215–216
  pitchers' comments, 87–92, 109, 122, 172
  telegram dispute, 119, 121–122, 131–132
Kuhn, Luisa, 203
Ku Klux Klan, 9, 41, 58, 64, 66

Landis, Kenesaw Mountain, 87, 90
Leigh, Vivian, 212
Lindbergh, Charles, 15, 25
Linz, Phil, 106
Littlefeather, Sacheen, 83
Locker, Bob, 134
Lockman, Whitey, 52
Long Winter of Henry Aaron, The, 182
Los Angeles Dodgers, 36–37, 42, 51, 71–72, 104, 153, 156, 162–163, 165, 166, 213–216, 218–222
Los Angeles Times, 65–66, 151, 224
Louis, Joe, 4
Lucas, Barbara, 23, 24, 141, 219
Lucas, Bill, 42, 82
Lum, Mike, 28, 134, 145, 171, 174, 204, 205, 210
Luzinski, Greg, 118, 224
Lynn, Loretta, 58

MacPhail, Lee, 215
Maddox, Lester, 41, 183
Magnavox, 169, 185, 201, 208, 214
Malcolm X, 49
Mantilla, Felix, 22, 129
Mantle, Mickey, 16, 17, 18, 27, 29, 57, 65, 70, 95, 96, 111, 177, 205
Marichal, Juan, 72, 86, 145
Maris, Richard, 103
Maris, Roger, 56, 92, 95–97, 102–103, 122, 214
Martin, Dean, 184
Martin, Louis, 224

Massell, Sam, 57
Mathews, Eddie, 57, 58, 67, 84, 105,
    153, 183, 184, 191–192, 207, 212,
    227
  on Aaron, 33–34, 57, 94, 97, 132,
    136, 137–138, 178
  lineup dispute, 182, 189, 197–198,
    200–202, 206, 208–210
  as a manager, 26–28, 31, 35, 44–45,
    52, 55, 89–90, 92, 101, 110,
    119–120, 130, 135, 142, 148, 152,
    154, 164, 167, 174, 196, 224
  as a player, 16, 27, 36, 48, 49, 72,
    100, 126
Mathis, Dawson, 216
Mayberry, John, 123
Mays, Willie, 4, 6, 16–18, 27, 32, 38,
    53, 55, 88, 104–111, 113, 121, 159,
    169, 170, 177, 181, 195, 208, 218,
    228
McCovey, Willie, 38, 98, 104
McGraw, Tug, 86, 88, 90, 109–110
McGwire, Mark, 221, 226, 228
McHenry, Austin, 179
McLain, Denny, 30, 41
McMullen, Bobbie, 213
McMullen, Ken, 213
McQueen, Mike, 120
McSherry, John, 210
Meadows, Audrey, 184
Menton, Bill, 11
Merchant, Larry, 189
Messersmith, Andy, 86, 88, 90
Milan, Felix, 48
Miller, Marvin, 196–197
Milwaukee, 47–49, 51, 128–131,
    183–184, 226
Milwaukee Braves, 12, 16, 23, 34,
    35–36, 87, 128–131
  move to Atlanta, 24, 47–49
Milwaukee Brewers, 128–131, 226
Minshew, Wayne, 166
Mitchell, Margaret, 116
Mobile, Alabama, 7–11, 38, 67, 69, 81,
    112–115, 134, 146, 162, 169,
    186–188, 204, 205, 220, 225, 227
Mobile Beacon, 187
Mobile Bears, 9
Mobile Black Bears, 11–12, 110
Mobile *Register and Press*, 115
Money, Don, 131
Money, Sharon, 131
Montreal Expos, 135–136, 230
Montreal Royals, 8

Morgan, Joe, 46, 143, 210–211
Morris Brown College Choir, 217
Morris, Greg, 156
Morton, Carl, 30, 35, 153, 205
Mota, Manny, 72
Mullen, John, 220
Murphy, Reg, 190, 192
Murray, Jim, 65, 214
Musial, Stan, 80, 110, 136, 177, 193

NAACP, 9, 11
Nashville Tennessean, 140
National Baseball Hall of Fame, 32,
    129, 200
NBC, 65, 114, 116, 148, 209, 213
Negro leagues, 4, 8, 10, 11, 12, 43, 111
New York, 68, 104
New York Daily News, 55, 189, 208
New York Giants, 104
New York Mets, 52–56, 69, 92, 99, 107,
    109–110, 180–181
New York Post, 189
New York Times, 65, 68, 136, 151, 189
New York Yankees, 15, 42
Newcombe, Don, 4, 12
Newsday, 35
Newsweek, 65, 115, 137, 151, 158, 201
Niekro, Joe, 154
Niekro, Phil, 72, 117, 212
Nixon, Richard, 4, 82–83, 180, 188,
    207–208, 221, 223
Norman, Fred, 36
Norton, Ken, 144, 157

Oakland A's, 6, 180–181
Oates, John, 29, 30, 53, 89, 120
Odom, John "Blue Moon," 6
Office, Rowland, 196
Operation PUSH, 76, 78
Osteen, Claude, 37, 162, 166
Otis, Amos, 38, 123
Ott, Mel, 195
Outlar, Jesse, 166, 213
Ozark, Danny, 119

Pacific Bell Stadium, 229
Paige, Leroy "Satchel," 7, 8
Palmer, Arnold, 212
Pappas, Milt, 93
Parsons, Bill, 131
Perez, Marty, 29, 143, 154, 157, 196
Perez, Tony, 46
Philadelphia Phillies, 57, 115, 117–119
Pirone, Dorothy, see Ruth, Dorothy

Pittsburgh Courier, 224
Pittsburgh Pirates, 74–76, 99–100, 137
Playboy, 230
Plimpton, George, 156, 167
Pompidou, Georges, 207–208
Ponce de Leon Park, 66
Pravda, 224
Presley, Elvis, 225, 229
Preston, Billy, 77
Psychology Today, 95
Pursley, David, 98–100

Quilici, Frank, 84

racism, 12, 22, 49, 50, 55–59, 63–65,
    73, 83–84, 93, 108–109, 152
Radcliffe, Ted "Double Duty," 8
Rader, Doug, 176
Rau, Doug, 166
Rawls, Lou, 184
Reasoner, Harry, 194
Reed, Ron, 120
Reedy, Fleming "Junior," 22
Reese, "Pee Wee," 4
Reuschel, Rick, 52
Reuss, Jerry, 169–172
Richard, James Rodney, 195
Richards, Paul, 79
Richert, Pete, 86
Richman, Milton, 63
Riggs, Bobby, 83, 144, 154–155, 156
Ripken, Cal, Jr., 226
Rippy, Rodney Allen, 184
Riverfront Stadium, 46, 146, 148–149,
    199, 202
Riverside Church, 3, 6, 10, 12, 13
Rizzo, Frank, 116
Roberts, Dave, 86, 157, 169–170,
    173–174
Robinson, Brooks, 55
Robinson, Craig, 196
Robinson, Eddie, 82, 153, 201
Robinson, Frank, 80, 230
Robinson, Gloria (Aaron), 169, 170,
    173, 220
Robinson, Jackie, 22, 25, 57, 66, 71,
    76, 78–80, 82, 102, 108–109,
    230
  funeral, 3–7, 11, 13
  impact on Aaron, 8–13, 56, 70, 121,
    150, 159, 186, 227, 231
Rojas, Cookie, 123
Romo, Vicente, 142
Rooker, Jim, 99–100

Rose, Pete, 46, 121, 143–144, 147, 166,
    205, 206, 226
Ross, Gary, 150
Rothenberg, Fred, 86
Russell, Bill (basketball star), 4
Russell, Bill (Dodger), 220, 222
Russell, Herman, 80
Russell, Horace (the Rev.), 182
Russell, Nipsey, 184–185
Ruth, Claire, 24, 25, 91–92, 96, 208,
    224
Ruth, Dorothy, 23–24, 25
Ruth, George Herman "Babe," 7–8,
    14–16, 90, 92, 95–96, 111, 122,
    135, 159, 170, 195–196, 204, 208,
    228
  and Aaron, 13, 18–25, 31, 32, 55–57,
    58, 84, 91, 102, 125–126, 133, 136,
    150, 162, 177–178, 181, 185, 205,
    224, 227, 229–230
  home-run record, 27, 65, 104, 106,
    124
  popularity, 63, 64, 130, 201
Ruth, Helen, 21, 23, 24
Ryan, Nolan, 121

St. Louis Cardinals, 99, 136
Sally (Southern) League, 22, 55
San Diego Padres, 70, 88, 89, 126,
    142–143
San Francisco Chronicle, 151
San Francisco Giants, 37–39, 72, 104,
    145
Sanguillen, Manny, 75
Santana, Carlos, 41
Saturday Evening Post, 18
Sayers, Gale, 77
Scarce, Mac, 115
Schmidt, Mike, 228
Schoendienst, Red, 99
Schueler, Ron, 143
Schulz, Charles, 65
Scott, Alfredia (Aaron), 169, 178, 220
Scott, David, 167
Scott, Ed, 11–12, 114, 220
Seals Stadium, 142
Seaver, Tom, 52–53, 54, 55, 158, 161,
    173, 180
Secretariat, 84–85, 144, 157, 168
Selig, Ben, 129
Selig, Bud, 129, 183, 221, 226
Shea Stadium, 68, 91, 92, 104, 107
Shore, Dinah, 182
Silvestri, Ken "Hatch," 205

Singleton, Ken, 135
Sisler, George, 15
Siwoff, Seymour, 137
Slayback, Bill, 116
Smith, Herman, 113
Smith, Red, 189
Smith, Tommy, 49
Snider, Duke, 16, 111
Sosa, Sammy, 231
Spahn, Warren, 16, 128–129, 130
Speaker, Tris, 14
Spinks, Scipio, 99
Spitz, Mark, 158, 168
Sport magazine, 17, 18
Sports Illustrated, 17, 27, 65, 156,
    195–196
Sporting News, 18, 91, 117
Staple Singers, 194
Stargell, Willie, 6, 28, 70, 73, 75–76,
    127, 161, 165
Staub, Rusty, 181
Stensland, Gary, 58, 144–145, 163, 218
Stone, George, 92
Stoneman, Bill, 135
Sutton, Don, 76, 162–163
Sutton, Shelby, 187

Tepedino, Frank, 129
Theodore, George, 107
Thomson, Bobby, 16, 23
Three Rivers Stadium, 74
Time magazine, 65, 115, 151
Titus, Pete, 140, 146–147, 149, 220
Tolan, Bobby, 46
Torre, Joe, 48, 126, 231
Toulminville, 8, 112
Tribbitt, Sherman, 167
Troedson, Rich, 36, 142
Turner, Ted, 151, 227
TV Guide, 137
Twitchell, Wayne, 115

Vargo, Ed, 52, 145, 205
Veterans Stadium, 64

Wagner, Dick, 204, 206
Wagner, Honus, 14
Wahoo Club, 215
Walker, Joe, 166

Walker, Luke, 74
Wall Street Journal, 18
Wallace, George, 41, 188
Walter, Eugene, 9
Wardlaw, Calvin, 67, 164, 186–187,
    192, 194, 195, 220, 222–223, 227
Washington, Harriet, 29
Washington Post, 18, 65
Washington Senators, 42
Watson, Bob, 157
Welch, Charles, 115
Welch, Raquel, 184
William Morris Agency, 158, 168
Williams, Bernie, 82
Williams, Bill, 142, 163
Williams, Billy, 38, 121
Williams, Billye, 59–61, 78, 117, 164,
    167, 173, 183, 187–188, 192, 195,
    199–201, 206, 225
  engagement and wedding, 61, 115,
    182
  at games, 163, 169, 171, 205, 220, 222
Williams, Ceci, 60, 192, 195
Williams, Earl, 6, 48, 221
Williams, Samuel, 60, 61
Williams, Ted, 16, 27, 54, 55, 100, 111,
    159
Wills, Maury, 230
Wilson, Don, 173–175
Wilson, Flip, 181–182
Winborne, Robert, 118, 119
Winfield, Dave, 76
Wise, Rick, 184
Woodford, Helen, see Ruth, Helen
Woods, Tiger, 230
World Series, 17, 21; (1954) 105; (1957)
    23, 35–36, 42, 53; (1972) 5; (1973)
    110, 150, 180–181
Wrigley Field, 47, 51, 69, 77
Wynn, Jimmy, 221

Xenia, Ohio, 200, 203

Yankee Stadium, 19, 91, 96
Young, Andrew, 80, 194, 217
Young, Dick, 55–56, 91, 96, 166, 189,
    193

Zimmer, Don, 70, 89, 126, 128

When he crossed the color barrier with the Brooklyn Dodgers, Jackie Robinson became an instant idol to tens of thousands of black youths, including thirteen-year-old Hank Aaron. (Detroit Public Library/Burton Historical Collection)

When Jackie Robinson visited Mobile,
he often appeared on Davis Avenue,
the geographical heart of the African
American community. (Julius E. Marx
Collection, University of South Alabama
Archives)

Negro League teams like the Black Yankees drew crowds to Hartwell Field, where
Aaron's hero, Jackie Robinson, played scrimmages with the Brooklyn Dodgers and
barnstorming teams. (University of South Alabama Archives)

The Mobile Bears, a Double-A minor-league team, played in the 1930s before segregated crowds at Hartwell Field. (Eric Overbey Collection, University of South Alabama Archives)

LEFT: *Hank Aaron broke in with the Milwaukee Braves in 1954, capitalizing on an injury to outfielder Bobby Thomson.* (Detroit Public Library/Burton Historical Collection)

ABOVE: *Fans and writers often compared Willie Mays and Hank Aaron. But for a few thousand dollars, the two Alabama natives might have spent their careers together as Giants.* (Detroit Public Library/Burton Historical Collection)

ABOVE: *Hank Aaron and Eddie Mathews, pictured with Joe Adcock (right), hit more home runs than any other pair of teammates in baseball history. Mathews was manager of the Braves when Aaron made his final push for the record.*
(Detroit Public Library/Burton Historical Collection)

In the late 1950s, Eddie Mathews and Mickey Mantle were considered more likely than Aaron to surpass Babe Ruth. The Braves and Yankees met in two championship series. (Detroit Public Library/Burton Historical Collection)

In 1957 at age twenty-three, Henry Aaron won the Most Valuable Player Award, belted the home run that captured the pennant, and led Milwaukee to its first world championship. (Detroit Public Library/Burton Historical Collection)

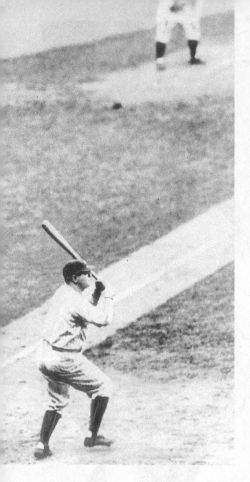

Babe Ruth reigned as all-time home-run king for more than a half century before Hank Aaron surpassed him in 1974. Ruth's widow, Claire, was alive at the time. (Detroit Public Library/Burton Historical Collection)

Despite being hounded by the media and fans, Aaron contended he felt no pressure pursuing the record. (Courtesy of the National Baseball Hall of Fame Library, Cooperstown, NY)

Hank Aaron launches an Al Downing pitch toward the Braves bullpen in left field, claiming the all-time home-run crown. (Courtesy of the National Baseball Hall of Fame Library, Cooperstown, NY)

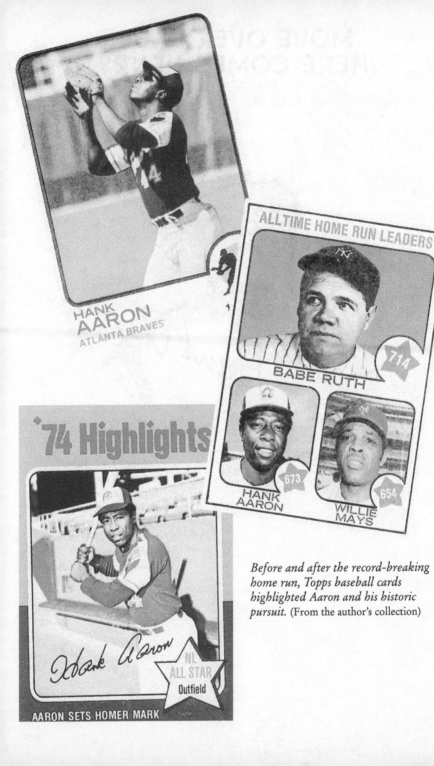

HANK
AARON
ATLANTA BRAVES

ALLTIME HOME RUN LEADERS

714

BABE RUTH

HANK
AARON 673

WILLIE
MAYS 654

'74 Highlights

Hank Aaron

NL
ALL STAR
Outfield

AARON SETS HOMER MARK

Before and after the record-breaking home run, Topps baseball cards highlighted Aaron and his historic pursuit. (From the author's collection)

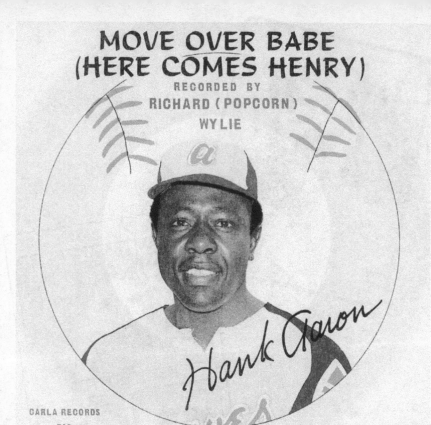

MOVE OVER BABE
(HERE COMES HENRY)

RECORDED BY

RICHARD (POPCORN)

WYLIE

CARLA RECORDS
715

"Move Over, Babe,"
composed by broadcaster
Ernie Harwell and pitcher
Bill Slayback, was the best
known of several songs
released in 1973 in honor
of Hank Aaron.
(From the author's collection)

Dusty Baker (12) greets Hank Aaron after he tagged Steve Renko for home run 703 before an enthusiastic crowd in Montreal. (Courtesy of the National Baseball Hall of Fame Library, Cooperstown, NY)

ABOVE: *Media interest was so great in the chase that the Atlanta Braves issued a press guide devoted solely to Aaron.* (From the author's collection)

BELOW: *On his first swing of the 1974 campaign, Hank Aaron ties the record against Jack Billingham. The Braves opened the year in Cincinnati. Bowie Kuhn had ordered them to play Aaron in two of three games.* (Courtesy of the National Baseball Hall of Fame Library, Cooperstown, NY)

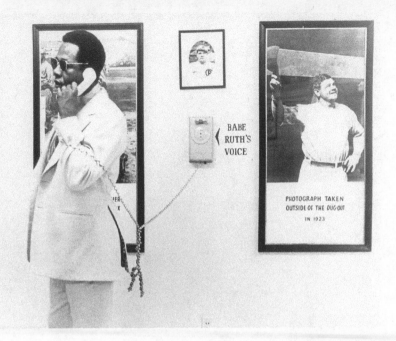

ABOVE: *Hank Aaron listens to a recording of Babe Ruth's voice in an August 1974 visit to the National Baseball Hall of Fame in Cooperstown, NY.* (Courtesy of the National Baseball Hall of Fame Library, Cooperstown, NY)

RIGHT: *Hank Aaron, pictured with wife, Billye, found himself on the cover of numerous national magazines. But the Aaron portrayed in black publications like* Ebony *and* Jet *often came off as more outspoken.* (From the author's collection)

CPSIA information can be obtained
at www.ICGtesting.com
Printed in the USA
LVHW040044260121
677442LV00018B/3616

9 780060 722906